Modern American Remedies:
Cases and Materials

2017 Supplement

2017 Supplement

Modern American Remedies:

Cases and Materials

Fourth Edition

Douglas Laycock

Robert E. Scott Distinguished Professor of Law,
Class of 1963 Research Professor In Honor of
  Graham C. Lilly and Peter W. Low
Professor of Religious Studies
University of Virginia

Alice McKean Young Regents Chair in Law Emeritus
The University of Texas at Austin

SUSTAINABLE FORESTRY INITIATIVE   Certified Sourcing
www.sfiprogram.org
SFI-00756

About Wolters Kluwer Legal & Regulatory U.S.

Wolters Kluwer Legal & Regulatory U.S. delivers expert content and solutions in the areas of law, corporate compliance, health compliance, reimbursement, and legal education. Its practical solutions help customers successfully navigate the demands of a changing environment to drive their daily activities, enhance decision quality and inspire confident outcomes.

Serving customers worldwide, its legal and regulatory portfolio includes products under the Aspen Publishers, CCH Incorporated, Kluwer Law International, ftwilliam.com and MediRegs names. They are regarded as exceptional and trusted resources for general legal and practice-specific knowledge, compliance and risk management, dynamic workflow solutions, and expert commentary.

Contents

PREFACE

This Supplement includes decisions through the end of the Supreme Court's term on June 27, including its very important 2011 opinion on the scope of injunctions in the California prison litigation, and selected developments in the lower courts through the first half of July. Professors should look at the supplement to page 709, on constructive trusts in bankruptcy, at least a few days before they get to it in class; they need to tell their students what to read. And at page 733, there is a much clearer statement of the facts in Mort v. United States; on that assignment, students should start with the Supplement before going to the main volume.

Students, just as no one expects you to memorize all the information in the main volume (see the preface to the main volume), no one expects you to memorize all the recent decisions. But reviewing recent developments helps give you a sense of the field and its trajectory. The continuing flow of remedies litigation, especially in the Supreme Court of the United States, illustrates the continuing importance of these issues and the remarkable variety and novelty with which they appear. Thinking about these recent developments will cast further light on the issues raised by the book's principal cases.

I am grateful to David Gremling for research assistance.

Douglas Laycock
Charlottesville
July 2017

Modern American Remedies:
Cases and Materials

2017 Supplement

CHAPTER TWO

PAYING FOR HARM: COMPENSATORY DAMAGES

A. The Basic Principle: Restoring Plaintiff to His Rightful Position

Page 15. At the end of the first paragraph of note 3, add:
   3. More facts in *Hatahley*. . . .
The Threedy article is now published at 34 Am. Indian L. Rev. 1 (2010).

B. Value as the Measure of the Rightful Position

Page 22. Before note 1, add:
   0.1. Appeals. The World Trade Center's appeals, which had to await a final judgment resolving all the issues in the case, have at last been decided. In re September 11 Litigation, 802 F.3d 314 (2d Cir. 2015). The court vacated and remanded for further consideration of damages. There is a new opinion of the district court on remand, resolving some preliminary calculation issues for the guidance of the expert witnesses for each side. In re September 11 Litigation, 2017 WL 1287141 (S.D.N.Y. April 6, 2017).
   The Second Circuit held that the measure of damages is the difference between the value of the 99-year leasehold before and after the destruction of the towers. An outright owner would not recover the cost of replacing the towers, and the plaintiff's contractual obligation to rebuild as required by the lease should not change that result. So on the points that principally concern us, the Second Circuit opinion is entirely consistent with the district court's original opinion.
   Judge Straub would have certified the issues concerning replacement cost to the New York Court of Appeals. The state had filed an amicus brief arguing that the towers were special purpose property, more valuable to the public than to the market. And there were New York tort cases awarding consequential damages arising out of the plaintiff's contractual obligations, including a case involving a lease. The stakes were radically different, and the issue was not replacement cost. A plaintiff whose leased car was destroyed in a collision recovered the value of the car plus the early termination fees on the lease. Plouffe v. Rogers, 534 N.Y.S.2d 731 (App. Div. 1988).
   Beyond that, the Second Circuit vacated and remanded on grounds that do not concern us, deep into the nitty gritty of calculating the value of the leasehold. The World Trade Center case is here because it has dramatic facts and it illustrates the lesser-of-two rule, which widely applies to far more prosaic facts. I have long told my own students not to worry about the details of the 99-year lease. Just treat the $2.8 billion present value as the purchase price, and as evidence of the value before destruction. And just assume that value after the buildings were destroyed is zero at best, and maybe less if plaintiff was responsible for clearing the wreckage. Is the rightful position the difference between those two values, or does the rightful position include the cost of replacing the towers? That is the question for our purposes, and the complexities of the Second Circuit opinion do not change that question. They change the method of calculation, and they may eventually change the bottom line

number, but quite possibly not by much. There also appears to be some tension between the Second Circuit's opinion and the district court's understanding of the facts on remand. But those disagreements, if they exist, do not go to the issues that matter here, and are far too complex to be worth explaining.

Page 28. At the end of note 7, add:
  7. **Value to the owner less than market? . . .**
  A similar issue reached the Supreme Court in Horne v. Department of Agriculture, 135 S. Ct. 2419 (2015). To support the price of raisins, the government required growers to give a substantial percentage of each year's crop to the government — 30% and 47% in the two years at issue in *Horne*. The Court held that this was a taking of property that required just compensation. So this was a constitutional takings case, not a tort case. The Court said that the "clear and administrable rule for just compensation" in takings cases is "the market value of the property at the time of the taking." *Id.* at 2432, quoting United States v. 50 Acres of Land, 469 U.S. 24, 29 (1984).
  Three dissenters argued that without the government's price-support program, the market value of the raisins would have been much less. They pointed to a line of cases in which the government takes part of a piece of land for a project — say a highway interchange — that increases the value of the owner's remaining land. The increase in the value of the remainder is offset against the just compensation due for the part taken. And while the dissenters didn't say so, the part taken is generally valued as of before the announcement of the government's project. The dissenters thought this case was the same; the government's taking of nearly half the raisins increased the value of both the half taken and the half that remained. The majority distinguished those cases on grounds that are far from clear, but appear to be based in takings law rather than remedies law.

Page 34. After note 3, add:
  4. **Injured pets.** The general rule is that the owner of a pet who is killed can recover only the market value of the pet as property. See note 2.e. at page 176 of the main volume. But if the pet is injured, owners can recover the costs of medical care. A handful of cases are collected in Kimes v. Grosser, 126 Cal. Rptr. 3d 581 (Ct. App. 2011), where defendant shot plaintiff's cat with a pellet gun, and plaintiff spent $36,000 on veterinary care. Plaintiff conceded that the cat had no market value. But the court said he was entitled to go to the jury on whether it was reasonable to spend $36,000 to save the cat. No doubt the willfulness of the wrong would influence the jury, but it did not appear to be part of the reasoning of the court.
  The court applied *Kimes* to a negligence case (veterinary malpractice) in Martinez v. Robledo, 147 Cal. Rptr. 3d 921 (Ct. App. 2012).

C. Expectancy and Reliance as Measures of the Rightful Position

Page 38. At the end of note 3, add:
   3. Lost-volume sellers and the common law. . . .
   The state supreme court has affirmed the judgment, specifically including the finding that Dr. Gianetti was a lost-volume seller. Gianetti v. Norwalk Hospital, 43 A.3d 567 (Conn. 2012).

Page 42. At the end of the first paragraph of note 2, add:
   2. Academic alternatives. . . .
   The Triantis article is now published at 60 U. Toronto L.J. 643 (2010).

Page 52. At the end of note 3, add:
   3. *Dura* and its impact. . . .
   The Court unanimously held that plaintiffs need not prove loss causation at the class certification stage. Erica P. John Fund, Inc. v. Halliburton Co., 563 U.S. 804 (2011). The Court summarized loss causation as requiring "a plaintiff to show that a misrepresentation that affected the integrity of the market price *also* caused a subsequent economic loss," *id.* at 812, and further explained that the subsequent price decline must have resulted from public correction of the misrepresentation and not from other factors influencing the market.
   3.1. Fraud on the market. The *Halliburton* litigation came back to the Court, this time presenting a more fundamental question. Halliburton Co. v. Erica P. John Fund, Inc., 134 S. Ct. 2398 (2014). A securities-fraud plaintiff must prove a material misrepresentation or omission, scienter (knowledge that the statement was false or that the omission was material), a purchase or sale of a security, reliance, economic loss, and loss causation. If each investor had to individually prove that she read the false or misleading statements and relied on them before investing, few if any class actions for securities fraud could ever proceed. Individual proof of reliance would overwhelm the issues common to the class.
   In Basic Inc. v. Levinson, 485 U.S. 224 (1988), the Court held that individualized proof of reliance is not required. New information about a security, whether true or false, affects the market price, and all investors rely on the integrity of the market price — on the view that the market price is an honest price not distorted by fraudulent misrepresentations. This is the fraud-on-the-market theory. It raises a rebuttable presumption of reliance; defendant can rebut the presumption by proving that the alleged misrepresentations did not affect the market price.
   To invoke the fraud-on-the-market theory, *Basic* requires plaintiff to prove that the misrepresentations were publicly known, that they were material, that the security traded in a reasonably efficient market, and that the plaintiff bought or sold the stock before the truth came out, while the price was influenced by the misrepresentations. "Efficient market" is sometimes taken to mean that the market price is the right price, *accurately* reflecting all available information. But markets often over react, under react, or react emotionally and irrationally, so it is hard to sustain the belief that markets are efficient in that sense. All that most efficient-market theorists really claim is that individual investors cannot know when a stock is over or under priced,

so they cannot systematically make money by betting against the market price. Another way to describe efficient markets, more directly relevant to *Basic*, is that the market price is determined by the individual decisions of many investors, and their reaction to all available information is reflected in the market price. Their reaction need not be wise or accurate.

Halliburton asked the Court to overrule *Basic* and abolish the fraud-on-the-market theory. It took efficient markets to mean that the market price is the right price, and it argued that markets are clearly not efficient in that sense. And it argued that many investors — it particularly emphasized value investors, who try to buy stocks when they are cheap — do not believe that the market price is the right price; they believe that they can sometimes recognize when the market price is wrong. Halliburton's argument was an invitation to abolish class actions for securities fraud, although some commentators thought there would still be ways to make them work.

The Court reaffirmed *Basic*, emphasizing stare decisis and a more realistic account of what investors rely on. Investors need not rely on a belief that the market price is the right price, or the true value; they rely on the belief that whatever forces are affecting the market price, fraud is not among them. Or as the Court phrased it, they rely on "the integrity of the market price." *Halliburton*, 134 S. Ct. at 2412, 2414.

Defendants can rebut the fraud-on-the-market presumption by showing that their allegedly false statements did not affect the market price. And the Court held that they can offer that proof at the class-certification stage; they need not wait for the trial on the merits. Chief Justice Roberts wrote the opinion; Justices Thomas, Scalia, and Alito would have overruled *Basic*.

D. Consequential Damages

Page 58. At the end of the first paragraph of note 9, add:
  9. Actual damages. . . .
  The Supreme Court resolved the issue in favor of the government in Federal Aviation Administration v. Cooper, 566 U.S. 284 (2012). The majority collected cases interpreting "actual damages" in a remarkable variety of ways. Emphasizing that the Privacy Act creates a cause of action against the United States, and invoking the principle that waivers of sovereign immunity must be narrowly construed, the Court concluded that "actual damages" means "special damages for proven pecuniary loss," *id.* at 1452, not including emotional distress and apparently (this is implicit rather than explicit) not including loss of reputation unless the harm to reputation causes a loss of income or the like. Three dissenters argued that "actual damages" simply means no presumed damages. Justice Kagan did not participate.

  There are lengthy discussions of the meaning of special damages and general damages, both generally and in the special context of defamation and privacy torts, responding in part to a congressional decision not to authorize "general damages" in the Privacy Act. The majority argued that emotional distress is a form of general damages, which is generally true; the dissenters argued that general damages for defamation can be presumed, and that it is that meaning of general damages — presumed damages — that Congress declined to authorize.

E. Limits on Damages

1. The Parties' Power to Specify the Remedy

Page 78. At the end of note 5.b, add:
  b. Cell phone termination fees. . . .
The court of appeal affirmed. In re Cellphone Fee Termination Cases, 122 Cal. Rptr. 3d 726 (Ct. App. 2011).

Page 81. After note 12, add:
  13. Alternative-performance clauses. Another way to draft around the problem is with an alternative-performance clause. Instead of saying that if a party breaches, he must pay liquidated damages, say that the party may perform the contract either by doing what the contract contemplates or by paying a sum of money. Mark Gergen, who teaches Contracts at Berkeley, has said in conversation that you can always draft a liquidated-damage clause as an alternative-performance clause.
  The Supreme Court of Washington upheld cellphone termination fees on this theory, holding that paying the fee is an alternative way of performing the contract and not a penalty for breach. Minnick v. Clearwire US LLC, 275 P.3d 1127 (Wash. 2012). The Washington court viewed the distinction as more than a drafting trick dependent on "a form of words;" it said that to qualify as an alternative-performance clause, the two options must "give the promisor a real choice between reasonably equivalent choices," viewed as of the time of contracting. *Id.* at 1131.
  But there did not seem to be much content in the court's enforcement of these criteria. The court said the termination fee was not significantly different in amount from paying the monthly charge for the remaining term of the contract, so the choices were reasonably equivalent. But as the four dissenters pointed out, consumers got nothing for the termination fee; they got cellphone service for paying the remaining monthly charges.

2. Avoidable Consequences, Offsetting Benefits, and Collateral Sources

Page 95. After note 4, add:
  5. Takings of property. The Court summarily rejected a seemingly straightforward offsetting-benefits argument in Horne v. Department of Agriculture, 135 S. Ct. 2419 (2015), summarized in this supplement to page 28.

Page 99. At the end of note 3, add:
  3. What counts as a collateral source? . . .
  New York eventually passed the amendment to eliminate the illustrations of collateral sources. The law now says that the court must take account of "any collateral source," except for life insurance and those payments as to which there is a statutory right of reimbursement." N.Y. C.P.L.R. §4545(a) (LexisNexis Supp. 2017). The exception for charitable donations still appears in §4545(b). Collateral source is undefined. The legislature has not done anything to change the matching requirement announced in *Oden*.

Page 101. At the end of note 7, add:
    7. Subrogation in practice. . . .
    The problem of under compensation in *Ahlborn* is widespread and gets too little attention in the main volume. Coverage limits, litigation risks, difficulties of proof, attorneys' fees, statutory caps on damages, and other problems often cause plaintiff's net recovery to be less than the reasonable value of her injuries — sometimes dramatically less. Many judgments and some settlements are never fully collected. In all these cases, there is no double recovery in the absence of subrogation, and subrogation aggravates the plaintiff's under compensation. Some of these sources of under compensation can be identified and measured; some are hard to address.
    Many states addressed at least what could be measured with a make-whole rule: no insurer could claim subrogation rights unless the injury victim was fully compensated. A modern example is Fischer v. Steffen, 797 N.W.2d 501 (Wis. 2011); older cases are collected in Brendan S. Maher & Radha A. Pathak, *Understanding and Problematizing Contractual Tort Subrogation*, 40 Loy. U. Chi. L.J. 49, 64-65 (2008). But the make-whole rule is undermined by statutes and contract provisions like the Arkansas Medicaid law in *Ahlborn*, providing that the subrogated insurer gets paid first and in full before the injury victim keeps anything.
    7.1. Another Medicaid example. Wos v. E.M.A., 568 U.S. 627 (2013), did not have stipulations like those in *Ahlborn*. E.M.A. was profoundly injured in the process of being born; she will require skilled nursing care for her entire life. Her expert witness estimated the cost of this care at $37 million. She and her parents also claimed other expenses, loss of earning capacity, pain and suffering, and emotional distress. The case settled for $2.8 million, based principally on the policy limits of defendants' malpractice coverage. The settlement did not allocate that total among various items of damage.
    North Carolina, which was paying for her medical care, had a statute that irrebuttably attributed one-third of her recovery to medical expenses. The Court held that the Medicaid Act requires a case-by-case allocation, to be based on "how likely E.M.A. and her parents would have been to prevail on [each individual claim] at trial and how much they reasonably could have expected to receive on each claim if successful, in view of damages awarded in comparable tort cases." *Id.* at 1400. The Court believed that individual hearings had not been burdensome in states that held them, and suggested, without holding, that rebuttable presumptions might be permissible.
    7.2. The impact of ERISA. Many health-insurance policies are provided by employers and are subject to the Employee Retirement Income Security Act. ERISA gives employers power to write employee-benefit plans, makes those plans enforceable, and allows the terms of the plan to preempt most contrary state law. The Act authorizes "appropriate equitable relief" — but not legal relief — to enforce the terms of a plan. 29 U.S.C. §1132(a)(3) (2012). The plans typically provide for subrogation, and the Court has held, under the label "equitable lien by agreement," that the plan's claim to reimbursement out of the proceeds of a judgment or settlement is "appropriate equitable relief." Sereboff v. Mid Atlantic Medical Services, Inc., 547 U.S. 356 (2006). An equitable lien is a restitutionary remedy closely related to subrogation and taken up in section 8.C.3.

An equitable lien normally attaches to specifically identifiable assets — in this case, the proceeds of the judgment or settlement. But employees who lost their income due to serious injuries often spend those proceeds rather quickly on living expenses and accumulated bills. And at least some try to hide any remaining proceeds from their employer's ERISA plan. In Great-West Life & Annuity Insurance Co. v. Knudson, 534 U.S. 204 (2002), the Court held that a claim to general assets — as distinguished from a claim to specific funds derived from the judgment or settlement — was legal, not equitable, and therefore unavailable under ERISA.

The Court reaffirmed that rule in Board of Trustees v. Montanile, 136 S. Ct. 651 (2016), a case where the personal injury victim had quickly spent most of the settlement proceeds. Justice Ginsburg dissented; she has rejected this whole line of cases as turning on distinctions that Congress knew nothing about and could not have intended. The issue is further discussed in the main volume and supplement at page 569.

A closely related issue is whether the subrogated insurer has to pay any share of the attorneys' fees that produced the recovery. The Court addressed this issue in the ERISA context in US Airways, Inc. v. McCutchen, 133 S. Ct. 1537 (2013). McCutchen suffered brain damage and permanent disability in an automobile accident. He recovered $110,000 from the other driver and the state's uninsured motorist fund, which may well have been grossly inadequate. From this amount, he paid 40 percent plus expenses to his attorneys. US Air had paid $66,000 of his medical expenses, and claimed a right to be fully subrogated to what remained of McCutchen's tort and uninsured motorist recovery. This would leave McCutchen with nothing except US Air's payment of his medical expenses. The court of appeals held that US Air's subrogation claim was a permitted equitable claim, but that US Air would be unjustly enriched if it recovered without contributing pro rata to the attorneys' fees that made the recovery possible — and that a judgment resulting in unjust enrichment would not be "appropriate" equitable relief. 663 F.3d 671 (3d Cir. 2011). The Supreme Court unanimously rejected that theory, holding that the ERISA plan controls.

Justice Kagan managed to affirm by interpreting the plan in light of the common-fund rule: those who recover out of a judgment or settlement obtained by another must contribute pro rata to the attorneys' fees required to obtain the judgment or settlement. But all the employers will presumably amend their plans to expressly override that rule. The common-fund rule is considered in section 10.B of the main volume.

7.3. Other sources of preemption. The Federal Employees Health Benefit Act, 5 U.S.C. §8901 *et seq.* (2012), provides for health insurance for federal employees. It contains preemption language much like ERISA's. And the Court unanimously held that this statute preempts a state-law ban on subrogation clauses in insurance contracts. Coventry Health Care v. Nevils, 137 S. Ct. 1190 (2017).

3. The Scope of Liability

Page 107. After note 7, add:

7.1. Intervening negligence. Another consideration that courts sometimes invoke is the intervening negligence of a third party. A recent illustration is Baumann v. Zhukov, 802 F.3d 950 (8th Cir. 2015), where two large trucks collided and blocked an interstate highway. Even at 4:00 a.m., traffic backed up for nearly a mile. A semi-tractor-trailer plowed into the cars at the end of the line, killing a family of four and their unborn baby. Applying Nebraska law, the court held that the drivers who caused the accident at the front of the line were not responsible for the accident at the back of the line. Many other drivers had stopped without incident, including truck drivers; the truck driver at the end of the line was fatigued and had not braked; he was the legal cause of the deaths, and his negligence was not foreseeable. The dissenter collected several cases from other states that had treated foreseeability on similar facts as a jury issue.

Page 108. After note 8.d, add:

8.1. Beyond RICO. The Court expanded *Hemi Group*'s approach beyond RICO in Bank of America Corp. v. City of Miami, 137 S. Ct. 1296 (2017). Miami sued the bank under the Fair Housing Act, which authorizes suits for damages by any "aggrieved person." 42 U.S.C. §3613 (2012). Miami alleged that the defendant banks discriminated on the basis of race in the terms of loans, in refinancing, and in foreclosures, causing many homes in minority neighborhoods to stand empty, lowering property values and tax revenues, and requiring additional expenditures for public safety. The Court held, in an opinion by Justice Breyer, that the city was an aggrieved person under precedents from the 1970s and 80s, precedent that Congress had implicitly reaffirmed when it amended the Act.

But the Court said that the foreseeability of Miami's harms was not enough to show proximate cause. Rather, there must be "some direct relation between the injury asserted and the injurious conduct alleged," quoting *Holmes*. And once again, "'[t]he general tendency' in these cases, 'in regard to damages at least, is not to go beyond the first step,'" quoting *Hemi Group*. It is hard to see how Miami's claims can survive this emphasis on "the first step," but the Court remanded to the Eleventh Circuit to apply its test in the first instance. The Court was unanimous on this approach to proximate cause. Three dissenters would have held that Miami was not an aggrieved person under the Act, and that no remand was needed because it could never show proximate cause under the Court's test.

8.2. 71,000 causes. The Supreme Court faced an insoluble variant on the problem of multiple causation in Paroline v. United States, 134 S. Ct. 1710 (2014). The context was criminal, but the Court drew heavily on common law tort principles.

Criminal sentences commonly include orders to pay compensation to the victim; these orders are typically called "restitution," and they are very briefly considered at page 857 in the main volume. The federal child-pornography law has its own victim-restitution provision, which says that a convicted defendant shall be ordered to pay "the full amount of the victim's losses." 18 U.S.C. §2259(b)(1) (2012). Related provisions, and Supreme Court precedent, specify that this means the losses caused by the offense of which defendant was convicted, and that the government bears the burden of proving that amount by a preponderance of the evidence. 18 U.S.C. §3664(e) (2012).

Defendant Paroline was convicted of possession of child pornography. Among the many images on his computer were two images of a young woman known to the courts as Amy Unknown. Amy Unknown says that she will require counseling throughout her life, because images of her sexual abuse by her uncle are among the most widely traded and viewed child-pornography images in the world. She somehow estimated that 71,000 offenders, most of whom will probably never be convicted, have images of her sexual abuse. She lives with that knowledge and with the fear that she will be recognized. And her expert calculated — the Court does not say how — that she will lose nearly $3 million in income over her lifetime because the images of her abuse are being shared on the internet. And her future counseling would cost $500,000, so her total loss was $3.4 million. Accepting all that, how much of those losses is a proximate result of Paroline's offense?

The victim, and Justice Sotomayor, dissenting, said that Paroline was liable for the whole $3.4 million. This was a case of an indivisible injury inflicted by joint wrongdoers, and each wrongdoer was liable for the entire loss. Of course Paroline did not know most of the other 71,000 offenders, but he knew that he was part of an organized network for distributing and trading child pornography. The federal statutes on victim restitution provide for payment schedules based on defendant's means, and Sotomayor thought this was sufficient to protect Paroline from a ruinous or unfair share of the total liability.

The majority acknowledged joint and several liability in the cases of multiple sufficient causes, such as two negligently caused fires, either of which would have destroyed plaintiff's house. But they thought that Paroline's two images were plainly not a sufficient cause of Amy Unknown's total loss. They also acknowledged joint and several liability in the cases of joint tortfeasors cooperating to inflict an indivisible harm, as when a gang beats somebody up. But the Court thought that this case "stretches the fiction of aggregate causation to the breaking point." 134 S. Ct. at 1729. The Court was unwilling to say that all 71,000 offenders were working together, or that Paroline's two images added any measurable increment to the victim's harm, or that Paroline should be liable for all the harm caused by all the others. "The premise of her argument is that because it is in a sense a fiction to say Paroline caused $1,000 in losses, $10,000 in losses, or any other lesser amount, it is necessary to embrace the much greater fiction that Paroline caused all the victim's losses from the ongoing trade in her images." *Id.* at 1728. The Court suggested, without deciding, that liability for the entire $3.4 million might violate the Excessive Fines Clause.

The Court said that courts should apportion the victim's losses based on the causal significance of an offender's contribution to her loss. It emphasized that this apportionment should not be "severe," given defendant's minimal contribution to the total harm, nor should it result in "a token or nominal amount." *Id.* at 1727. The victim's $3.4 million loss, divided by 71,000 offenders, was $47, and the Court clearly rejected that number.

Chief Justice Roberts, joined by Justices Scalia and Thomas, thought that these problems were insuperable — that the government could not prove any amount of loss attributable to Paroline's crime. The Court's "sensible" search for a solution could not be reconciled with the statute, the government could not prove any amount of losses attributable to defendant's offense, and "it is not possible to do anything more than pick an arbitrary number for that 'amount.' And arbitrary is not good enough for the criminal law." *Id.* at 1730 (Roberts, C.J., dissenting). They would have awarded no restitution and waited for Congress to fix the statute.

Amy Unknown has diligently pursued her right to restitution; as of late 2013, she had obtained restitution orders against 182 defendants. The lower courts had largely anticipated the Supreme Court's solution; these awards ranged from $50 to $530,000, and most were under $5,000. Her uncle, the primary wrongdoer, was ordered to pay $6,325.

Other victims apparently have not been so diligent. The problem before the Court would have been even more complex if fifty victims with comparable restitution claims had been before the Court. No Justice mentioned that possibility. Justice Sotomayor would presumably hold defendant responsible for the full loss of every victim filing a claim; the majority would presumably apportion losses for each of them. Then maybe defendant's payments would be divided pro rata among all the victims who filed.

Page 109. After note 9, add:

10. Business disparagement. The Court allowed what it appeared to view as a third-party claim in Lexmark International, Inc. v. Static Control Components, Inc., 134 S. Ct. 1377 (2014). But it's not clear they had to view it that way; the plaintiff was the direct target of the alleged wrongdoing.

Lexmark sells printers, and toner cartridges for its printers, and it recharges used toner cartridges. It attempts to kill any competitive market for recharged cartridges in two ways. It puts a notice on new cartridges stating that the buyer has received a price discount in return for an obligation to return the used cartridge to Lexmark. And it places a chip in the cartridge that prevents a recharged cartridge from working unless Lexmark replaces the chip.

Static Control sells toner and equipment needed to recharge toner cartridges, and it developed a chip that mimics the Lexmark replacement chip. Lexmark sued Static Control; it also told its customers that the Static Control products were illegal. Static Control counterclaimed under the false-advertising provisions of the Lanham Trademark Act. 15 U.S.C. §1125(a)(1)(B) (2012).

As the Court viewed the case, Lexmark and Static Control were not direct competitors. Lexmark sells recharged toner cartridges; Static Control does not. But Static Control had sufficiently alleged that its damages were proximately caused by Lexmark's conduct, for two reasons. First, Lexmark directly disparaged Static Control's product. And second, any loss of business to the companies that recharged cartridges (companies that *were* direct competitors of Lexmark) corresponded one-to-one with loss of business to Static Control; if the direct competitors recharged fewer cartridges, they would buy fewer replacement chips, and Static Control was the only source of those chips. This distinguished cases like *Anza* in note 8.b, where it was hard to know how much plaintiff's business was affected.

Along the way, the Court said that what it had long called "prudential" rules of standing were not part of the law of standing at all, but part of the cause of action, and that unless Congress indicated otherwise, a claim for damages caused by violation of a federal statute must include a showing that plaintiff's damages are within the zone of interests protected by the statute and were proximately caused by the violation of the statute.

11. The Federal Employers' Liability Act. The Federal Employers' Liability Act, 45 U.S.C. §51 *et seq.* (2012), makes railroads liable for on-the-job injuries to employees "resulting in whole or in part" from the employer's negligence. Since Rogers v. Missouri Pacific Railroad Co., 352 U.S. 500 (1957), this language has been understood to dispense with any requirement of proximate cause. Apparently inspired by the RICO cases, by *Dura Pharmaceuticals*, described in the main volume at page 51, and by causation decisions in antitrust cases, the railroad unsuccessfully challenged this rule in CSX Transportation, Inc. v. McBride, 564 U.S. 685 (2011).

The majority thought that "resulting in whole or in part" from the employer's negligence means that it is enough that the employer's negligence played any role, however slight, in causing the injury. But this had not led to absurd results, because there is no negligence unless injury is a foreseeable consequence of the employer's conduct, and because some cases had been dismissed for lack of cause in fact. The Court criticized the great diversity of judicial formulations of proximate cause, and seemed to endorse (but did not adopt) the *Restatement*'s change of vocabulary. The Court also cited studies finding that many or most jurors do not understand instructions on proximate cause.

Chief Justice Roberts, dissenting for himself and Justices Scalia, Thomas, and Alito, thought that both the statutory language and the Court's decision in *Rogers* were aimed only at the defense of contributory negligence, not at proximate cause. They offered extreme hypotheticals in which some injury was foreseeable and the railroad's negligence was a but-for cause of the remote and wholly unforeseeable injury that actually happened.

12. Injury or death to employees. Cantor Fitzgerald is a major financial-services and bond-trading firm. Its offices were at the top of the World Trade Center, and it lost 658 employees on September 11. It sued the airlines for property damage and business-interruption damage. Following what appears to be a quite general rule, the court held that the firm could recover for the losses caused by damage to its property, including its leasehold in the office space, but that it could not recover for damages caused by the loss of its employees. In re September 11 Litigation, 760 F. Supp. 2d 433 (S.D.N.Y. 2011). The claim eventually settled for $135 million. *Cantor Fitzgerald Settles 9/11 Suit Against American Airlines for $135 Million*, N.Y. Times (Dec. 17, 2013).

The stated rule is that defendants owed no duty to the employer not to kill or injure its employees. Stated in more explanatory terms, the employer did not own its employees, who were free to quit at any time. When the employees were killed, the employer's claim is really a form of wrongful death action, but the wrongful death acts specify next of kin or dependents as the proper plaintiffs. The rule appears to be equally settled when the employees are only injured.

Page 109. At the end of note 1, add:
   1. The basics. . . .
Catherine Sharkey traces the decline of the privity rule and the ensuing rise of the economic-loss rule in *The Remains of the Citadel (Economic Loss Rule in Products Cases)*, 100 Minn. L. Rev. 1845 (2016).

Page 110. At the end of note 4, add:
   4. A doctrinal twist? . . .
   The American Law Institute has adopted something like the New York vocabulary, which it says is more widespread than the main volume implies. "Except as provided elsewhere in this Restatement, there is no liability in tort for economic loss caused by negligence in the performance or negotiation of a contract between the parties." *Restatement (Third) of Torts: Liability for Economic Harm* §3 (Tent. Draft 1, 2012). This rule is defined to be the economic-loss rule. All the other applications of the broad principle stated in note 1 in the main volume are also being restated, but they will be stated as separate rules.

Page 110. After note 6, add:
   6.1. The BP oil spill. The Oil Pollution Act requires a party responsible for an oil spill in navigable waters to "establish a procedure for the payment or settlement of claims for interim, short-term damages." 33 U.S.C. §2705 (2012). These payments do not preclude later recovery for "damages not reflected in the paid or settled partial claim." *Id.*
   This provision is the original basis for the much publicized Gulf Coast Claims Facility, a $20-billion fund administered by Kenneth Feinberg, who also administered the September 11 claim fund. The Gulf Coast fund paid more than $6 billion in interim and permanent settlements. It was praised by some as efficient and generous, and condemned by others as standardless and unsupervised. For the former view, see Joe Nocera, *The Phony Settlement*, N.Y. Times (March 10, 2012); for the latter, see George W. Conk, *Diving into the Wreck: BP and Kenneth Feinberg's Gulf Coast Gambit*, 17 Roger Williams L. Rev. 137 (2012).
   Some plaintiffs went to court instead of to the fund. In 2013, the court approved class settlements of all claims of individuals and businesses for property damage, economic loss, or medical harms. In re Oil Spill by the Oil Rig "Deepwater Horizon," 295 F.R.D. 112 (E.D. La. 2013) (medical harms); 910 F. Supp. 2d 891 (E.D. La. 2012) (property damage and economic loss). The medical settlement creates a matrix of objective criteria of injury linked to specified cash awards. Class members will have to show where they fit on the matrix, and prove the objective criteria for eligibility, but issues of liability, causation, measurement of damages, and the like have been reduced to these objective criteria. The property-damage and economic-loss settlement is structurally similar; some class members have to prove causation individually, but many need prove only that their business is in a defined geographic area and that it took in less revenue after the spill than before. Some claimants,

including BP employees, governmental entities, casinos, real estate developers, and financial institutions, are excluded from the class and left to separate litigation. According to press accounts, BP valued the combined settlements at $7.8 billion, but they have no cap. John Schwartz, *Accord Reached Settling Lawsuit over BP Oil Spill*, N.Y. Times (March 3, 2012).

BP later claimed that the lawyer administering the settlement (who also has the title Claims Administrator) was misinterpreting its terms and paying out much more money than anticipated, much of it for "fictitious claims" unconnected to the spill. The Fifth Circuit rejected these arguments. As it read the settlement, claimants must attest under penalty of perjury that all statements on their claim form are true, including a preprinted statement that the form is for businesses "that assert economic loss due to the spill." In re Deepwater Horizon, 744 F.3d 370, 376 (5th Cir. 2014). But they do not need to offer any evidence beyond the objective facts of location and reduced revenue that bring them within the scope of the settlement. "There is nothing fundamentally unreasonable about what BP accepted but now wishes it had not." 744 F.3d at 377.

Awards by the settlement's Claims Administrator are subject to discretionary review in the district court, and the district court's decisions can be appealed. In re Deepwater Horizon, 785 F.3d 986 (5th Cir. 2015). Following similar precedent elsewhere, the court held that when a settlement provides a mechanism for further processing of claims, and that mechanism includes review in the district court, then there is also a right of appeal unless the settlement agreement expressly waives that right.

On July 2, 2015, BP and the government announced an $18.7 billion settlement with the United States, the five Gulf Coast states, and more than 400 local governments along the coast. Campbell Robertson, *et al.*, *BP to Pay $18.7 Billion for Deepwater Horizon Oil Spill*, N.Y. Times (July 3, 2015). This sum includes civil penalties and compensation for economic and environmental damage. The amount was later increased to $20 billion, and the court approved the settlement, to be paid over sixteen years. *Judge Approves Settlement of $20 Billion in BP Oil Spill*, N.Y Times (April 5, 2016). BP estimates its total costs related to the spill at more than $61 billion. Steven Mufson, *BP's Big Bill for the World's Largest Oil Spill Reaches $61.6 Billion*, Washington Post (July 14, 2016). This includes criminal fines; clean-up costs; civil settlements with individuals, businesses, and governments; money paid through the Gulf Coast Claims Facility; and settlements with BP investors mislead about the magnitude of the disaster.

4. Substantive Policy Goals

Page 123. At the end of note 3, add:
3. The loss of illegal employment. . . .
A survey of reported cases finds that *Hoffman Plastics* has gotten a generally hostile reception in the lower courts. Employers have invoked it in all sorts of employment litigation, but just five percent of those cases find an employer substantively liable but refuse monetary relief because of the plaintiff's immigration status. Michael H. LeRoy, *Remedies for Unlawful Alien Workers: One Law for the*

Native and for the Stranger Who Resides in Your Midst? An Empirical Perspective, 28 Geo. Immigration L.J. 623 (2013).

5. The Requirement of Reasonable Certainty

Page 129. At the end of note 2, add:
2. **Resolving uncertainty against the wrongdoer, but requiring reasonable certainty. . . .**

The problem of uncertain damages is extensively analyzed, with many examples from reported cases, in Tun-Jen Chiang, *The Information-Forcing Dilemma in Damages Law*, 59 Wm. & Mary L. Rev. --- (forthcoming 2017), available at http://ssrn.com/abstract=2829179. He argues that the tension in the rules is inherent in the problem courts face. If they award zero because plaintiff failed to prove his damages with sufficient certainty, they do an injustice in the individual case. But if they award their best guess (or let a jury award its best guess), even when the damages are seriously uncertain, they undermine incentives for future plaintiffs to prove their damages more precisely. Courts have said inconsistent things over the years depending on which of these problems loomed larger.

He proposes that courts require as much evidence of damages as it is cost-efficient to produce and require that it be provided by the party who can provide it less expensively. This specifies in economic terms the suggestion in the main volume that plaintiffs prove their damages with as much certainty as is reasonable under the circumstances.

F. Damages Where Value Cannot Be Measured in Dollars

1. Personal Injuries and Death

Page 137. At the end of note 1, add:
1. **A persistent split. . . .**

What appears to be the most detailed survey of jurisdictions is reported in John Campbell, Bernard Chao, & Christopher Robertson, *Time Is Money: Dollars for Days: An Empirical Assessment of Non-Economic Damages Arguments*, Wash. U. L. Rev. (forthcoming), available at http://ssrn.com/abstract=2770616. They report that twenty-three states and the District of Columbia allow a total demand supported by a per diem calculation. Nine states allow a lump sum demand but do not allow a per diem calculation. Two states allow plaintiff to argue for per diem calculations without assigning a value to the unit of time suggested. Four states allow neither a per diem argument nor the mention of a total demand. The remaining states either leave these issues to the discretion of the trial judge or have no identifiable rule. An appendix collects the authorities for each jurisdiction; of course these authorities are clear in some states and fuzzy in others. Campbell and Chao's empirical study is described in supplement to page 140.

Page 140. After note 10, add:

   10.1. More experiments. Campbell and Chao, cited in supplement to note 1, created a forty-minute video of the high points of a medical malpractice trial: expert testimony, jury instructions, and opening and closing argument. The case was designed to be close on liability. They created four variations, with and without a per diem argument and with or without a lump sum demand. So in version 1, the lawyer showed that plaintiff's remaining life expectancy, which would be spent disabled and in pain, was 4,979,520 minutes and asked for $5 million. In version 2, the lawyer said that life expectancy was nine and a half years, and asked for $5 million. In version 3, the lawyer said that he could not suggest a number, but the number should be fair, and he showed that life expectancy was 4,979,520 minutes. And in version 4, the lawyer said that he could not suggest a number, but that it should be fair for the life expectancy of nine and a half years.

   The per diem calculation increased awards modestly; suggesting $5 million increased awards much more dramatically. Awards greater than $5 million were reduced to $5 million in calculating the statistics that follow. The mean award in versions 1 and 2 (with the lump sum anchor) were $2,042,006 and $1,887,500. The mean awards in versions 3 and 4 (without the lump sum) were $714,317 and $473,489. The medians were $1 million, $1 million, $275,000, and $225,000. In a regression equation, the effect of per diem arguments on awards was not statistically significant. These were the awards of individual mock jurors; there was no opportunity for deliberation with others. The authors collect other studies also suggesting that plaintiffs get more when they ask for a big lump sum. This is the anchoring effect described by Professor King and others.

   Mock jurors who heard per diem arguments were more likely to rule for the plaintiff (59 percent of mock jurors versus 51 percent of mock jurors), and that effect was statistically significant. Per diem arguments also had a statistically significant effect on the expected value of the case — the percentage of plaintiff wins times the mean award when plaintiff won.

   A similar study tested high and low anchors and alternatives for how defense counsel might respond. John Campbell, Bernard Chao, Christopher Robertson and David V. Yokum, *Countering the Plaintiff's Anchor: Jury Simulations to Evaluate Damages Arguments*, 101 Iowa L. Rev. 543 (2016). Half the plaintiff's counsel asked for $250,000; half asked for $5 million, which the experimenters thought was unrealistically high on the facts. One third of defense counsel ignored the lump sum demand; one third countered, arguing that there was no liability but if the jury disagreed, damages should not exceed $50,000; and one third ridiculed plaintiff's demand and argued that it showed that the jury could not trust anything the plaintiff and his lawyer said. And this time, the authors used sophisticated statistical methods to simulate jury deliberation, which tended to moderate the responses of individual mock jurors.

   The $5 million demand increased damages from a mean of $65,000 to a mean of $278,000 in the simulated jury deliberations. But the high demand did affect plaintiff's credibility; it significantly reduced the percentage of verdicts for plaintiff. The effect on the magnitude of damages was much bigger than the effect on winning or losing, so the $5 million demand increased the expected value of the case. That makes the unrealistically high demand clearly in the interest of the lawyer, who can average out his experience over many cases. The interests of the client are different. He has only one case, and recovering nothing is a disaster. How to balance the risk of losing against the chance of increasing the verdict is a more complex choice than simply calculating expected values.

When plaintiff asked for $250,000, countering with $50,000 appeared to reduce the size of verdicts and reduce the number of plaintiff verdicts. And most of the differences were statistically significant. Many defense lawyers fear that suggesting a number will be taken to concede liability; this experiment suggests otherwise.

None of the three defense strategies made a statistically significant difference when plaintiff asked for $5 million, perhaps because the variance in the simulated juries' responses was so great that statistical significance was hard to achieve. Just eyeballing the results, countering with the $50,000 figure appeared to substantially reduce the size of verdicts and slightly increase the percentage of plaintiff wins.

Page 140. After note 11, add:

12. History. For a succinct review of the doctrinal evolution of intangible damages, including pain and suffering, emotional distress, and the harms from defamation, see Robert L. Rabin, *Intangible Damages in American Tort Law: A Roadmap*, available at http://ssrn.com/abstract=2727885.

Page 142. At the end of note 5, add:
5. The value of decedent's life to himself. . . .

The Georgia rule appears to have mattered to a recent jury verdict. An SUV with a plastic gas tank mounted behind the rear axle burst into flame in a rear-end collision; a four-year-old boy was burned to death. The jury awarded $30 million for the boy's pain and suffering and $120 million for the value of his life. Punitive damages were not at issue, but the jury found that Chrysler acted with reckless disregard for human life, and the verdict may contain a large punitive element.

Chrysler's motion for new trial said that the wrongful death award was more than eleven times the largest award previously upheld in Georgia, and that the largest previous pain and suffering award was $7 million for a plaintiff who was hospitalized for months, paralyzed, and in severe pain. It argued that $30 million for one minute of suffering, however intense, is irrational. The plaintiffs indicated willingness to accept a remittitur in an amount determined by the court, but they opposed a new trial.

The trial judge reduced the award to $10 million for pain and suffering and $30 million for the value of the child's life. He refused to grant a new trial, calling the evidence at the first trial "overwhelming."

These facts were taken from news accounts. *Judge Cuts Award to Family of Boy Killed in Jeep Crash*, N.Y. Times (July 29, 2015); Mike Spector, *Family Rejects New Jeep-Fire Trial*, Wall St. J. (June 9, 2015); *Fiat Chrysler Seeks New Trial in Georgia Jeep Fire Case*, N.Y. Times (May 8, 2015); *Jury Makes Chrysler Pay $150 Million to Family of Boy Killed in Jeep Grand Cherokee*, N.Y. Times (Apr. 3, 2015).

Page 150. After note 2, add:

    2.1. An update. If I read the docket sheet correctly, all the wrongful death, personal injury, and property damage claims against the airlines were settled or resolved in the district court by summer of 2014 — thirteen years after the events. There is a separate set of claims by first responders, clean-up workers, and neighboring property owners who were injured by hazardous materials at the site. Many of these claims have settled, some with the help of a claims administrator. See, e.g., In re World Trade Center Disaster Site Litigation, 124 F. Supp. 3d 281 (S.D.N.Y. 2015). Others are still pending, and two questions of state law were recently certified to the New York Court of Appeals. In re World Trade Center Lower Manhattan Disaster Site Litigation, 846 F.3d 58 (2d Cir. 2017).

2. The Controversy over Tort Law

Page 159. At the end of note 1, add:
    1. More recent decisions. . . .
    Overruling an earlier decision, the Missouri court has held that the state's $350,000 cap on "noneconomic" damages violates the state's right to jury trial. Watts v. Lester E. Cox Medical Centers, 376 S.W.3d 633 (Mo. 2012). The jury had awarded $1,450,000 in damages subject to the cap, plus $3.4 million in future medical expenses, to a child born with catastrophic brain injuries. The Kansas court upheld that state's $250,000 cap on "noneconomic" damages. Miller v. Johnson, 289 P.3d 1098 (Kan. 2012). And the Fifth Circuit, applying its prediction of Mississippi law, has upheld that state's damage cap on "noneconomic" damages against jury trial and separation of powers challenges. Learmonth v. Sears, Roebuck and Co., 710 F.3d 249 (5th Cir. 2013).

    The Florida court struck down a million-dollar cap on "noneconomic" damages in cases of medical malpractice resulting in death or "catastrophic" injury; the cap was $500,000 in lesser cases. Estate of McCall v. United States, 134 So.2d 894 (Fla. 2014). And the Oregon court upheld a $3 million cap on total damages in suits against the state, without relying on sovereign immunity, but simply applying the state's right to jury trial and right to a remedy. Horton v. Oregon Health & Science University, 376 P.3d 998 (Or. 2016). The jury had awarded just over $12,000,000, half of it for "economic" damages.

    The Maryland court has invalidated, under a remedy-for-every-wrong clause, a statute granting immunity to landlords for damages caused by lead-based paint. Jackson v. Dackman Co., 30 A.3d 854 (Md. 2011). The court said that the legislature could abolish common law remedies and substitute statutory remedies, but that here, the statutory remedy was "totally inadequate and unreasonable." *Id.* at 868. The plaintiff child had suffered permanent brain damage; the statutory remedy could provide a maximum of $17,000 in compensation if it applied, and in this case, it appeared not to apply. This reasoning suggests that reasonable damage caps may be permitted, and that unreasonably low damage caps may be unconstitutional.

    A fair number of courts and commentators have attempted to collect the state supreme court cases upholding or invalidating damage caps. Most of these lists contain cases that others missed. Some courts distinguish different kinds of caps, as in *Arbino*, and some courts have overruled earlier decisions. So no simple count of cases will ever be entirely accurate. But for a general indication, I compiled the cases cited in several recent sources. The most recent decision in 20 states upheld caps; the most recent decision in 12 states struck down caps. Five other state constitutions expressly prohibit damage caps, sometimes with an exception for workers' compensation. In two more states, the state constitution expressly prohibits caps in wrongful death cases.

Federal courts have generally treated damage caps and other tort reform measures as economic regulation subject to deferential review. The Eighth Circuit collected some of the federal cases in the course of upholding Nebraska's $1.75 million cap on total compensation (not just on "noneconomic" damages) in a case where a jury awarded $17 million to a baby with profound brain damage. Schmidt v. Ramsey, 2017 WL 2674339 (8th Cir. June 22, 2017).

Page 164. After note 6, add:

6.1. A medical malpractice update. New studies using the federal database of malpractice payouts on behalf of physicians find substantial declines in the number of claims and stability or modest decline in the size of payouts. The database begins in 1992. Claims declined gradually from 1992 to 2001, mostly because of a very substantial drop in small claims resulting in payouts under $50,000. Claims of all sizes declined more substantially after 2001. The effect was large in states that had not enacted caps on damages, and larger in states that had. Overall, claims paid per physician declined 57 percent from 1992 to 2012.

The mean payout in large claims (that is, excluding all those under $50,000) was $416,000 in 1992 and $426,000 in 2012, both in 2011 dollars. This number increased modestly in states without caps or with caps already in effect before 1992; it declined by 21 percent in states with newly enacted caps. The combined result of fewer claims and stable payouts in large claims is a sharp drop in annual malpractice payments per physician. This number was $7500 in 1992, peaked at $8200 in 2001, and dropped to $3850 in 2012 — 0.11 percent (11/100 of one percent) of total spending on health care. Myungho Paik, Bernard Black, & David A. Hyman, *The Receding Tide of Medical Malpractice Litigation: Part 1 — National Trends*, 10 J. Empirical Legal Stud. 612 (2013).

Newly enacted caps on damages reduce both the number of claims and the payout per claim, and as would be expected, the effect is concentrated on larger claims. Other tort reform provisions had no measurable effect on claims or payouts. Myungho Paik, Bernard Black, & David A. Hyman, *The Receding Tide of Medical Malpractice Litigation: Part 2 — Effect of Damage Caps*, 10 J. Empirical Legal Stud. 639 (2013).

The decline in claims and payouts in states without damage caps indicates that something else is going on — changed behavior by actors in the system. Maybe physicians and hospitals have improved their safety practices; maybe jurors are bringing in smaller verdicts; maybe insurers are bargaining harder over settlements; maybe some combination of these or of other less obvious possibilities.

Page 165. After note 8, add:

   8.1. The significance of the defendant. Defendant's apparent wealth is legally irrelevant, but in practice, it is highly significant. This tension was at issue in Hand v. Howell, Sarto & Howell, 131 So.3d 599 (Ala. 2013). Hand was seriously injured in a collision with a reporter for the Montgomery *Advertiser*, a newspaper owned by Gannett, a major publishing company. The reporter was on the job and clearly at fault. Hand's original lawyers sued only the reporter, and the case settled for $625,000. Hand sued those lawyers, alleging that it was malpractice not to name the *Advertiser* as an additional defendant.

   An accountant retained to testify for Hand estimated his "economic" losses — medical expenses and lost income — at $872,000. The personal injury lawyers who represented him after he fired the original lawyers estimated the settlement value of the case against the *Advertiser* at $1 to $1.2 million. The reporter was covered by Gannett's $5 million insurance policy, so the lost settlement value was not a result of policy limits. The new lawyers simply said that a claim against an individual was worth far less than the same claim against the newspaper, which a jury would perceive as a deep pocket. In the malpractice case, Hand said that "every trial lawyer in the country" would agree with this assessment. *Id.* at 603.

   The majority said that was irrelevant even if true. The court "must presume that juries will follow the law," and under the law, the identity, wealth, and corporate status of the defendant are all irrelevant. *Id.* Three dissenters (on a court of eight) voted for reality over theory.

Page 168. At the end of note 2, add:

   2. The value of a statistical life. . . .

   Each federal agency sets its own number for the value of a human life, and there is considerable variation from agency to agency. But in general, agencies in the Obama Administration used higher numbers than agencies in the George W. Bush Administration. Binyamin Appelbaum, *As U.S. Agencies Put More Value on Life, Businesses Fret*, N.Y. Times (Feb. 17, 2011). The Obama people said they were just applying the most recent studies and adjusting for inflation; business groups accused them of inflating the numbers to justify more regulations. Kip Viscusi, a long-time advocate of these statistical methods, said that "[a]gencies have been using numbers that I thought were just too low." The increases began flipping political biases; businesses that liked statistical valuations when they showed that life was cheap were souring on the method. Labor and consumer groups said they still didn't like the method, but that if it is going to be used, then it should set higher values.

   Illustrative numbers cited by the *Times*: the Environmental Protection Agency valued a human life at $6.8 million during the Bush years, but $9.1 million in 2010. The Food and Drug Administration valued a life at $5 million in 2008, but $7.9 million in 2010. And some agencies began suggesting that some deaths may be worth more than others. The EPA said that people might pay more to avoid a slow death from cancer, and perhaps somewhat inconsistently, the Department of Homeland Security said people might pay more to avoid sudden deaths from terrorism.

Page 170. At the end of note 4, add:
4. Trading incommensurables and the feasible level of safety. . . .
The Masur & Posner article is now published at 77 U. Chi. L. Rev. 657 (2010).

3. Dignitary and Constitutional Harms

Page 174. At the end of note 1, add:
1. The strip-search cases. . . .
The law had been against the jailers in these cases, but the law has changed. Florence v. Board of Chosen Freeholders, 566 U.S. 318 (2012), upheld routine strip searches of all arrestees who are placed in the jail's general population, no matter how trivial the offense. There were four dissents.

The Court reserved judgment on whether arrestees held briefly and separately from the general population (which appear to have been the facts in *Levka*) could be strip searched without reasonable suspicion. And nothing in *Florence* suggests that it would be lawful to strip search women but not men, as in *Levka*. So *Levka* may still be good law even on liability. However that turns out, the opinion is still a great vehicle for exploring the difficulties of proving, rebutting, and measuring damages for emotional distress.

Page 176. Add the following additional examples in note 2:
2. Other examples. . . .
e. . . .
The Texas Supreme Court has unanimously reaffirmed the traditional rule in a substantial and wide-ranging opinion. The court characterized the emotional loss from the death of a pet as a form of loss of consortium, which is recoverable in Texas only by statute and only by spouses and children. It would be anomalous if one could recover for the death of a pet but not for the death of a sibling. And a majority of pet-welfare groups argued against liability, fearing a litigation burden on veterinarians and animal shelters that would raise the cost of pet ownership and ultimately result in more abandoned or euthanized pets. The court authorized recovery of the pet's value to the owner, not including emotional value. Medlen v. Strickland, 397 S.W.3d 184 (Tex. 2013).

But there are cases allowing emotional-distress damages against persons who intentionally kill or injure a pet. Plotnik v. Meihaus, 146 Cal. Rptr. 3d 585, 600-601 (Ct. App. 2012) (allowing such damages and collecting cases). For cases allowing recovery of the medical expenses of caring for an injured pet, see supplement to page 33. . . .
g. . . .
A student on Staten Island was killed in an auto accident. The medical examiner for the county performed an autopsy and then released the body to the family for burial. Two months later, forensic-science students from decedent's high school took a field trip to the county morgue. One of them saw decedent's brain, labeled with his name, sitting in a jar on a shelf. It was soon revealed that the county had retained the brain and parts of other internal organs for later examination. The family's priest said

that the burial was not proper without the brain; the family attended a second funeral and burial.

A jury awarded each parent $500,000 for violation of their common law right to have the body for burial. The Appellate Division reduced this to $300,000 each — $600,000 in all — with little explanation. Shipley v. City of New York, 963 N.Y.S.2d 692 (App. Div. 2013). The facts are taken from the opinion of the Court of Appeals, which reversed on the ground that no rights had been violated. 37 N.E.3d 58 (N.Y. 2015). . . .

    h. . . .

There's a good chance that you already read somewhere that a Florida jury awarded $140 million — $55 million for economic harm, $60 million for emotional distress, and $25 million punitives — to retired wrestler Hulk Hogan against Gawker Media, for posting on the web a brief clip from a surreptitiously shot video of Hogan having sex with his best friend's wife. Nick Madigan and Ravi Somaiya, *Hulk Hogan Awarded $115 Million in Privacy Suit Against Gawker*, N.Y. Times (March 18, 2016); Steven Perlberg, *Gawker Begins Appeal of $140 Million Hulk Hogan Verdict*, Wall St. J. (April 5, 2016). The "friend" had urged his wife to have sex with Hogan and the "friend" had set up the camera. Gawker filed for bankruptcy, sold its business to Univision, and settled with Hogan for $31 million. Sydney Ember, *Gawker and Hulk Hogan Reach $31 Million Settlement*, N.Y. Times (Nov. 2, 2016). Such post-verdict settlements are common. Plaintiff accepts less than the jury awarded in exchange for defendant dropping its appeal. . . .

    j. The Second Circuit has upheld $1,320,000 in compensatory damages for management's failure to protect a black employee from a three-year campaign of unusually severe racial harassment; many examples are set out in the opinion. Turley v. ISG Lackawanna, Inc., 774 F.3d 140 (2d Cir. 2014). The emotional damage may be permanent. The victim had once been happy and confident, but at the time of trial, he suffered from panic attacks, depression, and post-traumatic stress disorder; one witness described him as a "broken" man. The court said the award "tests the boundaries," but under the "exceptional and egregious facts of this case," it was "fair and reasonable." *Id.* at 163. The opinion collects somewhat similar cases from elsewhere.

G. Taxes, Time, and the Value of Money

2. Interest on Past Damages

Page 200. At the end of note 7, add:

7. Postjudgment interest. . . .

In Gianetti v. Norwalk Hospital, 43 A.3d 567 (Conn. 2012), the trial court denied both prejudgment and postjudgment interest, and the state supreme court found no abuse of discretion. The court found that defendant litigated in good faith, and that the damages could not be calculated until the lost-volume-seller issue (supplement to page 38) was finally resolved in 2012. Connecticut appears to take a rather narrow view of when to award interest.

This is the third decision in the state supreme court; the doctor was discharged in 1983, and the first judgment on liability was entered in 1987. Apart from the repeated appeals, I have not been able to learn why a simple suit for breach of contract took twenty-nine years to resolve. The court did not appear to blame the litigation delays on either side.

Page 200. After note 10, add:

11. Substance and procedure. The Second Circuit has reaffirmed its rule that prejudgment interest is substantive, so that state law controls interest on state-law claims. In re September 11 Litigation, 802 F.3d 314 (2d Cir. 2015). This seems clearly right; the interest rate directly affects the amount of compensation for plaintiff's state-law injuries. But it does not appear to be a settled rule.

There is a federal statute on postjudgment interest, which is generally treated as procedural in diversity cases. Cappiello v. ICD Publications, Inc., 720 F.3d 109 (2d Cir. 2013). This also affects the amount of compensation, but courts have said that the statute is at least arguably procedural. It controls the effect of a federal judgment and, at least when interest rates are higher, tends to deter frivolous appeals in federal courts.

The federal statute that creates the claim in the September 11 cases requires the application of state substantive law, and a New York statute requires 9 percent interest, both pre and postjudgment, on contract claims and claims for property damage. N.Y. C.P.L.R. §§5001 to 5004 (LexisNexis 2003). Nine percent under the New York statute is vastly better for plaintiffs than the Treasury bill rate under federal law.

3. The Net Present Value of Future Damages

Page 214. At the end of note 2, add:
2. The "tort reform" proposals. . . .
A Missouri statute provides that future damages may be paid, "in whole or in part," in installments over the plaintiff's life expectancy, plus interest at the 52-week Treasury-bill rate. That rate has been extremely low for years; in May 2011, when judgment was entered, it was 0.26 percent. The Missouri court held that it was an abuse of discretion to pay any part of the damages for future medical expenses over fifty years at that interest rate. Watts v. Lester E. Cox Medical Center, 376 S.W.3d 633 (Mo. 2012). The court noted that medical inflation would be much greater, and that the judgment guaranteed that plaintiff would not have adequate funds for medical care.

CHAPTER THREE

PUNITIVE REMEDIES

A. Punitive Damages

1. Common Law and Statutes

Page 226. At the end of note 1, add:
1. Why punitive damages? . . .
The Calandrillo article is now published at 78 Geo. Wash. L. Rev. 774 (2010).

Page 232. At the end of note 6, add:
6. Should wealth matter? . . .
The mandamus petition in *Jacobs* was dismissed. The judgment in *Motorola* remains uncollected; for an update, see this supplement to page 841.

Page 233. After note 7, add:
8. **Other federal claims.** Punitive damages are available for federal constitutional claims and for some statutory claims. *Exxon*'s general approach applies to these claims unless there is some more specific statutory provision. An example is Turley v. ISG Lackawanna, Inc., 774 F.3d 140 (2d Cir. 2014), a racial-harassment case more fully described in this supplement to page 176. The claims were based on state and federal civil rights laws and intentional infliction of emotional distress. The jury awarded $24 million in punitives, which the trial court reduced to $5 million. Reviewing this amount first under "federal common law," and then under the Constitution, the court of appeals ordered a further remittitur to two times compensatories, or $2.5 million against the corporate defendants. *Id.* at 164. The court said a 2:1 ratio was appropriate, despite the very large and ill-defined compensatories, because of "the extreme nature of defendants' conduct." *Id.* at 167. An award of $1,250 against a supervisor was not disturbed.

Claims of race discrimination can be brought under 42 U.S.C. §1981 (2012), which has no damages cap. Claims of discrimination based on sex, religion, national origin, or disability can be brought under 42 U.S.C. §1981a (2012), which caps compensatory and punitive damages combined at $300,000 for large employers and various smaller amounts for smaller employers. Plaintiffs in these categories can often join a claim under a state civil rights law with their federal claims, and many of the state laws have no caps.

Where the $300,000 combined cap applies, the Ninth Circuit recently held that it displaces the Supreme Court's analysis of ratios. The combined cap reverses the logic of ratios; the larger the compensatories, the smaller the possible punitives. The injuries are sometimes emotional and hard to value, and if the jury awards nominal damages plus punitives, the nominals do not attempt to measure the actual damages. The jury in a sexual-harassment case awarded $1 in nominal damages and $868,750 in punitives, which the trial court reduced to the $300,000 cap. Finding defendant's conduct sufficiently reprehensible to justify a maximum award, the court of appeals affirmed. Arizona v. ASARCO LLC, 773 F.3d 1050 (9th Cir. 2014) (en banc).

2. The Constitution

Page 240. At the end of note 5, add:
5. Ratios. . . .
In Hamlin v. Hampton Lumber Mills, Inc., 246 P.3d 1121 (Or. 2011), the court upheld $6,000 in compensatory damages and $175,000 in punitives in an employment-discrimination case. The majority collected cases from around the country upholding high ratios, and concluded that ratios are "of limited assistance" when compensatories are small and do not "already serve an admonitory function." *Id.* at 1128. The dissenters thought that the Supreme Court's approval of greater-than-single-digit ratios in cases with small compensatories was confined to cases of "egregious misconduct." *Id.* at 1132 (Gillette, J., dissenting).

Page 247. At the end of note 6.a, add:
a. The Florida tobacco litigation. . . .
The Supreme Court of Florida held that the class action findings were claim preclusive, not issue preclusive, but it seems to have really meant a sort of hybrid. The issues decided in the class action went to defendants' conduct, and on those issues, all arguments actually litigated or that could have been litigated were barred. But each plaintiff still had to prove class membership, causation, and damages; class membership required proof that he smoked because he was addicted. Philip Morris USA, Inc. v. Douglas, 110 So.3d 419 (Fla. 2013). Both the Florida court and the Eleventh Circuit rejected the argument that this use of claim preclusion violates due process. *Douglas*; Graham v. R.J. Reynolds Tobacco Co., 857 F.3d 1169 (11th Cir. 2017) (en banc); Walker v. R.J. Reynolds Tobacco Co., 734 F.3d 1278 (11th Cir. 2013) (panel). The Supreme Court has repeatedly denied cert on the tobacco companies' due process claims.

The cases are reviewed in Martina S. Barash, *Settlement Prospects Uncertain, Cases Still Numerous in Tobacco Products*, 83 U.S.L.W. 1391 (Mar. 24, 2015). A Morgan Stanley report found 124 cases tried to verdict, with 77 plaintiff wins and 47 wins for the tobacco companies, and total awards of $515 million, or about $6.7 million per successful plaintiff. Of course there was a very wide range on either side of this mean. The remaining 415 federal cases had recently settled for $100 million, or about $240,000 each. Thousands of cases were still pending in state court, where judges have imposed less pressure to try the cases quickly.

Both the en banc Eleventh Circuit and the Florida Supreme Court have rejected the argument that giving preclusive effect to the *Engle* findings makes it a violation of a state-law tort duty for any tobacco company to sell a cigarette in Florida, and that the *Engle*-progeny litigation is therefore preempted by the congressional decision not to ban cigarettes. *Graham*; R.J. Reynolds Tobacco Co. v. Marotta, 214 So.3d 590 (Fla. 2017). Cert petitions are to be expected.

A lawyer commenting on the *Graham* decision said that plaintiffs have been winning about two-thirds of the cases, typically for seven or eight figures. But plaintiff verdicts have varied in amount from zero to billions. Lawyers for both sides agreed that the tobacco companies are reluctant to settle and that the three- to four-thousand remaining cases are likely to drag on. Martina Barash, *Florida Tobacco Plaintiffs, Health Advocates Breathe Easier*, 85 U.S.L.W. 1666 (June 1, 2017).

Page 248. At the end of note 8, add:
   8. Sharing punitives with the state. . . .

The Indiana court has again upheld a statute awarding 75 percent of punitive damages to the state, and capping punitive damages at three times compensatories or $50,000, whichever is greater. State v. Doe, 987 N.E.2d 1066 (Ind. 2013). Indiana is one of the six states counted in the Sharkey survey cited in the main volume.

   9. The state's share in *Philip Morris*. An Oregon statute makes 60 percent of all punitive damage awards payable to the state. Philip Morris refused to pay the state's share on the ground that the state had released its claim in a 1998 global tobacco settlement of state claims for medical expenses incurred by smokers and paid by states through Medicaid benefits or employee health-insurance plans. The court rejected that defense, holding that Oregon's right to a share of the punitive award to Williams arose from the statute and the private tort judgment, and was not included in the 1998 release of claims for medical expenses. Williams v. RJ Reynolds Tobacco Co., 271 P.3d 103 (Or. 2011).

The opinion also revealed a joint litigation agreement between the Williams family and the state, in which they agreed to cooperate to ensure that Philip Morris paid the entire judgment, and to divide the judgment in different ways depending on the course of the litigation. None of the agreed splits matched the 60/40 split specified by statute. *Id.* at 107 n.7.

B. Other Punitive Remedies

1. Statutory Recoveries by Private Litigants

Page 258. After note 1.d, add:
   e. No standing? The business community tried to use standing doctrine to generalize a rule that no plaintiff could recover statutory damages without first proving actual damages. The Court did not go so far, but it gave defendants part of what they wanted in Spokeo, Inc. v. Robins, 136 S. Ct. 1540 (2016). Users can search for anybody's name on Spokeo, and it will search public records for that name and provide a report. It is not clear that it makes any effort to distinguish individuals with the same name; it certainly does not try very hard. Spokeo reported lots of false information about Robins, but it said he hadn't been harmed because the false information was positive. It reported him married, wealthy, and highly educated, when none of that was true. He said the report hurt his job searches by making him appear over qualified. And he said it didn't matter whether he had been injured. The Fair Credit Reporting Act, 15 U.S.C. §1681 *et seq.* (2012), authorized a recovery of $100 to $1000 for each violation, plus attorneys' fees, without proof of actual damages. He alleged not just that Spokeo had failed to use reasonable care to avoid

errors, but also that it had violated several of the Act's procedural requirements. And he filed it as a class action.

The Court said that standing requires "injury in fact," which must be "concrete and particularized," and that these were two requirements, not one. Congress can create new statutory rights, and violations of those rights can be an injury in fact, but not automatically. Robins's alleged injuries were particularized; the false information was about him, and people searching his name had not received required notices about him. But the Court was skeptical about whether all these injuries were concrete, and it remanded for further inquiry. It said that intangible injuries can be concrete. But it noted that a report of a mistaken Zip Code could not inflict concrete injury, so false information was not automatically enough, and it doubted that the procedural violations had inflicted concrete injury. This holding clearly undermines many applications of statutory minimum recoveries; to what extent remains to be seen.

f. The Patent Act. The Patent Act provides that the court or jury "shall award the claimant damages adequate to compensate for the infringement, but in no event less than a reasonable royalty," and that "the court may increase the damages up to three times the amount found or assessed." 35 U.S.C. §1984 (2012). The statutory text gives no guidance as to when damages should be increased or how much.

The Court interpreted this provision in light of a long line of decisions under similar provisions dating back to the Patent Act of 1836. Halo Electronics, Inc. v. Pulse Electronics, Inc., 136 S. Ct. 1923 (2016). Enhanced damages should be reserved for "egregious cases of culpable behavior." *Id.* at 1932, The Court put the focus on the infringer's "subjective willfulness" and on what the infringer knew and intended, and not on the "objective" unreasonableness that was the first step in the Federal Circuit's three-part test. *Id.* at 1933. As administered by the Federal Circuit, objective unreasonableness meant that even egregiously willful infringers were protected if their lawyer could think of a non-frivolous argument in response to the suit for infringement. The Court heard two cases, and remanded both for application of its new approach.

Page 259. After note 2.c, add:

3. Constitutionality. Defendants sued for sharing files of copyrighted music have argued, without much success so far, that statutory recoveries should be subject to the Court's constitutional limits on punitive damages. The leading Supreme Court case on constitutional limits on statutory recoveries is still St. Louis, Iron Mountain & Southern Railway v. Williams, 251 U.S. 63 (1919). For what it is worth, the Court said:

> That [the Due Process Clause] places a limitation upon the power of the states to prescribe penalties for violations of their laws has been fully recognized, but always with the express or tacit qualification that the states still possess a wide latitude of discretion in the matter, and that their enactments transcend the limitation only where the penalty prescribed is so severe and oppressive as to be wholly disproportioned to the offense and obviously unreasonable.

Id. at 66-67.

The court of appeals applied this deferential standard to a file-sharing case in *Capitol Records, Inc. v. Thomas-Rassett*, 692 F.3d 899 (8th Cir. 2012). It refused to apply the three "guideposts" from the Supreme Court's punitive damages cases. The statute gives notice of the possible penalty, thus addressing one of the Supreme Court's concerns about punitive damages. Statutory recoveries for copyright infringement could not be proportioned to compensatory damages; they were enacted because compensatory damages are so hard to measure. They could not be compared to statutory civil penalties; they *were* the statutory civil penalty.

The Copyright Act authorizes statutory damages of not less than $750 nor more than $150,000 for each willful violation. 17 U.S.C. §504(c) (2012). Is that any better notice than the common law of punitive damages? The amount is to be determined in the discretion of the finder of fact, and either side has a right to jury trial. In *Thomas-Rassett*, the record companies proved 24 violations. For reasons not relevant here, the case was tried three times to three different juries, which brought in verdicts of $222,000, $1,920,000, and $1,500,000. Thomas-Rassett may have hurt herself with the juries by destroying her hard drive and giving implausible testimony that might have been perceived as perjury. The district court held that any award greater than $54,000 ($750 per violation, trebled) would be unconstitutional, and entered judgment for that amount. The court of appeals reversed, and reinstated the $222,000 verdict. The record companies did not ask it to reinstate either of the million-dollar-plus verdicts.

There is a similar holding, with less detailed reasoning, in Sony BMG Music Entertainment v. Tenenbaum, 719 F.3d 67 (1st Cir. 2013). The court upheld a jury verdict of $675,000, apparently based on $22,500 per song for each of the 30 songs that Sony pursued at trial. Defendant had distributed many more songs than those 30; this fact influenced the court and probably the jury as well.

The emergence of subscription plans at reasonable prices has reportedly led to dramatic declines in amateur online piracy, so this issue may fade away.

Page 261. At the end of note 5, add:
    5. Statutory reform. . . .
The Court has interpreted the underlying statute to preclude joint-and-several liability. Each member of a conspiracy can be required to forfeit the crime proceeds that he received, but he cannot be required to pay an amount equal to the crime proceeds that others received. Honeycutt v. United States, 137 S. Ct. 1626 (2017).

CHAPTER FOUR

PREVENTING HARM: THE MEASURE OF INJUNCTIVE RELIEF

A. The Scope of Injunctions

1. Preventing Wrongful Acts

Page 268. After note 9, add:

9.1. How high a standard? *Almurbati* says only that the threatened injury cannot be "remote and speculative." Putting the point more affirmatively, the Court said in *Lyons* that plaintiff must be "realistically threatened." *Id.* at 109. I used a similar formulation without attribution in note 8: there must be "a substantial or realistic threat."

In Clapper v. Amnesty International, USA, 568 U.S. 398 (2013), the Court emphasized that the threatened injury "must be *certainly* impending." *Id.* at 409. It cited several cases for this proposition; it also acknowledged a similar number of cases saying that a "substantial risk" is sufficient. *Id.* at 414 n.5. Justice Breyer, dissenting for four, compiled a longer list of cases requiring substantial risk or some similar formulation, and argued that the Supreme Court had never required literal certainty in a holding. In *Clapper*, the majority said that plaintiffs also failed to satisfy the substantial-risk test, and it characterized their threatened injury as "highly speculative" and "highly attenuated." *Id.* at 410.

Supreme Court ripeness doctrine is widely viewed as inconsistent and highly manipulable, so the variety of formulations is no surprise. In *Clapper*, the Court was visibly influenced by the national-security context; plaintiffs sought to challenge key parts of the government's monitoring of electronic communications in its search for terrorists.

In Susan B. Anthony List v. Driehaus, 134 S. Ct. 2334 (2014), the Court returned to the standard of "a credible threat" of injury — in that case, of prosecution for conduct that was allegedly constitutionally protected. *Clapper*'s standard was quoted as injury "certainly impending" *or* a "substantial risk." *Driehaus* is further described in this supplement to 597.

9.2. Constitutional and remedial ripeness. Ripeness is a constitutional and jurisdictional doctrine as well as a remedial doctrine. The principal cases in the main volume are written in terms of the law of injunctions; *Clapper* is written in terms of the law of standing to sue. The doctrines are related, and a case that is not ripe under one doctrine is unlikely to be ripe under the other. But the doctrines emphasize different purposes, and at least in theory, those purposes might occasionally suggest different results.

Constitutional ripeness emphasizes separation of powers, limiting the jurisdiction of courts, and reducing the occasions on which they interfere with judgments committed to the other two branches of government. Remedial ripeness emphasizes the competing interests of plaintiff and defendant and whether an injunction is really needed. These may just be two ways of talking about substantially the same thing, but the choice at least affects the tone of the opinions.

Page 269. After note 13, add:

   14. The merits in *Almurbati*. The Supreme Court subsequently held that courts must defer to a determination of the executive branch that a detainee is not likely to be tortured if transferred to a foreign country. Munaf v. Geren, 553 U.S. 674, 702 (2008). There are issues that remain open after *Munaf*, but this holding would pose another major obstacle to relief to any plaintiffs who succeed in showing a ripe threat of transfer.

Paged 274. After note 7, add:

   8. Leveling up or leveling down? Statutes sometimes openly discriminate, extending some government benefit to one set of people but not to others claiming to be similarly situated. When a court finds such discrimination unconstitutional, a recurring issue is whether to extend the benefit to those excluded or take it away from those preferred. Either will remedy the discrimination, but the latter will not give the plaintiff what he wanted.

   The Court returned to this issue in Sessions v. Morales-Santana, 137 S. Ct. 1678 (2017). The issue was the citizenship status of children born abroad to one parent who was a U.S. citizen and one who was not. If the parents were married, or if they were unmarried and the U.S. citizen was the father, the citizen parent had to have been physically present in the United States for a continuous *five*-year period at sometime (anytime) prior to the birth. But if the parents were unmarried and the U.S. citizen was the mother, the child was a citizen if the mother had been physically present in the United States for a continuous *one*-year period at sometime prior to the birth. However such a bizarre distinction emerged, the Court held that it was unconstitutional sex discrimination.

   The Court said that the choice of remedy depends on legislative intent, which almost certainly will not have been stated. "Ordinarily," the proper remedy is to extend the benefit to the disadvantaged class. But here, Congress seemed to care more about physical attachment to the country than about blood lines alone. The class subject to the five-year rule — all married parents and all unmarried parents where the father was the citizen — was larger than the class subject to the one-year rule. And Congress surely would not want to discriminate only against married parents, So the Court decided that the appropriate remedy on these facts was to apply the five-year rule to all children born abroad to citizen/non-citizen parents. No doubt the Court was also influenced by the importance of conferring citizenship, a benefit that cannot be revoked or repealed by later legislation.

   Justices Thomas and Alito thought the decision to refuse a remedy made it unnecessary to decide the merits. Sometimes in situations like this, the Court gives a remedy to the first litigant to bring the issue to the Supreme Court, even as it denies a remedy to future litigants similarly situated. See note 5 at pages 497-498 of the main volume.

Page 275. After note 8, add:

   8.1. The Securities and Exchange Commission. The SEC, and probably some other government agencies too, are great fans of obey-the-law injunctions in civil-enforcement litigation. And they often get them. But the Eleventh Circuit held that

SEC cases are subject to Rule 65(d)(1), more or less like any other case. SEC v. Goble, 682 F.3d 934 (11th Cir. 2012).

The court said that some provisions of some statutes are sufficiently specific that an injunction tracking the terms of such a statute complies with the Rule. This was the court's explanation of McComb v. Jacksonville Paper Co., 336 U.S. 187 (1949), discussed in the main volume at pages 823 and 826-827. *McComb* enforced an injunction that largely restated key provisions of the Fair Labor Standards Act, and it seems to me to have turned more on the egregiousness and variety of the violations than on the specificity of the statute.

On its reading of *McComb*, the Eleventh Circuit thought it obvious that the broad anti-fraud provisions of the securities laws are not sufficiently specific to support an obey-the-law injunction. And even for two statutory sections that it viewed as more specific, the court refused to approve an injunction that simply said to obey section such and such. Instead, it required that the specific terms of the provision be set out in the injunction.

Page 276. At the end of the Note on Individual and Class Injunctions, add:

In Monsanto Co. v. Geertson Seed Farms, 561 U.S. 139 (2010), the Court said that "Respondents in this case do not represent a class, so they could not seek to enjoin [enforcement of] such an [administrative agency] order on the ground that it might cause harm to other parties." *Id.* at 163. This is not quite the same question as who the injunction might explicitly protect, but it is related. Justice Stevens, in a solitary dissent, responded that "although we have not squarely addressed the issue, in my view '[t]here is no general requirement that an injunction affect only the parties in the suit.'" *Id.* at 181 n.12, quoting Bresgal v. Brock, 843 F.2d 1163, 1169 (9th Cir. 1987). This was a minor point in each opinion, but definitely part of the rationale for resolving at least one issue in the case. The principal issues in *Monsanto* are described in this supplement to page 428.

Much of the confusion in the same-sex marriage cases around the country arose from a striking neglect of this issue. These cases were nearly all filed as individual actions by one or a few couples; there were few class certifications. Yet federal district judges repeatedly issued statewide injunctions protecting all same-sex couples, and so far as I am aware, only Alabama officials ever raised the issue. We repeatedly saw dozens or hundreds of couples getting married in the first days after a district court's order, often while defendants scrambled to get a stay of that order. Defendants might have done better to focus the district court's attention on the scope of the order it should issue in the first place. Couples not party to the litigation would get the protection of precedent once a judgment is affirmed on appeal, and all couples throughout the country are now protected by the precedential effect of the Supreme Court's marriage decision. Obergefell v. Hodges, 135 S. Ct. 2584 (2015). With all but the most obstreperous defendants, unambiguous precedent is good enough. But a trial court opinion has no precedential effect; only the judgment is binding. So the scope of the injunction was a critical issue that both sides neglected.

Professor Bray views the marriage cases not as an example of neglecting a rule limiting relief to the plaintiffs, but as an example of increasingly routine acceptance of injunctions *not* limited to the plaintiffs. Samuel L. Bray, *Multiple Chancellors:*

Reforming the National Injunction, 131 Harv. L. Rev. --- (forthcoming) available at https://ssrn.com/abstract=2864175. He focuses on nationwide injunctions against enforcement of allegedly unconstitutional federal regulations. He argues that such injunctions reward forum shopping; conservatives plaintiffs sought nationwide injunctions against Obama regulations in Texas, and liberal plaintiffs sought nationwide injunctions against Bush regulations in California. And when a nationwide injunction against enforcement of a federal regulation issues, the Supreme Court is more or less forced to review the first case, without waiting for a circuit split and broader and deeper exploration of the issue in the courts of appeals.

Page 279. After note 3, add:

    3.1. Change of administration. The Court applied the voluntary cessation doctrine without controversy in Trinity Lutheran Church v. Comer, 137 S. Ct. 2012 (2017). The church initially qualified for a state grant to improve playground safety, but state officials then decided that it was ineligible because of a provision in the state constitution barring the expenditure of public funds in aid of any church. After the case was fully briefed in the Supreme Court, a new Governor and Attorney General, both Republicans, replaced their Democratic predecessors. Six days before oral argument, the Governor announced that he had "instructed" the relevant department to give equal treatment to future applications from religious organizations. This announcement did not fund the church's playground, because that grant application was from the 2012 funding cycle, and that money was all gone. The Attorney General's office recused itself from the case, and the case was argued by the Solicitor General from the previous administration, who had filed the briefs.

    A flurry of online commentary, mostly from opponents of funding who feared an adverse decision, insisted that the case was now moot. It seems unlikely that the new administration would voluntarily reverse its position, but it had not disabled itself from doing so. It had not even issued a regulation, but only a press release announcing an unpublished "instruct[ion]." More fundamentally, the state constitutional provision barring the funds remained in effect, and no governor could change that. Opponents of funding could sue to enforce the state constitution, and the state courts could overturn the new administration's position. The Court said that no one had "carried the 'heavy burden' of making 'absolutely clear' that [the state] could not revert" to the challenged policy. *Id.* at 2019 n.1, quoting Friends of the Earth, Inc. v. Laidlaw Environmental Services (TOC), Inc., 528 U.S. 167, 189 (2000). No one had tried to carry that burden; both sides agreed that the case was not moot.

    The Court did not make the seemingly obvious point that there was still a live dispute about the money that the church had never received. The church had not asked the federal courts to order state officials to give it the money, because the state has sovereign immunity from money judgments in federal court. See section 5.C.1 in the main volume. The church had asked for a declaratory judgment that it had been unconstitutional to withhold the money and an injunction ordering that it henceforth be given equal treatment with secular grant applicants.

    3.2. Deterrence. The Court rather easily accepted a special master's finding that there was no "cognizable danger of recurrent violations," quoting *W.T. Grant*, in an interstate water dispute. Kansas v. Nebraska, 135 S. Ct. 1042, 1059 (2015). Nebraska had knowingly and recklessly, but not deliberately, taken more than its share of the water in the Republican River, and the Court had awarded a substantial monetary remedy, in excess of actual damages. Meanwhile, Nebraska had adopted new compliance measures that would suffice if adhered to. The Court believed that the risk of renewed monetary liability would likely keep those new measures in place. The case is more fully described in this supplement to page 686.

Page 280. After the first paragraph of note 6, add:
   6. Mootness and monetary relief. . . .
   Knox v. Service Employees International Union, 567 U.S. 298 (2012), was a suit to recover the proportion of union dues devoted to political purposes. After cert was granted, the union offered a full refund to any member who asked. Even though plaintiffs sought only a refund, and sought no prospective relief of any kind, the Court said the case was not moot. It cited the voluntary cessation cases for the proposition that "maneuvers designed to insulate a decision from review by this Court must be viewed with a critical eye." *Id.* at 307. The offer of a refund came with conditions designed to make it difficult to collect. An application for refund had to have an original signature and social security number; fax and e-mail applications were not accepted. "The union is not entitled to dictate unilaterally the manner in which it advertises the availability of the refund." *Id.* at 308. Four justices disagreed with all or much of what the Court did on the merits, but there was no dissent from the mootness holding.

Page 280. After note 6, add:
   7. Unaccepted offers of full compensation. The defendant cannot moot an alleged class action by offering to fully compensate the named plaintiff, unless the named plaintiff accepts the offer. Campbell-Ewald Co. v. Gomez, 136 S. Ct. 663 (2016). If defendants could moot class claims by offering modest sums to buy off the class representatives, then few lawyers would take these cases; both the individual claims and the class claims would wither away. That is what was at stake; what the Court said was that an unaccepted offer is a nullity, both in first-year Contracts and explicitly in Federal Rule 68 on offers of judgment. Rule 68 says that an offer not accepted within fourteen days is considered withdrawn. and that the party rejecting the offer is liable for costs if she eventually obtains a judgment less favorable than the offer.
   Chief Justice Roberts dissented on the ground that once the defendant offered full relief, the case was moot and no case or controversy remained. Justices Scalia and Alito joined this dissent. Justice Thomas concurred on the ground that an offer was not enough to moot a case under the common law of tenders; defendant had to actually tender the sum offered in an unconditional manner. Rule 68 was derived from this body of law, and he would construe Article III of the Constitution in light of common law practice at the founding. The majority reserved judgment on a case in which a defendant pays the offered amount into court, or deposits it in an account in plaintiff's name, and the court enters judgment for that amount.
   This appears to dispose of a bizarre case in which the plaintiff rejected an offer of full compensation, the court held that the mere offer mooted the case, and then

dismissed the case with the plaintiff never receiving the amount offered. Genesis Healthcare Corp. v. Symczyk, 133 S. Ct. 1523 (2013). The Supreme Court affirmed on the ground the plaintiff had failed to preserve her objection to the holding that her individual claim was moot, and that because the individual claim became moot before a class was certified, the class allegations were also dismissed.

8. Enforceability. The likelihood that any judgment will be unenforceable, as where defendant is insolvent or no longer within the jurisdiction, does not make a case moot. The Court collects diverse authorities to this effect in Chafin v. Chafin, 568 U.S. 165 (2013), a child-custody dispute in which the child had been returned to her mother in Scotland pursuant to a trial-court decision in the United States, and a Scottish court had ordered the American father not to remove the child from Scotland. The Supreme Court of the United States did not assume that Scottish authorities would be uncooperative if the American judgment were reversed, and did not think the case would be moot if it assumed the contrary.

2. Preventing Lawful Acts That Might Have Wrongful Consequences

Page 283. After note 6, add:

6.1. Ripeness and claim and issue preclusion. Note 6 assumes that the neighbors could bring a second lawsuit later, if the halfway house turns out to be a nuisance in practice. That is probably uncontroversial if the first case is explicitly dismissed on ripeness grounds, clearly not reaching the merits. But what if the court is unclear about that? Or what if it simply says that plaintiff has made "an insufficient factual showing." Reread the last paragraph of *Nicholson*.

The Supreme Court fought over this issue in Whole Woman's Health v. Hellerstedt, 136 S. Ct. 2292 (2016). Texas passed a statute requiring every doctor performing an abortion to have admitting privileges at a local hospital and requiring all abortion clinics to meet the same standards as ambulatory surgical centers. Just "days before" the law took effect, abortion clinics and doctors filed a suit alleging that the requirement of hospital admitting privileges would force many abortion clinics to close and thus impose an undue burden on the right to abortion. Planned Parenthood v. Abbott, 748 F.3d 583, 587 (5th Cir. 2014). The district court held a hurried hearing with "a few witnesses and . . . numerous affidavits," *id.* at 588, and permanently enjoined enforcement of the requirement of admitting privileges. The court of appeals reversed on the merits, holding that the district court had applied the wrong legal standard and that under the correct standard, plaintiffs had failed to prove an undue burden on the right to choose abortion. *Id.* at 590-600. The clinics did not petition for certiorari.

Then many of the same clinics filed a new lawsuit, challenging the admitting privileges requirement for some clinics and the surgical center requirement for all clinics. They proved that many clinics had in fact closed when the admitting-privileges requirement took effect, and the clinics and the state agreed that when the surgical-center requirement was fully enforced, only seven or eight clinics would remain in the state. There had been forty clinics before the challenged legislation, although the state offered evidence that some had closed for unrelated reasons. The district court held both requirements unconstitutional and enjoined their enforcement as to all the clinics in the state, including those who had participated in the first lawsuit.

The Supreme Court held that the second lawsuit, challenging the law after it took effect and in light of actual experience, was a different claim from the first lawsuit, challenging the law before it took effect and based on predictions of what might happen. And therefore, the first lawsuit did not preclude the second. This is important, and surely right as a general proposition.

But as Justice Alito argued for three dissenters: "The Court of Appeals did not hold that the [first] challenge was premature. It held that the evidence petitioners offered was insufficient." 136 S. Ct. at 2335. Alito said that this was a ruling on the merits.

Ripeness and insufficiency of evidence can be closely related. The state had argued in the first case that the clinics' predictions that they would be forced to close did not prove that they really would close. Actual experience is far more persuasive than predictions of doom. But Justice Alito said that the actual closing of the clinics was just new evidence, and new evidence is not a basis for creating exceptions to claim or issue preclusion. He also argued that the clinics in the first case could have produced better evidence than they had.

Justice Breyer for the majority said that Alito was "simply wrong," *id.* at 2306, and Alito said the majority was "plainly wrong," *id.* at 2332. What seems to have been plainly wrong was that the district court issued a final judgment in the first case when there had not been reasonable time for preparation and full litigation. The law of preliminary injunctions, taken up in chapter 5, is designed to avoid that problem; the court grants or refuses interim relief based on probable outcomes determined in a preliminary hearing. And it is settled that a decision granting or denying a preliminary injunction is not claim or issue preclusive in later litigation in the same case over a permanent injunction. The clinics should have vigorously opposed converting their hurried hearing into a hearing on a permanent injunction, which results in a final judgment.

The next day, Alito, writing for the same three Justices, dissented from denial of certiorari in Stormans v. Wiesman, 136 S. Ct. 2433 (2016). Petitioners had challenged certain regulations as unconstitutional, after a threat of enforcement but before any actual enforcement. The cert denial ended nine years of litigation, including a preliminary injunction hearing, an appeal, a twelve-day trial, and a second appeal. Justice Alito ended his dissent with this footnote: "The Court's denial of certiorari does not, of course, preclude petitioners from bring a future as-applied challenge to the Board's regulations." *Id.* at 2440 n.6.

He might have cited *Whole Woman's Health* for this proposition. Or he might have explained how this footnote was consistent with his dissent in *Whole Woman's Health*. But he did neither.

Page 284. After note 7, add:

8. A federal example. In Already, LLC v. Nike, Inc., 568 U.S. 85 (2013), Nike accused Already of trademark infringement, Already counterclaimed for a declaratory judgment that the trademark was invalid, and Nike sought to moot the case by filing with the court a covenant not to sue. Already argued that the case was not moot, in part because investors were refusing to invest additional funds because of fear of further trademark litigation with Nike. Applying the voluntary cessation doctrine, the Court held that there was no reasonable prospect of Nike resuming its trademark litigation. And then it said that irrational fears by potential investors could not suffice to keep a moot case alive.

The dissenters in *Gomez*, in supplement to page 280, relied on *Already*. Nike had offered full relief, Already had refused the offer, and the Court had held the case moot. The majority distinguished *Already* on the ground that plaintiff had actually received the offered relief. Nike had not merely offered; it had actually reduced the risk of further litigation to levels too small to sustain a case or controversy.

Page 288. After note 2, add:

2.1. The Defend Trade Secrets Act of 2016. Trade secret has always been a matter of state law, but now Congress has enacted federal remedies for misappropriation of trade secrets "related to a product or service used in, or intended for use in, interstate or foreign commerce." 18 U.S.C.A. §1836(b)(1) (Supp. 2017). The federal act does not authorize the *Pepsico* remedy. A federal court may grant an injunction:

> to prevent any actual or threatened misappropriation . . . on such terms as the court deems reasonable, provided the order does not —
>> (1) prevent a person from entering into an employment relationship, and that conditions placed on such employment shall be based on evidence of threatened misappropriation and not merely on the information the person knows.

18 U.S.C. §1836(b)(3)(A). Nothing in the Act appears to preempt state law; a federal court in diversity jurisdiction can still grant the *Pepsico* remedy under state law, as the Seventh Circuit did. But the new statute may have a persuasive influence.

Page 290. After note 8, add:

8.1. File sharing. The court of appeals held it an abuse of discretion not to issue a prophylactic injunction in Capitol Records, Inc. v. Thomas-Rassett, 692 F.3d 899 (8th Cir. 2012), more fully described in supplement to page 259. The district judge ordered Thomas-Rassett not to download or upload any copyrighted music. The court of appeals directed the judge to add an injunction against making any copyrighted music available for others to upload from Thomas-Rassett's computer and then download to their own. The court assumed (the legal issue was disputed) that simply making music available is not an infringement if no one uploads it. But actual uploading can be difficult to prove, and Thomas-Rassett was a willful infringer who had attempted to conceal her misconduct and thus had demonstrated "a proclivity for unlawful conduct," and these facts justified the prophylactic provision. *Id.* at 906. She did not oppose the broadening of the injunction.

4. Ending Complex Violations — and Their Consequences — in Large Institutions

a. A Case Study: School Desegregation

Page 325. At the end of note 10, add:
10. Continued enforcement. . . .

The Missouri court rejected Kansas City's state-law challenges to the funding of charter schools, holding that the diversion of state aid from the KCMSD to the charters was not an indirect diversion of KCMSD funds. School District v. State, 317 S.W.3d 599 (Mo. 2010).

b. Other Examples, and the Current Law in the Supreme Court

Pages 325-336. Delete Hutto v. Finney, Lewis v. Casey, and the accompanying notes, and substitute the following:

BROWN v. PLATA
563 U.S. 493 (2011)

Justice KENNEDY delivered the opinion of the Court.

This case arises from serious constitutional violations in California's prison system. The violations have persisted for years. They remain uncorrected. . . .

After years of litigation, it became apparent that a remedy for the constitutional violations would not be effective absent a reduction in the prison system population. The authority to order release of prisoners as a remedy to cure a systemic violation of the Eighth Amendment is a power reserved to a three-judge district court, not a single-judge district court. 18 U.S.C. §3626(a) (2006). [Appeals from such a three-judge district court lie directly to the Supreme Court.]

The appeal presents the question whether the remedial order issued by the three-judge court is consistent with requirements and procedures set forth in . . . the Prison Litigation Reform Act of 1995 (PLRA). 18 U.S.C. §3626 (2006). . . .

I

A

The degree of overcrowding in California's prisons is exceptional. California's prisons are designed to house a population just under 80,000, but at the time of the three-judge court's decision the population was [about 156,000.] The State's prisons had operated at around 200% of design capacity for at least 11 years. Prisoners are crammed into spaces neither designed nor intended to house inmates. As many as 200 prisoners may live in a gymnasium, monitored by as few as two or three correctional officers. As many as 54 prisoners may share a single toilet. . . .

Prisoners in California with serious mental illness do not receive minimal, adequate care. Because of a shortage of treatment beds, suicidal inmates may be held for prolonged periods in telephone-booth sized cages without toilets. A psychiatric expert reported observing an inmate who had been held in such a cage for nearly 24 hours, standing in a pool of his own urine, unresponsive and nearly catatonic. Prison officials explained they had "'no place to put him.'" Other inmates awaiting care may be held for months in administrative segregation, where they endure harsh and isolated conditions and receive only limited mental health services. Wait times for mental health care range as high as 12 months. In 2006, the suicide rate in California's prisons was nearly 80% higher than the national average for prison populations; and a court-appointed Special Master found that 72.1% of suicides involved "some measure of inadequate assessment, treatment, or intervention, and were therefore most probably foreseeable and/or preventable."

Prisoners suffering from physical illness also receive severely deficient care. California's prisons were designed to meet the medical needs of a population at 100% of design capacity and so have only half the clinical space needed to treat the current population. A correctional officer testified that, in one prison, up to 50 sick inmates may be held together in a 12- by 20-foot cage for up to five hours awaiting treatment. The number of staff is inadequate, and prisoners face significant delays in access to care. A prisoner with severe abdominal pain died after a 5-week delay in referral to a specialist; a prisoner with "constant and extreme" chest pain died after an 8-hour delay in evaluation by a doctor; and a prisoner died of testicular cancer after a "failure of MDs to work up for cancer in a young man with 17 months of testicular pain."[3] Doctor Ronald Shansky, former medical director of the Illinois state prison system, surveyed death reviews for California prisoners. He concluded that extreme departures from the standard of care were "widespread," and that the proportion of "possibly preventable or preventable" deaths was "extremely high."[4] . . .

B

These conditions are the subject of two federal cases. The first to commence, *Coleman v. Brown*, was filed in 1990. *Coleman* involves the class of seriously mentally ill persons in California prisons. . . . [A]fter a 39-day trial, the *Coleman* District Court found "overwhelming evidence of the systematic failure to deliver necessary care to mentally ill inmates" in California prisons. Coleman v. Wilson, 912

---

[3] Because plaintiffs do not base their case on deficiencies in care provided on any one occasion, this Court has no occasion to consider whether these instances of delay — or any other particular deficiency in medical care complained of by the plaintiffs — would violate the Constitution . . . if considered in isolation. Plaintiffs rely on systemwide deficiencies in the provision of medical and mental health care that, taken as a whole, subject sick and mentally ill prisoners in California to "substantial risk of serious harm" . . . . Farmer v. Brennan, 511 U.S. 825, 834 (1994).

[4] [Preventable or more-likely-than-not preventable deaths in the prison system totaled 66 in 2006, 68 in 2007, 66 in 2008, and 46 in 2009. Only data through 2007 was available to the three-judge court.] The three-judge court could not have anticipated [the apparent improvement in 2009], and it would be inappropriate for this Court to evaluate its significance for the first time on appeal. The three-judge court should, of course, consider this and any other evidence of improved conditions when considering future requests by the State for modification of its order.

F. Supp. 1282, 1316 (E.D. Cal. 1995). . . . The court appointed a Special Master to oversee development and implementation of a remedial plan of action.

In 2007, 12 years after his appointment, the Special Master in *Coleman* filed a report stating that, after years of slow improvement, the state of mental health care in California's prisons was deteriorating. The Special Master ascribed this change to increased overcrowding. . . . [E]xisting programming space and staffing levels were inadequate to keep pace. . . . [T]he need to house the expanding population had also caused a "reduction of programming space now occupied by inmate bunks." . . . The Special Master concluded that many early "achievements have succumbed to the inexorably rising tide of population, leaving behind growing frustration and despair."

C

The second action, *Plata* v. *Brown*, involves the class of state prisoners with serious medical conditions. After this action commenced in 2001, the State conceded that deficiencies in prison medical care violated prisoners' Eighth Amendment rights. The State stipulated to a remedial injunction. The State failed to comply with that injunction, and in 2005 the court appointed a Receiver to oversee remedial efforts. The court found that "the California prison medical care system is broken beyond repair," resulting in an "unconscionable degree of suffering and death." The court found: "[I]t is an uncontested fact that, on average, an inmate in one of California's prisons needlessly dies every six to seven days due to constitutional deficiencies in the [California prisons'] medical delivery system." . . .

Prisons were unable to retain sufficient numbers of competent medical staff, and would "hire any doctor who had 'a license, a pulse and a pair of shoes.'" Medical facilities lacked "necessary medical equipment" and did "not meet basic sanitation standards." "Exam tables and counter tops, where prisoners with . . . communicable diseases are treated, [were] not routinely disinfected."

In 2008, three years after the District Court's decision, the Receiver described continuing deficiencies in the health care provided by California prisons . . . .

The Receiver explained that "overcrowding, combined with staffing shortages, has created a culture of cynicism, fear, and despair which makes hiring and retaining competent clinicians extremely difficult." "[O]vercrowding, and the resulting day to day operational chaos of the [prison system], creates regular 'crisis' situations which . . . take time [and] energy . . . away from important remedial programs." Overcrowding had increased the incidence of infectious disease, and had led to rising prison violence and greater reliance by custodial staff on lockdowns, which "inhibit the delivery of medical care and increase the staffing necessary for such care." . . .

D . . .

The three-judge court heard 14 days of testimony and issued a 184-page opinion, making extensive findings of fact. The court ordered California to reduce its prison population to 137.5% of the prisons' design capacity within two years. Assuming the State does not increase capacity through new construction, the order requires a population reduction of 38,000 to 46,000 persons. Because it appears all but certain that the State cannot complete sufficient construction to comply fully with the order, the prison population will have to be reduced to at least some extent. The court did not order the State to achieve this reduction in any particular manner. Instead, the court ordered the State to formulate a plan for compliance and submit its plan for approval by the court. . . .

II

As a consequence of their own actions, prisoners may be deprived of rights that are fundamental to liberty. Yet the law and the Constitution demand recognition of certain other rights. . . .

Just as a prisoner may starve if not fed, he or she may suffer or die if not provided adequate medical care. A prison that deprives prisoners of basic sustenance, including adequate medical care, is incompatible with the concept of human dignity and has no place in civilized society.

If government fails to fulfill this obligation, the courts have a responsibility to remedy the resulting Eighth Amendment violation. Courts must be sensitive to the State's interest in punishment, deterrence, and rehabilitation, as well as the need for deference to experienced and expert prison administrators faced with the difficult and dangerous task of housing large numbers of convicted criminals. . . . [But courts] may not allow constitutional violations to continue simply because a remedy would involve intrusion into the realm of prison administration.

Courts faced with the sensitive task of remedying unconstitutional prison conditions must consider a range of available options, including appointment of special masters or receivers . . . . When necessary to ensure compliance with a constitutional mandate, courts may enter orders placing limits on a prison's population. . . .

Before a three-judge court may be convened [to consider such an order], a district court first must have entered an order for less intrusive relief that failed to remedy the constitutional violation and must have given the defendant a reasonable time to comply with its prior orders. §3626(a)(3)(A). . . .

The three-judge court must then find by clear and convincing evidence that "crowding is the primary cause of the violation of a Federal right" and that "no other relief will remedy the violation of the Federal right." 18 U.S.C. §3626(a)(3)(E). As with any award of prospective relief under the PLRA, the relief "shall extend no further than necessary to correct the violation of the Federal right of a particular plaintiff or plaintiffs." §3626(a)(1)(A). The three-judge court must therefore find that the relief is "narrowly drawn, extends no further than necessary . . . , and is the least intrusive means necessary to correct the violation of the Federal right." *Id.* In making this determination, the three-judge court must give "substantial weight to any adverse impact on public safety or the operation of a criminal justice system caused by the relief." *Id.* Applying these standards, the three-judge court found a population limit appropriate, necessary, and authorized in this case.

This Court's review of the three-judge court's legal determinations is *de novo*, but factual findings are reviewed for clear error. . . .

A

The State contends that it was error to convene the three-judge court without affording it more time to comply with the prior orders in *Coleman* and *Plata*. . . .

2 . . .

When the three-judge court was convened, 12 years had passed since the appointment of the *Coleman* Special Master, and 5 years had passed since the approval of the *Plata* consent decree. The State does not claim that either order achieved a remedy. . . .

The State claims instead that . . . other, later remedial efforts should have been given more time to succeed. [There were new orders, or proposals, for construction of new facilities, hiring of new staff, and implementation of new procedures in each case in 2006 and later.]

[T]he failed consent decree in *Plata* had called for . . . new procedures and . . . additional staff; and the *Coleman* Special Master had issued over 70 orders directed at achieving a remedy through construction, hiring, and procedural reforms. . . .

Having engaged in remedial efforts for 5 years in *Plata* and 12 in *Coleman*, the District Courts were not required to wait to see whether their more recent efforts would yield equal disappointment. When a court attempts to remedy an entrenched constitutional violation through reform of a complex institution . . ., it may be necessary in the ordinary course to issue multiple orders directing and adjusting ongoing remedial efforts. Each new order must be given a reasonable time to succeed, but reasonableness must be assessed in light of the entire history of the court's remedial efforts. . . .

The *Coleman* and *Plata* courts had a solid basis to doubt that additional efforts to build new facilities and hire new staff would achieve a remedy. . . . A report filed by the *Coleman* Special Master in July 2009 describes ongoing violations, including an "absence of timely access to appropriate levels of care at every point in the system." A report filed by the *Plata* Receiver in October 2010 likewise describes ongoing deficiencies in the provision of medical care and concludes that there are simply "too many prisoners for the healthcare infrastructure." The *Coleman* and *Plata* courts acted reasonably when they convened a three-judge court without further delay.

B

Once a three-judge court has been convened, the court must find additional requirements satisfied before it may impose a population limit. The first of these requirements is that "crowding is the primary cause of the violation of a Federal right." 18 U.S.C. §3626(a)(3)(E)(i).

1

The three-judge court found the primary cause requirement satisfied by the evidence at trial. The court found that overcrowding strains inadequate medical and mental health facilities; overburdens limited clinical and custodial staff; and creates violent, unsanitary, and chaotic conditions that contribute to the constitutional violations and frustrate efforts to fashion a remedy. The three-judge court also found that "until the problem of overcrowding is overcome it will be impossible to provide constitutionally compliant care to California's prison population." . . .

The record documents the severe impact of burgeoning demand on the provision of care. At the time of trial, vacancy rates for medical and mental health staff ranged as high as 20% for surgeons, 25% for physicians, 39% for nurse practitioners, and 54.1% for psychiatrists. These percentages are based on the number of positions budgeted by the State. Dr. . . . Shansky . . . concluded that these numbers understate the severity of the crisis because the State has not budgeted sufficient staff to meet demand. . . .

Even on the assumption that vacant positions could be filled, the evidence suggested there would be insufficient space for the necessary additional staff to perform their jobs. . . . Staff operate out of converted storage rooms, closets, bathrooms, shower rooms, and visiting centers. These makeshift facilities impede the effective delivery of care and place the safety of medical professionals in jeopardy, compounding the difficulty of hiring additional staff.

This shortfall of resources relative to demand contributes to significant delays in treatment. . . .

Prisons have backlogs of up to 700 prisoners waiting to see a doctor. A review of referrals for urgent specialty care at one prison revealed that only 105 of 316 pending referrals had a scheduled appointment, and only 2 had an appointment scheduled to occur within 14 days. Urgent specialty referrals at one prison had been pending for six months to a year.

Crowding also creates unsafe and unsanitary living conditions that hamper effective delivery of medical and mental health care. . . . Cramped conditions promote unrest and violence . . . .

Increased violence . . . requires increased reliance on lockdowns to keep order, and lockdowns further impede the effective delivery of care. In 2006, prison officials instituted 449 lockdowns. The average lockdown lasted 12 days, and 20 lockdowns lasted 60 days or longer. During lockdowns, staff must either escort prisoners to medical facilities or bring medical staff to the prisoners. Either procedure puts additional strain on already overburdened medical and custodial staff. Some programming for the mentally ill even may be canceled altogether during lockdowns, and staff may be unable to supervise the delivery of psychotropic medications.

The effects of overcrowding are particularly acute in the prisons' reception centers, intake areas that process 140,000 new or returning prisoners every year. Crowding in these areas runs as high as 300% of design capacity. . . . Inmates spend long periods of time in these areas awaiting transfer to the general population. Some prisoners are held in the reception centers for their entire period of incarceration.

Numerous experts testified that crowding is the primary cause of the constitutional violations. [The Court quoted testimony by the former warden of San Quentin and three current or former heads of prison systems in other large states.]

2

The State attempts to undermine the substantial evidence presented at trial, and the three-judge court's findings of fact, by complaining that the three-judge court did not allow it to present evidence of current prison conditions. This suggestion lacks a factual basis. . . .

[B]oth parties presented testimony related to current conditions, including understaffing, inadequate facilities, and unsanitary and unsafe living conditions. . . .

It is true that the three-judge court established a cutoff date for discovery a few months before trial. . . . The court also excluded evidence not pertinent to the issue whether a population limit is appropriate under the PLRA, including evidence relevant solely to the existence of an ongoing constitutional violation. . . .

Both rulings were within the sound discretion of the three-judge court. . . .

The State does not point to any significant evidence that it was unable to present and that would have changed the outcome of the proceedings. . . .

3

The three-judge court acknowledged that the violations were caused by factors in addition to overcrowding and that reducing crowding in the prisons would not entirely cure the violations. . . . [E]ven a significant reduction in the prison population would not remedy the violations absent continued efforts to train staff, improve facilities, and reform procedures. The three-judge court nevertheless found that overcrowding was the primary cause in the sense of being the foremost cause of the violation. . . .

Overcrowding need only be the foremost, chief, or principal cause of the violation. If Congress had intended to require that crowding be the only cause, it would have said so . . . .

As this case illustrates, constitutional violations in conditions of confinement are rarely susceptible of simple or straightforward solutions. In addition to overcrowding the failure of California's prisons to provide adequate medical and mental health care may be ascribed to chronic and worsening budget shortfalls, a lack of political will in favor of reform, inadequate facilities, and systemic administrative failures. . . . *See also* Hutto v. Finney, 437 U.S. 678, 688 (1978) (noting "the interdependence of the conditions producing the violation," including overcrowding). Only a multifaceted approach aimed at many causes, including overcrowding, will yield a solution. . . .

A reading of the PLRA that would render population limits unavailable in practice would raise serious constitutional concerns. A finding that overcrowding is the "primary cause" of a violation is therefore permissible, despite the fact that additional steps will be required to remedy the violation.

C

The three-judge court was also required to find by clear and convincing evidence that "no other relief will remedy the violation of the Federal right." §3626(a)(3)(E)(ii).

The State argues that the violation could have been remedied through a combination of new construction, transfers of prisoners out of State, hiring of medical personnel, and continued efforts by the *Plata* Receiver and *Coleman* Special Master. The order in fact permits the State to comply with the population limit by transferring prisoners to county facilities or facilities in other States, or by constructing new facilities to raise the prisons' design capacity. . . . If the State does find an adequate remedy other than a population limit, it may seek modification or termination of the three-judge court's order on that basis. . . .

Aside from asserting [that these remedies could still work], the State offers no reason to believe it is so. . . .

43

The common thread connecting the State's proposed remedial efforts is that they would require the State to expend large amounts of money absent a reduction in overcrowding. The Court cannot ignore the political and fiscal reality behind this case. California's Legislature has not been willing or able to allocate the resources necessary to meet this crisis absent a reduction in overcrowding. There is no reason to believe it will begin to do so now, when the State of California is facing an unprecedented budgetary shortfall. . . .

D

The PLRA states that no prospective relief shall issue with respect to prison conditions unless it is narrowly drawn, extends no further than necessary to correct the violation of a federal right, and is the least intrusive means necessary to correct the violation. 18 U.S.C. §3626(a). When determining whether these requirements are met, courts must "give substantial weight to any adverse impact on public safety or the operation of a criminal justice system." *Id.*

1

The three-judge court acknowledged that its order "is likely to affect inmates without medical conditions or serious mental illness." This is because reducing California's prison population will require reducing the number of prisoners outside the class through steps such as parole reform, sentencing reform, use of good-time credits, or other means to be determined by the State. Reducing overcrowding will also have positive effects beyond facilitating timely and adequate access to medical care, including reducing the incidence of prison violence and ameliorating unsafe living conditions. According to the State, these collateral consequences are evidence that the order sweeps more broadly than necessary.

The population limit imposed by the three-judge court does not fail narrow tailoring simply because it will have positive effects beyond the plaintiff class. Narrow tailoring requires a "'"fit"' between the [remedy's] ends and the means chosen to accomplish those ends.'" Board of Trustees v. Fox, 492 U.S. 469, 480 (1989). The scope of the remedy must be proportional to the scope of the violation, and the order must extend no further than necessary to remedy the violation. This Court has rejected remedial orders that unnecessarily reach out to improve prison conditions other than those that violate the Constitution. Lewis v. Casey, 518 U.S. 343, 357 (1996). But the precedents do not suggest that a narrow and otherwise proper remedy for a constitutional violation is invalid simply because it will have collateral effects.

Nor does anything in the text of the PLRA require that result. The PLRA states that a remedy shall extend no further than necessary to remedy the violation of the rights of a "particular plaintiff or plaintiffs." 18 U.S.C. §3626(a)(1)(A). This means only that the scope of the order must be determined with reference to the constitutional violations established by the specific plaintiffs before the court.

This case is unlike cases where courts have impermissibly reached out to control the treatment of persons or institutions beyond the scope of the violation. See Dayton Board of Education v. Brinkman, 433 U.S. 406 (1977) (*Dayton I*). Even prisoners with no present physical or mental illness may become afflicted, and all prisoners in

44

California are at risk so long as the State continues to provide inadequate care. Prisoners in the general population will become sick, and will become members of the plaintiff classes, with routine frequency; and overcrowding may prevent the timely diagnosis and care necessary to provide effective treatment and to prevent further spread of disease. Relief targeted only at present members of the plaintiff classes may therefore fail to adequately protect future class members who will develop serious physical or mental illness. Prisoners who are not sick or mentally ill do not yet have a claim that they have been subjected to care that violates the Eighth Amendment, but in no sense are they remote bystanders in California's medical care system. They are that system's next potential victims.

A release order limited to prisoners within the plaintiff classes would, if anything, unduly limit the ability of State officials to determine which prisoners should be released. As the State acknowledges in its brief, "release of seriously mentally ill inmates [would be] likely to create special dangers because of their recidivism rates." . . .

In reaching its decision, the three-judge court gave "substantial weight" to any potential adverse impact on public safety from its order. The court devoted nearly 10 days of trial to the issue of public safety, and it gave the question extensive attention in its opinion. Ultimately, the court concluded that it would be possible to reduce the prison population "in a manner that preserves public safety and the operation of the criminal justice system."

The PLRA's requirement that a court give "substantial weight" to public safety does not require the court to certify that its order has no possible adverse impact on the public. A contrary reading would depart from the statute's text by replacing the word "substantial" with "conclusive." . . . A court is required to consider the public safety consequences of its order and to structure, and monitor, its ruling in a way that mitigates those consequences while still achieving an effective remedy of the constitutional violation.

This inquiry necessarily involves difficult predictive judgments regarding the likely effects of court orders. Although these judgments are normally made by state officials, they necessarily must be made by courts when those courts fashion injunctive relief to remedy serious constitutional violations in the prisons. These questions are difficult and sensitive, but they are factual questions and should be treated as such. Courts can, and should, rely on relevant and informed expert testimony when making factual findings. . . .

The three-judge court credited substantial evidence that prison populations can be reduced in a manner that does not increase crime to a significant degree. Some evidence indicated that reducing overcrowding in California's prisons could even improve public safety [by reducing the extent to which the prison system made criminals worse than when they entered.]

Expert witnesses produced statistical evidence that prison populations had been lowered without adversely affecting public safety in a number of jurisdictions, including certain counties in California, as well as Wisconsin, Illinois, Texas,

Colorado, Montana, Michigan, Florida, and Canada.[11] . . .

The court found that various available methods of reducing overcrowding would have little or no impact on public safety. Expansion of good-time credits would allow the State to give early release to only those prisoners who pose the least risk of reoffending. Diverting low-risk offenders to community programs such as drug treatment, day reporting centers, and electronic monitoring would likewise lower the prison population without releasing violent convicts. The State now sends large numbers of persons to prison for violating a technical term or condition of their parole, and it could reduce the prison population by punishing technical parole violations through community-based programs. . . .

III

Establishing the population at which the State could begin to provide constitutionally adequate medical and mental health care, and the appropriate time frame within which to achieve the necessary reduction, requires a degree of judgment. The inquiry involves uncertain predictions regarding the effects of population reductions, as well as difficult determinations regarding the capacity of prison officials to provide adequate care at various population levels. Courts have substantial flexibility when making these judgments. "'Once invoked, "the scope of a district court's equitable powers . . . is broad, for breadth and flexibility are inherent in equitable remedies."'" *Hutto*, 437 U.S. at 687 n.9, quoting Milliken v. Bradley, 433 U.S. 267 (1977) (*Milliken II*), quoting Swann v. Charlotte-Mecklenburg Board of Education, 402 U.S. 1 (1971).

Nevertheless, the PLRA requires a court to adopt a remedy that is "narrowly tailored" to the constitutional violation and that gives "substantial weight" to public safety. 18 U.S.C. §3626(a). When a court is imposing a population limit, this means the court must set the limit at the highest population consistent with an efficacious remedy. The court must also order the population reduction achieved in the shortest period of time reasonably consistent with public safety.

A

The three-judge court concluded that the population of California's prisons should be capped at 137.5% of design capacity. This conclusion is supported by the record. Indeed, some evidence supported a limit as low as 100% of design capacity . . . . Other evidence supported a limit as low as 130%. . . .

Although the three-judge court concluded that the "evidence in support of a

---

[11] Philadelphia's experience in the early 1990's with a federal court order mandating reductions in the prison population was less positive, and that history illustrates the undoubted need for caution in this area. One congressional witness testified that released prisoners committed 79 murders and multiple other offenses. See Hearing on S. 3 *et al.* before the Senate Committee on the Judiciary, 104th Cong., 1st Sess. 45 (1995) (statement of Lynne Abraham, District Attorney of Philadelphia). Lead counsel for the plaintiff class in that case responded that "[t]his inflammatory assertion has never been documented." *Id.* at 212 (statement of David Richman). . . .

130% limit is strong," it found that some upward adjustment was warranted in light of "the caution and restraint required by the PLRA." . . . [T]he State's Corrections Independent Review Panel had found that 145% was the maximum "operable capacity" of California's prisons, although the relevance of that determination was undermined by the fact that the panel had not considered the need to provide constitutionally adequate medical and mental health care, as the State itself concedes. After considering, but discounting, this evidence, the three-judge court . . . imposed a limit of 137.5%.

This weighing of the evidence was not clearly erroneous. . . . The plaintiffs' evidentiary showing was intended to justify a limit of 130%, and the State made no attempt to show that any other number would allow for a remedy. . . . The three-judge court made the most precise determination it could in light of the record before it. The PLRA's narrow tailoring requirement is satisfied so long as these equitable, remedial judgments are made with the objective of releasing the fewest possible prisoners consistent with an efficacious remedy. In light of substantial evidence supporting an even more drastic remedy, the three-judge court complied with the requirement of the PLRA in this case.

B

The three-judge court ordered the State to achieve this reduction within two years. . . .

The State first had notice that it would be required to reduce its prison population in February 2009, when the three-judge court gave notice of its tentative ruling after trial. The 2-year deadline, however, will not begin to run until this Court issues its judgment. When that happens, the State will have already had over two years to begin complying with the order of the three-judge court. The State has used the time productively. At oral argument, the State indicated it had reduced its prison population by approximately 9,000 persons since the decision of the three-judge court. After oral argument, the State filed a supplemental brief indicating that it had begun to implement measures to shift "thousands" of additional prisoners to county facilities.

Particularly in light of the State's failure to contest the issue at trial, the three-judge court did not err when it established a 2-year deadline for relief. [Later, when the State submitted its plan to implement the court's order, it said that it could not safely comply in two years, but that it could safely comply in five years. The three-judge court approved the State's plan without considering whether the specific measures contained within it would substantially threaten public safety. The three-judge court had left the choice of how best to comply to state prison officials, and the Supreme Court said that the three-judge court was not required to second-guess the state's exercise of that discretion.]

The three-judge court, however, retains the authority, and the responsibility, to make further amendments to the existing order or any modified decree it may enter as warranted by the exercise of its sound discretion. . . . [T]he three-judge court must remain open to a showing . . . by either party that the injunction should be altered to ensure that the rights and interests of the parties are given all due and necessary protection. . . .

The State may wish to move for modification of the three-judge court's order to extend the deadline for the required reduction to five years from the entry of the judgment of this Court . . . . The three-judge court may grant such a request provided that the State satisfies necessary and appropriate preconditions designed to ensure that measures are taken to implement the plan without undue delay. . . .

If significant progress is made toward remedying the underlying constitutional violations, that progress may demonstrate that further population reductions are not necessary or are less urgent than previously believed. Were the State to make this showing, the three-judge court in the exercise of its discretion could consider whether it is appropriate to extend or modify this timeline. . . .

These observations reflect the fact that the three-judge court's order, like all continuing equitable decrees, must remain open to appropriate modification. They are not intended to cast doubt on the validity of the basic premise of the existing order. The medical and mental health care provided by California's prisons falls below the standard of decency that inheres in the Eighth Amendment. This extensive and ongoing constitutional violation requires a remedy, and a remedy will not be achieved without a reduction in overcrowding. The relief ordered by the three-judge court is required by the Constitution and was authorized by Congress in the PLRA. The State shall implement the order without further delay.

The judgment of the three-judge court is affirmed. . . .

Justice SCALIA, with whom Justice THOMAS joins, dissenting.

Today the Court affirms what is perhaps the most radical injunction issued by a court in our Nation's history . . . .

There comes before us, now and then, a case whose proper outcome is so clearly indicated by tradition and common sense, that its decision ought to shape the law, rather than vice versa. One would think that, before allowing the decree of a federal district court to release 46,000 convicted felons, this Court would bend every effort to read the law in such a way as to avoid that outrageous result. . . .

The proceedings that led to this result were a judicial travesty. I dissent because the institutional reform the District Court has undertaken violates the terms of the governing statute, ignores bedrock limitations on the power of Article III judges, and takes federal courts wildly beyond their institutional capacity.

I

A . . .

What has been alleged here . . . is the running of a prison system with inadequate medical facilities. That may result in the denial of needed medical treatment to "a particular [prisoner] or [prisoners]," [paraphrasing the statutory focus on the rights of "a particular plaintiff or plaintiffs' — ED.], thereby violating (according to our cases) his or their Eighth Amendment rights. But the mere existence of the inadequate system does not subject to cruel and unusual punishment the entire prison population in need of medical care, including those who receive it.

The Court acknowledges that the plaintiffs "do not base their case on deficiencies in care provided on any one occasion"; rather, "[p]laintiffs rely on systemwide deficiencies . . ." *Ante* n.3. But our judge-empowering "evolving standards of decency" jurisprudence (with which, by the way, I heartily disagree) does not prescribe (or at least has not until today prescribed) rules for the "decent" running of schools, prisons, and other government institutions. It forbids . . . the *denial of medical care* to those who need it. And the persons who have a constitutional claim for denial of medical care are those who are denied medical care — not all who face a "substantial risk" (whatever that is) of being denied medical care. . . .

[I]t is inconceivable that anything more than a small proportion of prisoners in the plaintiff classes have personally received sufficiently atrocious treatment that their Eighth Amendment right was violated . . . .

[W]hat procedural principle justifies certifying a class of plaintiffs so they may assert a claim of systemic unconstitutionality? I can think of two possibilities, both of which are untenable. The first is that although some or most plaintiffs in the class do not *individually* have viable Eighth Amendment claims, the class as a whole has collectively suffered an Eighth Amendment violation. That theory is contrary to the bedrock rule that the sole purpose of classwide adjudication is to aggregate claims that are individually viable. . . .

The second possibility is that every member of the plaintiff class *has* suffered an Eighth Amendment violation merely by virtue of being a patient in a poorly-run prison system, and the purpose of the class is merely to aggregate all those individually viable claims. . . . Under this theory, each and every prisoner who happens to be a patient in a system that has systemic weaknesses . . . has suffered cruel or unusual punishment, even if that person cannot make an individualized showing of mistreatment. Such a theory of the Eighth Amendment is preposterous. And we have said as much in the past: "If . . . a healthy inmate who had suffered no deprivation of needed medical treatment were able to claim violation of his constitutional right to medical care . . . simply on the ground that the prison medical facilities were inadequate, the essential distinction between judge and executive would have disappeared: it would have become the function of the courts to assure adequate medical care in prisons." *Lewis*, 518 U.S. at 350. . . .

B

Even if I accepted the implausible premise that the plaintiffs have established a systemwide violation of the Eighth Amendment, I would dissent from the Court's endorsement of a decrowding order. That order is an example of what has become known as a "structural injunction." . . . [S]tructural injunctions are radically different from the injunctions traditionally issued by courts of equity . . . .

Structural injunctions depart from [the] historical practice [of limiting mandatory injunctions to requiring "a single simple act" that requires no continuing supervision. They turn] judges into long-term administrators of complex social institutions such as schools, prisons, and police departments. Indeed, they require judges to play a role essentially indistinguishable from the role ordinarily played by executive officials. Today's decision not only affirms the structural injunction but vastly expands its use, by holding that an entire system is unconstitutional because it *may produce* constitutional violations. . . .

This case illustrates one of [the] most pernicious aspects [of structural injunctions]: that they force judges to engage in a form of factfinding-as-policymaking that is outside the traditional judicial role. The factfinding judges traditionally engage in involves the determination of past or present facts based . . . upon a closed trial record. . . . In a very limited category of cases, judges have also traditionally been called upon to make some predictive judgments: which custody will best serve the interests of the child, for example, or whether a particular one-shot injunction will remedy the plaintiff's grievance. When a judge manages a structural injunction, however, he will inevitably be required to make very broad empirical predictions necessarily based in large part upon policy views — the sort of predictions regularly made by legislators and executive officials, but inappropriate for the Third Branch.

This feature of structural injunctions is superbly illustrated by the District Court's proceeding concerning the decrowding order's effect on public safety. . . . Here, the District Court [made] the "factual finding" that "the state has available methods by which it could readily reduce the prison population to 137.5% design capacity or less without an adverse impact on public safety or the operation of the criminal justice system." It found the evidence "clear" that prison overcrowding would "perpetuate a criminogenic prison system that itself threatens public safety" . . . .

The District Court cast these predictions (and the Court today accepts them) as "factual findings," made in reliance on the procession of expert witnesses that testified at trial. Because these "findings" have support in the record, it is difficult to reverse them under a plain-error standard of review. And given that the District Court devoted nearly 10 days of trial and 70 pages of its opinion to this issue, it is difficult to dispute that the District Court has discharged its statutory obligation to give "substantial weight to any adverse impact on public safety."

But the idea that the three District Judges in this case relied solely on the credibility of the testifying expert witnesses is fanciful. *Of course* they were relying largely on their own beliefs about penology and recidivism. And *of course* different district judges, of different policy views, would have "found" that rehabilitation would not work and that releasing prisoners would increase the crime rate. I am not saying that the District Judges rendered their factual findings in bad faith. I am saying that it is impossible for judges to make "factual findings" without inserting their own policy judgments, when the factual findings *are* policy judgments. . . .

[T]he dressing-up of policy judgments as factual findings is not an error peculiar to this case. It is an unavoidable concomitant of institutional-reform litigation. When a district court issues an injunction, it must make a factual assessment of the anticipated consequences of the injunction. And when the injunction undertakes to restructure a social institution, assessing the factual consequences of the injunction is necessarily the sort of predictive judgment that our system of government allocates to other government officials. . . .

The District Court also relied heavily on the views of the Receiver and Special Master, and those reports play a starring role in the Court's opinion today. . . . The use of these reports is even less consonant with the traditional judicial role than the District Court's reliance on the expert testimony at trial. . . . Relying on the un-cross-examined findings of an investigator, sent into the field to prepare a factual report and give suggestions on how to improve the prison system, bears no resemblance to ordinary judicial decisionmaking. . . .

III

In my view, a court may not order a prisoner's release unless it determines that the prisoner is suffering from a violation of his constitutional rights, and that his release, and no other relief, will remedy that violation. Thus, if the court determines that a particular prisoner is being denied constitutionally required medical treatment, and the release of that prisoner (and no other remedy) would enable him to obtain medical treatment, then the court can order his release; but a court may not order the release of prisoners who have suffered no violations of their constitutional rights, merely to make it less likely that that will happen to them in the future. . . .

[M]y approach may invite the objection that the PLRA appears to contemplate structural injunctions in general and mass prisoner-release orders in particular. The statute requires courts to "give substantial weight to any adverse impact on public safety or the operation of a criminal justice system caused by the relief" and authorizes them to appoint Special Masters, §3626(a)(1)(A), (f), provisions that seem to presuppose the possibility of a structural remedy. It also sets forth criteria under which courts may issue orders that have "the purpose or effect of reducing or limiting the prisoner population," §3626(g)(4).

I do not believe that objection carries the day. In addition to imposing numerous limitations on the ability of district courts to order injunctive relief with respect to prison conditions, the PLRA states that "[n]othing in this section shall be construed to . . . repeal or detract from otherwise applicable limitations on the remedial powers of the courts." §3626(a)(1)(C). The PLRA is therefore best understood as an attempt to constrain the discretion of courts issuing structural injunctions — not as a mandate for their use. . . .

Justice ALITO, with whom Chief Justice ROBERTS joins, dissenting.

The decree in this case is a perfect example of what the Prison Litigation Reform Act of 1995 (PLRA) was enacted to prevent. . . .

The Eighth Amendment prohibits prison officials from depriving inmates of "the minimal civilized measure of life's necessities." Rhodes v. Chapman, 452 U.S. 337, 347 (1981). Federal courts have the responsibility to ensure that this constitutional standard is met, but undesirable prison conditions that do not violate the Constitution are beyond the federal courts' reach. . . .

I

Both the PLRA and general principles concerning injunctive relief dictate that a prisoner release order cannot properly be issued unless the relief is necessary to remedy an ongoing violation. . . .

The scope of permissible relief depends on the scope of any continuing violations, and therefore it was essential for the three-judge court to make a reliable determination of the extent of any violations as of the time its release order was issued. Particularly in light of the radical nature of its chosen remedy, nothing less than an up-to-date assessment was tolerable.

The three-judge court, however, relied heavily on outdated information and findings and refused to permit California to introduce new evidence. . . .

[B]y the date of the trial before the three-judge court, the death rate had been trending downward for 10 quarters, and the number of likely preventable deaths fell from 18 in 2006 to 3 in 2007, a decline of 83 percent. Between 2001 and 2007, the California prison system had the 13th lowest average mortality rate of all 50 state systems. . . .

II . . .

[The PLRA's remedial limitations] largely reflect general standards for injunctive relief aimed at remedying constitutional violations by state and local governments. "The power of the federal courts to restructure the operation of local and state governmental entities is not plenary. . . . Once a constitutional violation is found, a federal court is required to tailor the scope of the remedy to fit the nature and extent of the constitutional violation." *Dayton I.*

Here, the majority and the court below maintain that no remedy short of a massive release of prisoners from the general prison population can remedy the State's failure to provide constitutionally adequate health care. This argument is implausible on its face and is not supported by the requisite clear and convincing evidence. . . .

I do not dispute that general overcrowding *contributes* to many of the California system's healthcare problems. But it by no means follows that reducing overcrowding is the only or the best or even a particularly good way to alleviate those problems. . . . The release order is not limited to prisoners needing substantial medical care but instead calls for a reduction in the system's overall population. . . . Although some class members will presumably be among those who are discharged, the decrease in the number of prisoners needing mental health treatment or other forms of extensive medical care will be much smaller than the total number of prisoners released, and thus the release will produce at best only a modest improvement in the burden on the medical care system. . . .

The State proposed several remedies other than a massive release of prisoners, but the three-judge court, seemingly intent on attacking the broader problem of general overcrowding, rejected all of the State's proposals. In doing so, the court made three critical errors.

First, the court did not assess those proposals and other remedies in light of conditions proved to exist at the time the release order was framed. . . .

Second, the court failed to distinguish between conditions that fall below the level that may be desirable as a matter of public policy and conditions that do not meet the minimum level mandated by the Constitution. . . .

Third, the court rejected alternatives that would not have provided "'immediate'" relief. But nothing in the PLRA suggests that public safety may be sacrificed in order to implement an immediate remedy rather than a less dangerous one that requires a more extended but reasonable period of time.

If the three-judge court had not made these errors, it is entirely possible that an adequate but less drastic remedial plan could have been crafted. Without up-to-date information, it is not possible to specify what such a plan might provide, and in any event, that is not a task that should be undertaken in the first instance by this Court. But possible components of such a plan are not hard to identify. . . .

Sanitary procedures could be improved; sufficient supplies of medicine and medical equipment could be purchased; an adequate system of records management could be implemented; and the number of medical and other staff positions could be increased. Similarly, it is hard to believe that staffing vacancies cannot be reduced or eliminated and that the qualifications of medical personnel cannot be improved by any means short of a massive prisoner release. Without specific findings backed by hard evidence, this Court should not accept the counterintuitive proposition that these problems cannot be ameliorated by increasing salaries, improving working conditions, and providing better training and monitoring of performance.

While the cost of a large-scale construction program may well exceed California's current financial capabilities, a more targeted program, involving the repair and perhaps the expansion of current medical facilities (as opposed to general prison facilities), might be manageable. After all, any remedy in this case, including the new programs associated with the prisoner release order and other proposed relief now before the three-judge court, will necessarily involve some state expenditures.

Measures such as these might be combined with targeted reductions in critical components of the State's prison population. A certain number of prisoners in the classes on whose behalf the two cases were brought might be transferred to out-of-state facilities. . . .

Finally, as a last resort, a much smaller release of prisoners in the two plaintiff classes could be considered. . . .

III

Before ordering any prisoner release, the PLRA commands a court to "give substantial weight to any adverse impact on public safety or the operation of a criminal justice system caused by the relief." §3626(a)(1)(A). This provision unmistakably reflects Congress' view that prisoner release orders are inherently risky. . . .

[T]he three-judge court in this case concluded that loosing 46,000 criminals would not produce a tally like that in Philadelphia [see note 11 of the majority's opinion] and would actually improve public safety. . . .

This is a fundamental and dangerous error. When a trial court selects between the competing views of experts on broad empirical questions such as the efficacy of preventing crime through the incapacitation of convicted criminals, the trial court's choice is very different from a classic finding of fact and is not entitled to the same degree of deference on appeal. . . .

* * *

. . . I fear that today's decision, like prior prisoner release orders, will lead to a grim roster of victims. I hope that I am wrong.

In a few years, we will see.

1. The prison cases. Beginning in the 1970s, the federal courts supervised the reform of prisons, jails, and mental hospitals in nearly every state. The worst of cruel and unusual conditions were greatly improved, but money, institutional inertia, and political indifference remain substantial obstacles. And inevitably, some provisions of some of these decrees had unintended consequences that were counterproductive. The Supreme Court had issued narrow opinions in several prison cases, but remarkably, Brown v. Plata is the first Supreme Court case to grapple with the central problem presented by these cases.

2. The central issue. The central problem appears to be that California's voters are not willing to spend nearly enough money to provide facilities and medical care for all the people they wish to imprison. In 2009, with the state facing a projected $42 billion budget deficit, the receiver in *Coleman* asked for $8 billion to build seven new prison health care centers with a total of 10,000 beds. Malia Wollan, *California Asks Removal of Prison Overseer*, N.Y. Times (Jan. 29, 2009). Of course he didn't get the money.

The courts were patient. The *Coleman* litigation was twenty-one years old, and the *Plata* litigation ten, by the time of the Supreme Court's decision. The state was allowed to propose its own plans for reform and for compliance, and in *Plata* there is a consent decree. The evidence, and the fact finding, was massive and detailed. Justice Alito is new to the problem; he wants to give the state more time. But from the perspective of the district judges, and of the prisoners, the state has already had many years.

No doubt the courts are now deeply involved in what should be an executive branch function. And releasing tens of thousands of prisoners is no doubt an extraordinary remedy. What is the alternative? Should the court order tax increases under Missouri v. Jenkins, 495 U.S. 33 (1990) (*Jenkins II*), and earmark the money for prisons? Should the court give up and let the constitutional violations continue? And if the prisons need not provide medical care, what else do they not need to provide? Would the central issue be any different if the state provided no sanitary facilities? No food? In Hutto v. Finney, 437 U.S. 678 (1978), Arkansas prisoners were fed only 1000 calories a day, and nearly all were losing weight.

3. The Prison Litigation Reform Act. The Prison Litigation Reform Act, much discussed in *Plata*, codified remedial standards in prison cases. Its core provision, 18 U.S.C. §3626(a)(1)(A), is not confined to release orders. It requires that any prospective relief in a prison case "shall extend no further than necessary to correct the violation of the Federal right of a particular plaintiff or plaintiffs," that it be "narrowly drawn," that it extend "no further than necessary to correct the violation of the Federal right," and that it be "the least intrusive means necessary to correct the violation of the Federal right." Congress plainly thought that courts were engaged in free-wheeling equity in these cases, but it seems increasingly clear that the Court's view of appropriate injunctive remedies is not far from what Congress codified. The PLRA specifies multiple and sometimes redundant analytic steps, and the Court works its way through each of them. But do you get the sense at any point that the Court wishes it could do more than the Act permits?

The Act might be unconstitutional if it prohibited a remedy necessary to end an ongoing constitutional violation. Note the Court's brief allusion to that possibility in the fourth paragraph of part II.B.3 of the opinion.

Other provisions of §3626 deter prisoner litigation in other ways, with higher filing fees, limits on attorneys' fees, and elimination of all damage claims except for physical injury.

4. Substantial risk and threatened violations. The dissents raise issues about the judicial role in these cases that are both important and serious. But in their anger at what they believe to be an outrageous result and a process run amuck, they sometimes misstate what actually happened in the three-judge court. Justice Scalia thinks that no prisoner's constitutional right is violated until he is denied medical care (and maybe not even then), so that there can be no such thing as a systemic violation in this context. The phrase "substantial risk" (note 3 of the majority's opinion) comes from earlier cases holding that the Eighth Amendment is substantively violated by holding a prisoner in unsafe conditions that pose a substantial risk of injury. Helling v. McKinney, 509 U.S. 25 (1993). Justice Scalia dissented, and he plainly continued to reject that holding.

But even without that, injunctions are available to prevent threatened violations of law. That's the whole point of preventive injunctions. On the facts found by the district courts, doesn't California threaten to deprive every inmate of medical care every time he needs it? And given that litigation is slow, and that the need for medical care is often urgent, is there any imaginable way to effectively implement Justice Scalia's one-prisoner-at-a-time-after-he-gets-sick remedy?

5. Recent improvements. Justice Alito focuses on a decline in the death rate after the 2008 trial. Assuming these improvements are real, should we assume that less intrusive remedies are finally working after all these years? Or should we assume that the threat of a large prisoner release has finally gotten the state's attention and motivated more serious efforts?

Justice Alito also notes that California's overall prison death rate was relatively low compared to other states. The three-judge court considered that evidence, noting that it did not control for demographics, and that California's free population also had a low death rate, and concluded that this evidence of gross death rates did not overcome all the other evidence in the case. Coleman v. Schwarzenegger, 922 F. Supp. 2d 882, 941 (E.D. Cal. 2009).

6. Who would be released? The dissenters emphasize that California has been ordered to release 46,000 "convicted felons." But there is something very odd in the prison population statistics. The Court says that 140,000 prisoners enter the system every year. Yet there are only 156,000 prisoners altogether. If many of those prisoners are serving long terms, there must be tens of thousands of others who are passing through the system for less than a year at a time. Such short sentences do not suggest that California considers these people serious threats to public safety. Eliminating this enormous flow through of short-term prisoners is one potential source of substantial population reductions that may have only modest effects on public safety. The three-judge court did not say that prisoners can be released without danger to the public because rehabilitation works, as Justice Scalia seems to assume; rather, it principally said that many prisoners in the California system are not very dangerous in the first place and can safely be released earlier or dealt with by means other than incarceration.

7. The reports of the receiver and special master. Both sides introduced various reports of the receiver and special master without objection from the other side. *Id.* at 902 n.20. If the state had asserted its right to cross-examine the receiver, it is hard to imagine that the three-judge court would not have allowed that. But the state apparently never asked. The special master is more like an assistant judge; his findings of fact are reviewed de novo, unless the parties stipulate to a different standard. Fed. R. Civ. Proc. 53(f)(3).

In practice, the special master and the receiver appear to have functioned in similar ways; the special master gathered evidence not just by hearing testimony and receiving exhibits, but also by inspecting the prisons and gathering data. These methods are presumably more effective than passively receiving evidence submitted by the parties; the special master may be able to learn things that plaintiffs could not have learned through discovery. But this is not how judicial officers in our system usually function.

8. The remand. The Supreme Court's opinion came down in May 2011.

a. The 2011 orders. On June 30, the three-judge court ordered the state to reduce its prison population to 167 percent of design capacity by December, to 155 percent by June 2012, to 147 percent by December 2012, and to 137.5 percent by June 2013 (four years after the three-judge court's original order), and to file monthly progress reports. The state attempted to comply principally by authorizing the transfer of certain low-risk offenders to county jails. Most of these are also over crowded, and many of them are involved in separate litigation, but the effects at the state level were good. Another 9,000 prisoners were transferred to other states, which housed them at California's expense. The state also built additional facilities. The state met the 167-percent and 155-percent targets, but missed the 147-percent target. In May 2012, the state announced that it would not reduce the population to 137.5 percent of design capacity, and that it would move to modify the court's order. It also announced that it intended to terminate the out-of-state program, because it was expensive and it separated inmates from their families. This would take the prison population back up to 162 percent of design capacity.

b. The 2013 orders. On January 7, 2013, the state filed motions to vacate the court's orders and terminate the litigation. To the three-judge court, the state argued that crowding was no longer the primary cause of any deficiencies in medical care. To the single judge in *Coleman* (the mental-health case), the state argued that there was no continuing constitutional violation. It did not file a similar motion with the single judge in *Plata* (the general-medical case).

On January 8, Governor Jerry Brown issued an executive order terminating his emergency powers over the prisons. (I believe these powers originated in a 2006 declaration of emergency by Governor Arnold Schwarzenegger, but I haven't been able to connect all the dots.) The significance of revoking these emergency powers is that many possible steps to reduce crowding that the governor might have ordered, including the out-of-state program, would now require legislation. The court can order steps not authorized by state law, but only if it finds that "no other relief will correct the violation of the Federal right." 18 U.S.C. §3626(a)(1)(B)(iii) (2012).

The district court extended the deadline for reaching the 137.5-percent target to December 2013. Apart from that, it denied both motions in lengthy opinions from which I have taken these facts. Coleman v. Brown, 922 F. Supp. 2d 1004 (E.D. Cal. 2013) (three-judge court); Coleman v. Brown, 938 F. Supp. 2d 955 (E.D. Cal. 2013) (single judge). Both opinions found that there had been significant improvements, but that serious problems remained.

The single judge explicitly refused to rely on the "good faith" of California officials as a basis for terminating the decree. "There is overwhelming evidence in the record that much of defendants' progress to date is due to the pressure of this and other litigation." 938 F. Supp. 2d at 989. The three-judge court was more blunt. Apparently counting from the state's May 2012 announcement that it would not comply, the court found that "for approximately a year, defendants have acted in open defiance of this Court's Order" to reduce the prison population. 922 F. Supp. 2d at 1050. The state's conduct had been "openly contumacious" despite repeated admonitions to continue compliance efforts pending disposition of whatever motions the state planned to file. Id. at 1049. The court expressly questioned Governor Brown's good faith, id. at 1047, and later noted "the efforts made in good faith by Governor Brown's predecessors," id. at 1054. This is unusual language for a federal court. It cited Cooper v. Aaron, 358 U.S. 1 (1958), in which the Court insisted on the supremacy of judicial interpretations of the law, and in which the governor of Arkansas played a prominent and defiant role, and United States v. Barnett, 376 U.S. 681 (1964), in which the governor of Mississippi was held in criminal contempt.

Plaintiffs had filed repeated motions to hold defendants in contempt, but the court did not go there. "Being more interested in achieving compliance with our Order than in holding contempt hearings, this Court has exercised exceptional restraint." 922 F. Supp. 2d at 1050. The court issued a new and more detailed order aimed at reaching 137.5 percent of design capacity by December 31, 2013. The state was required to submit a list of all possible means of reducing prison population, ranked in order of the state's preference, with the estimated effect on population of each possibility, who within the state has authority to implement each possibility (legislature, governor, or a particular prison official), and other details. Increasingly detailed orders, and allusions to contempt without actual findings of contempt, are familiar tools of judges trying to extract compliance from resistant state officials.

The state submitted a plan that if fully implemented would get the prison population down to 142.6 percent by December 31, 2013. But most of the plan's elements required legislative approval, so the time line was open ended. The three-judge court ordered the plan into effect without legislative approval, making the required statutory finding that no lesser relief would correct the violation. It ordered that changes in good-time credits, which the state proposed to apply prospectively, also be applied retroactively. It ordered the state to compile a list of low-risk prisoners who would be released on December 31 if the other measures had not reduced the population to 137.5 percent of capacity. And it ordered defendants to report every two weeks instead of monthly. Coleman v. Brown, 952 F. Supp. 2d 901 (E.D. Cal. 2013).

With its budget much improved, the state proposed substantial new construction of prison medical facilities for the longer term. The court was also concerned with the longer term. It expressed doubt about the durability of any population reductions, noting that the inflow of new prisoners was increasing more rapidly than the state had projected.

Both the three-judge court and the Supreme Court denied a stay pending a renewed appeal to the Supreme Court. Coleman v. Brown, 960 F. Supp. 2d 1057 (2013); Brown v. Plata, 134 S. Ct. 1 (2013). The Supreme Court later dismissed the appeal for lack of jurisdiction. Brown v. Plata, 134 S. Ct. 436 (2013). The statute, 28 U.S.C. §1253 (2012), authorizes direct appeals to the Supreme Court from orders of three-judge courts granting or denying injunctions, but not from orders modifying or refusing to modify injunctions. The state should have taken its appeal to the Ninth Circuit under 28 U.S.C. §1292(a)(1) (2012). But it may well have thought that appealing there would be futile.

c. The legislature. The legislature then passed Senate Bill 105, http://leginfo.legislature.ca.gov/faces/billNavClient.xhtml?bill_id=201320140SB105 &search_keywords= [https://perma.cc/3HGG-KF36], which did several things. It provided for transfers to private, county, and out-of-state facilities. It provided incentive payments for counties that successfully supervised persons on probation and kept them out of prison. It created a Recidivism Reduction Fund "for activities designed to reduce the state's prison population." It directed studies, and reports to the legislature, on a long-term solution.

The state filed a motion to extend the deadline and told the three-judge court that if ordered to comply immediately, it would send thousands of prisoners to out-of-state facilities under this legislation.

d. The 2014 order. The three-judge court extended the deadline in an unreported order. Coleman v. Brown, No. 2:90-cv-020 (E.D. Cal. Feb. 10, 2014) (ECF No. 5060 and 5061). Population was to be reduced to 143 percent of capacity by June 30, 2014, to 141.5 percent by February 28, 2015, and to 137.5 percent by February 28, 2016. The number of inmates housed out of state was not to rise above the level at the time of the order. The court again ordered changes to good-time and parole practices, and an expanded re-entry program for prisoners being released.

The order created a new position, a Compliance Officer to be appointed by the court. If any of the three deadlines for population reduction is not achieved within thirty days of the deadline, the Compliance Officer shall, within seven days, order the release of specific prisoners in sufficient numbers to meet the population target. The Compliance Officer retains that authority after February 28, 2016 and until a "durable" remedy is achieved, and shall order the release of inmates if the population is above 137.5 percent of capacity in any two consecutive monthly reports. The prison authorities are ordered to maintain a list of low-risk offenders for use by the Compliance Officer if needed.

Perhaps most important but least enforceable, defendants represented to the court that they would not appeal the court's order, or any subsequent order necessary to implement it, or any order by the Compliance Officer; that they would not move to terminate the relief until "at least two years after the date of this order and such time as it is firmly established that compliance with the 137.5 percent design capacity benchmark is durable;" and that they would not support any such appeal or motion by an intervener. They further represented that they would "develop comprehensive and sustainable prison population-reduction reforms." The three-judge court recited that its extension of the deadline was in reliance on all of these representations.

e. A new era of cooperation? In February 2015, the state reported to the three-judge court says that it was in compliance with the court's orders, a year ahead of schedule, and that the prison population was at 136.6 percent of design capacity. It was still in compliance as of the most recent report, in June 2017; the prison population was at 136.7 percent of capacity. The reports do not assess the state of medical care. The monthly reports are available at http://www.cdcr.ca.gov/News/3-judge-panel.html.

The press reports "a remarkable series of court decisions and compromises between the Brown administration and lawyers for the inmates" during 2014. Sam Stanton & Denny Walsh, *Major Progress Cited in Prison Inmate Care*, Sacramento Bee (Dec. 20, 2014). A lead attorney for the prisoners says that "we went from total war . . . to where there's been a lot of cooperation and progress." Of course it is difficult to assess the reasons for such a change from the outside, but the key appears to be the appointment of Jeffrey Beard as head of the Department of Corrections and Rehabilitation. Beard had actually testified for the plaintiffs in 2010; when he took office in December 2012, he was described as "a vocal advocate of alternative sentencing laws that move non-serious criminals into community treatment programs rather than state lockup." *Jeff Beard: The New Name in California Corrections*, Correctional News (Jan. 2, 2013), available at http://www.correctionalnews.com/articles/2013/01/2/jeff-beard-the-new-name-in-california-corrections [https://perma.cc/9ZHY-22SK]. When the Supreme Court refused the governor's appeal in fall 2013, the new director was apparently freed to pursue his policy goals, which were much more in accord with the court's goals. The court had harsh words for the governor at times, but it was the governor who made this appointment. And the governor placed an initiative on the 2016 ballot to increase good-time credits and allow earlier parole for non-violent offenders; the state's district attorneys were opposed. *California Vote Sought for Prison Overhaul*, N.Y. Times (May 20, 2016). But the initiative, Proposition 57, passed by a lopsided margin. Election results are available at http://www.sos.ca.gov/elections/prior-elections/statewide-election-results/general-election-november-8-2016/statement-vote/.

f. What to make of all this. The repeated game of chicken between defendants and the court is not unusual in structural injunction cases, especially where there is political resistance to compliance. These issues are further addressed in units on modification of decrees, later in chapter 4, and on enforcement of judgments in chapter 9.

The population limit was adopted in part because it seemed more manageable, more achievable, than building facilities and improving care for all the inmates. But it was not achievable until the state decided to cooperate rather than resist. In theory the court could have just ordered a wholesale release of inmates on any one of its deadlines. Why didn't it do that?

There are many possible reasons. If the court appears unreasonable, it is more likely to get reversed. It might incur even greater wrath in public opinion. It cannot be sure of the facts; what if some of the released inmates really are dangerous? What if one or a few of those released commit spectacular crimes shortly after their release? It is safer to order process, and let the state be responsible for picking individual prisoners.

And what if the court ordered the immediate release of several thousand named prisoners — an order with no wiggle room or ambiguity — and the state just said no? Then the court has to either back down or impose serious contempt sanctions. Should the warden go to jail? The governor? Both the court and the defendants know that that is the ultimate end game; neither wants to get there. Plaintiffs file contempt motions to keep the pressure on; the court denies those motions without prejudice, to let the pressure simmer.

And it may be that California officials had backed themselves into a corner. Once they told the Supreme Court, and the press and the public, that the court order required them to release 46,000 dangerous felons, it might have been politically impossible to comply. Whether or not it was true, they had led the public to believe that it was true. There is little reason to think that California would have dramatically improved prison health care without the litigation. But it may also be that the high-profile litigation and the orders to reduce the prison population eventually became an obstacle to reducing the prison population. Now a new leader has found ways to release significant numbers of prisoners pursuant to new programs, and without the appearance of a wholesale release of prisoners.

9. Other prison litigation. It took some time for the Prison Litigation Reform Act to substantially reduce the flow of prison litigation, but it happened. There have been substantial declines in cases filed, cases filed per prisoner, and percentage of prisoners in an institution subject to a court order. Margo Schlanger, *Trends in Prison Litigation, as the PLRA Enters Adulthood*, 5 UC Irvine L. Rev. 153 (2015). Success rates are very low, in part because 95 percent of prisoner filings are pro se. Serious institutional-reform litigation requires dedicated lawyers, and data on all cases does not tell us what is happening with the most important cases. The article does not report on cases with lawyers, but a quick and preliminary look at the data shows substantial numbers of settlements. Plaintiffs appeared to get at least some relief in a modest majority of recent cases with lawyers.

10. Other legislation. The Civil Rights of Institutionalized Persons Act authorizes the Attorney General to sue states to correct "egregious or flagrant conditions" that violate constitutional rights of persons housed in prisons, mental hospitals, and similar institutions. 42 U.S.C. §1997a(a) (2012). Attorneys General of both parties have maintained an active practice under this section, more by negotiation than by litigation. An overview, with links to complaints, briefs, settlements, litigated decisions, and reports of investigations, is available at http://www.justice.gov/crt/about/spl/corrections.php [https://perma.cc/R8YR-TE4J].

11. School finance. Other showdowns between a reluctant legislature and a court enforcing an expensive remedy are going on in Kansas and Washington. See this supplement to page 847.

B. Modifying Injunctions

Page 354. After note 2, add:

2.1. The political-party litigation. In 1982, the Democratic National Committee and the Republican National Committee entered into a nationwide consent decree that limited the RNC's targeting of minority voters in its efforts to combat what it perceived as voter fraud. There have been repeated enforcement actions and repeated modifications over the years, but the decree remains in effect. The Third Circuit refused another motion to vacate the decree in Democratic National Committee v. Republican National Committee, 673 F.3d 192 (3d Cir. 2012). The court approved a modification under which the decree would expire in 2017 if no further violations were proved, and eight years after the date of the last violation if further violations *were* proved. The court took the standard for modification from *Rufo*, and from Third Circuit precedent interpreting *Rufo*. It cited Horne v. Flores only once, for the proposition that a decree should be vacated "if a durable remedy has been implemented." *Id.* at 212, quoting *Horne*, 557 U.S. 433, 450 (2009).

As of June 2017, the parties were engaged in discovery over alleged violations in the 2016 presidential campaign. The district court had preliminarily found that the DNC failed to prove those violations before the election. Democratic National Committee v. Republican National Committee, 2016 WL 6584915 (D.N.J. Nov. 5, 2016).

Page 355. After note 3, add:

3.1. The remand. On remand, the district court held a hearing that spread over 22 trial days from September 2010 to January 2011. More than two years after the hearing ended and nearly four years after the Supreme Court's remand, the court vacated the injunction and ordered the case dismissed. Flores v. Arizona, 2013 WL 10207656 (D. Ariz. Mar. 29, 2013). Two years after that, the court of appeals affirmed. Flores v. Huppenthal, 789 F.3d 994 (9th Cir. 2015).

The court of appeals' opinion noted substantial change in each of the four areas highlighted by the Supreme Court. The opinion does not say how much money was available for teaching English as a second language, but total funding per pupil in the Nogales district was up 44 percent from 2000 to 2010. The state had a clear plan for teaching English language learners, Nogales was implementing that plan, students in that program who were classified as proficient for two years were performing well academically, and more than 90 percent of them were graduating. But the opinion never says what percentage of English language learners achieved proficiency for two years.

The state's new plan for teaching English gave students four hours a day of structured English immersion, and the centerpiece of the litigation on remand appeared to be the plaintiffs' objections to this four-hour model. That part of the litigation had little connection to the Supreme Court's opinion, except that it did focus on educational methods, and to some extent, educational outcomes, and not on how much money was being spent.

The court of appeals held that plaintiffs lacked standing to assert a statewide violation, and in any event, implementation of the four-hour model varied from school district to school district, so that plaintiffs' objections could not be litigated on a statewide basis.

3.2. The motions to modify in the California prison litigation. The three-judge court in the California prison case viewed the state's 2013 motion to modify as simply an attempt to relitigate the order to reduce the prison population to 137.5 percent of design capacity. The changed circumstances to which the state pointed, at least by the court's account, were simply the passage of time, which was not a change at all; some reduction in prison population, which was wholly anticipated because it was court ordered; and some improvements in medical care, which the court found to be real but not nearly sufficient to end the constitutional violation. It also emphasized *Horne*'s reference to "a durable remedy;" nothing in California's improvements had yet been shown to be durable, and the state's recalcitrance cast serious doubt on the durability of anything that had been accomplished.

Page 356. At the end of note 1, add:
  1. The modification provisions of the PLRA. . . .
  The single judge in the California prison litigation treated the state's motion under the modification provisions of the PLRA and made the necessary findings. And then he said that *a fortiori*, the state was not entitled to relief under Rule 60(b)(5).

  The three-judge court (which included the single judge as one member) said that the PLRA provision did not apply, because California had not waited two years before filing its motion. Coleman v. Brown, 922 F. Supp. 2d 1004, 1025 n.23 (E.D. Cal. 2013). This argument treated the relevant order as the timetable order issued on June 30, 2011, and not the original order to reduce the prison population issued in 2009. In the alternative, this court also made the findings necessary to keep its orders in effect. But most of the three-judge court's opinion is written in terms of *Horne* and Rule 60(b)(5).

  Both opinions cite Ninth Circuit authority for the proposition that the burden of proof on a motion to modify or vacate a prison decree remains on defendants, even under the PLRA.

Page 357. At the end of note 2, add:
  2. Constitutionality. . . .
  For an example of prospective legislation to change the outcome in a single set of cases, see Bank Markazi v. Peterson, 136 S. Ct. 1310 (2016), described in supplement to page 847.

CHAPTER FIVE

CHOOSING REMEDIES

A. Substitutionary or Specific Relief

1. Irreplaceable Losses

a. Injunctions

Page 389. After note 1.d, add:

1.1. A Second Circuit formulation. "Harm may be irreparable where the loss is difficult to replace or measure, or where plaintiff should not be expected to suffer the loss." WPIX, Inc. v. ivi, Inc., 691 F.3d 275, 285 (2d Cir. 2012). The court affirmed a preliminary injunction against capturing over-the-air television signals and retransmitting them to subscribers over the internet. The damages would be hard to measure and defendant would be unable to pay any substantial award. A similar scheme made headlines when the Supreme Court held it illegal under the copyright laws. American Broadcasting Cos. v. Aereo Inc., 134 S. Ct. 2498 (2014).

The idea of losses that "plaintiff should not be expected to suffer" comes up in a variety of contexts, often involving some personal attachment or long investment of effort by the plaintiff. As Judge Friendly once put it, in a dispute over termination of a Ford dealership:

> Of course, Semmes' past profits would afford a basis for calculating damages for wrongful termination, and no one doubts Ford's ability to respond. But the right to continue a business in which William Semmes had engaged for twenty years and into which his son had recently entered is not measurable entirely in monetary terms; the Semmes want to sell automobiles, not to live on the income from a damages award.

Semmes Motors, Inc. v. Ford Motor Co., 429 F.2d 1197, 1205 (2d Cir. 1970),

b. Specific Performance of Contracts

Page 400. After note 13, add:

14. Business preferences. Professors Eisenberg and Miller examined contracts that were sufficiently significant to be attached to Form 8-K, on which publicly traded companies report "material events" to the Securities and Exchange Commission. Theodore Eisenberg & Geoffrey P. Miller, *Damages Versus Specific Performance: Lessons from Commercial Contracts*, 12 J. Empirical Legal Stud. 29 (2015). Thirty-one percent of these contracts provided for specific performance, including a majority of employment contracts and merger agreements. They take these provisions to indicate that sophisticated parties view specific performance as more efficient in these circumstances. Of course some of these contracting parties may also have assumed that specific performance would be available in appropriate circumstances without providing for it.

Page 406. At the end of note 5, add:
  5. The aftermath. . . .
The video has been taken down from YouTube. It is now available at http://vimeo.com/3002144.

2. Burdens on Defendant or the Court

Page 422. At the end of note 4, add:
  4. Balancing the injunction's burden and the legal remedy's inadequacy. . . .
  The Court said it again, quoting only the portion of the sentence about going much further to give relief, in Kansas v. Nebraska, 135 S. Ct. 1042, 1053 (2015), more fully described in this supplement to page 686.

3. Other Reasons (and More of the Same Reason)

Page 427. After note 4, add:
  4.1. The Federal Circuit. The Federal Circuit issued an extensive if belated response to *eBay* in Robert Bosch LLC v. Pylon Manufacturing Corp., 659 F.3d 1142 (Fed. Cir. 2011). The court held that *eBay* abolishes any presumption of irreparable injury in patent cases, but that the nature of the patent holder's property right remains relevant. "While the patentee's right to exclude alone cannot justify an injunction, it should not be ignored either." *Id.* at 1149. The court treated loss of market share and pricing power as irreparable injury; such damages would be difficult to prove and measure, although the court did not say that. The court also had some doubts about defendant's ability to pay a damage judgment. It reversed the district court's refusal to enter an injunction and ordered an injunction on remand. Judge Bryson would have remanded for further consideration.

  The court returned to the issue in Nichia Corp. v. Everlight Americas, Inc., 855 F.3d 1328 (Fed. Cir. 2017). Nichia produced products based on its patent and also licensed the patent to others, but it had not given a license to Everlight. The court affirmed a finding of no irreparable injury, based on two things. First, the willingness to license the invention cut against a finding of irreparable injury but could not be dispositive.

  Second, plaintiff had failed to prove damages. The ambiguous opinion can be read as saying that plaintiff wasn't injured at all, so there was no issue of whether any injury was irreparable. But plaintiff offered lots of evidence on damages, which the trial judge found insufficient to carry the burden of proof. This case looks more like a case in which damages weren't proved than a case in which the court could say with any confidence that there simply were no damages. Damages that are hard to prove and measure should be a reason for granting an injunction, not for withholding it. Compare Continental Airlines v. Intra Brokers at 387 of the main volume.

  4.2. A broader assessment of the impact of *eBay*. For a more complete analysis of *eBay*'s impact, see Mark P. Gergen, John M. Golden, & Henry E. Smith, *The*

Supreme Court's Accidental Revolution? The Test for Permanent Injunctions, 112 Colum. L. Rev. 203 (2012). They describe *eBay* as having "cataclysmic effect" in the lower federal courts. *Id.* at 205. Federal courts "have now repeatedly declared the *eBay* test to have swept aside long-settled presumptions about when injunctions should issue." *Id.*

Speaking in my own voice now: These presumptions were generally rebuttable, but they simplified litigation and embodied the practical meaning, derived from long experience, of such concepts as irreparable injury and balance of hardships. The reasons that gave rise to the presumptions could produce the same results in individual cases, but to some judges, that may seem like recreating the presumptions. The Supreme Court, of course, seems to have thought it was changing very little by invoking what it thought were "the traditional principles of equity." State courts have mostly ignored *eBay*, with a handful of exceptions.

Page 428. At the end of note 6, add:
   6. Fixing (or replacing) the damage remedy. . . .

The Federal Circuit understood in *Paice* that an ongoing royalty is an equitable remedy and not a measure of damages; it addressed the issue explicitly when it held that there is no right to jury trial on the amount of the royalty. Maybe a better way to explain this choice is that the court chooses an ongoing royalty instead of an injunction as a more appropriate equitable remedy. But it remains incoherent to explain a choice between two equitable remedies on the ground that there is an adequate remedy at law.

Page 428. After note 7, add:
   8. *Monsanto.* The Court reaffirmed "[t]he traditional four-factor test" from *eBay*, in an opinion joined by seven justices, in Monsanto Co. v. Geertson Seed Farms, 561 U.S. 139, 157 (2010). Even more clearly than in *eBay*, the Court was troubled by specific things about this injunction; the majority thought the injunction was overbroad, premature, and insufficiently deferential to the agency, and none of these problems cast much light on the meaning of the four-part "test." And once again, the Court appeared oblivious to any difference between permanent and preliminary injunctions.

   a. The facts. Monsanto manufactures Roundup, a widely used herbicide. The company has long worked to develop Roundup-resistant crops, so that farmers could spray the crop and kill only the weeds. This case arose when Monsanto received approval from the Department of Agriculture to sell genetically modified Roundup-resistant alfalfa. Alfalfa is a major forage crop, principally harvested as hay for feeding cattle and other grass-eating livestock; the human market for alfalfa sprouts is a negligible fraction of production.

   Plaintiffs included farmers who grow unmodified alfalfa for seed to sell to organic farmers and to farmers in countries where genetically modified crops are prohibited. They sued under the National Environmental Policy Act, 42 U.S.C. §4331 *et seq.* (2012), alleging that the agency must prepare an environmental impact statement before authorizing the sale, planting, or harvesting of Roundup-resistant alfalfa. The district court agreed. That court found that Roundup-resistant alfalfa posed no danger to humans or livestock, but that it posed serious risks to crops. The Roundup-resistant gene could easily be transmitted to unmodified alfalfa, because alfalfa is pollinated by bees with a range of up to ten miles. This genetic contamination could destroy the business of exporting alfalfa seed or selling seed to organic farmers. And the agency had not evaluated the risk that Roundup-resistant crops would encourage overuse and accelerate the evolution of Roundup-resistant weeds that would plague all farmers. By the time the case got to the Supreme Court, there were widespread reports of Roundup-resistant superweeds. William Neuman & Andrew Pollack, *Rise of the Superweeds*, N.Y. Times (May 4, 2010).

The district court enjoined any sale, planting, or harvesting of Roundup-resistant alfalfa, with a grandfather clause for crops planted before the injunction was issued, until the agency completed an environmental impact statement. The Supreme Court believed that this injunction went too far, erroneously precluding the agency from considering any partial deregulation in the interim, however limited and however harmless to plaintiffs. Suppose, in the Court's example, that the agency authorized the planting of Roundup-resistant alfalfa only in isolated areas far removed from any other alfalfa farm. Plaintiffs could not show a threat of irreparable injury from such a partial deregulation, because they could not show any threat of harm at all. Justice Stevens, dissenting, found such hypotheticals wholly implausible, because alfalfa seed is in fact grown in a few highly concentrated areas and because the agency lacked the capacity to enforce any regulations it might issue. Stevens dissented alone. Justice Breyer did not participate, because his brother was the trial judge.

b. Irreparable injury. The debate over the facts is interesting and important, but not our concern. With respect to the four-part test, the Court did *not* say that environmental harm could sometimes be adequately compensated in damages or that it might not be irreparable injury. Rather, it said that the injunction forbade potential agency action that might cause no harm to plaintiffs at all. And it said that if the agency partially deregulated Roundup-resistant alfalfa in a way that threatened irreparable harm to plaintiffs, they could file a new lawsuit and seek a preliminary injunction to prevent implementation of the new agency action.

c. Public interest. *Monsanto* revealed another ambiguity in the new four-part test. The Court said that the case was not a class action, so that plaintiffs could not rely on harm to other parties not before the Court. Although the Court emphasized its new four-part test, it appeared to treat as irrelevant the possibility that harm to alfalfa-seed farmers who were not plaintiffs might be harm to the public interest. What if such harm were widespread, or destroyed the export market for alfalfa seed? But in *eBay*'s formulation of the four-part test, quoted verbatim in *Monsanto*, plaintiff must show "that the public interest would not be disserved by a permanent injunction." *Monsanto*, 561 U.S. at 157. *EBay* does not explicitly say that the public interest can weigh in favor of issuing the injunction. Might this mean that benefits to the public interest cannot count in favor of issuing the injunction, but that harm to the public interest is an absolute reason not to issue it? Did Justice Thomas choose that phrasing deliberately in *eBay*, or might it be inadvertent?

Justice Stevens noted that the plaintiffs included organizations of farmers, consumers, and environmentalists. *Id.* at 181 n.12 (Stevens, J., dissenting). Organizations can represent their members without a class certification; his point appeared to be that harm to any member of one of these organizations was equivalent to harm to a party.

d. Permanent and preliminary injunctions again. *Monsanto* was a final judgment granting an injunction intended to last only until the agency completed its environmental impact statement. No preliminary injunction had been issued in the district court, and the litigation took two years before the permanent injunction was issued. So the permanent injunction features dominated, and the Court treated the injunction as permanent throughout its opinion. But it cited permanent and preliminary injunction cases without distinction. Thus it said that "[t]he traditional four-factor test applies when a plaintiff seeks a permanent injunction to remedy a NEPA violation," *id.* at 157, and that "[a]n injunction should issue only if the traditional four-factor test is satisfied," *id.*, citing for each statement Winter v. Natural Resources Defense Council, 555 U.S. 7, 31-33 (2008). *Winter*, reprinted at page 440 in the main volume, is a preliminary injunction case involving a four-factor test that is somewhat different in its verbal formulation and has historically been substantially different in its application. The Court also repeated the old shibboleth that "[a]n injunction is a drastic and extraordinary remedy, which should not be granted as a matter of course," *id.* at 165, citing Weinberger v. Romero-Barcelo, 456 U.S. 305, 311-312 (1982). *Romero-Barcelo* was another final judgment designed to preserve the environmental status quo pending resolution of administrative proceedings, but in *Romero-Barcelo*, the Court treated the injunction as though it were preliminary.

9. More supportive views. Professor Janutis reads *eBay* with great charity and finds little that is new or surprising. Courts have always had discretion to refuse injunctive relief to avoid undue hardship, and she sees little more than that going on. Rachel M. Janutis, *The Supreme Court's Unremarkable Decision in eBay Inc. v. Mercexchange, L.L.C.*, 14 Lewis & Clark L. Rev. 597 (2010). If the Court had simply said that, scholarly reaction would have been much different.

Professor Bray reviews *eBay*, *Monsanto*, and nine other cases, most of which will appear later in the main volume or this supplement, and finds a strong recommitment to the separation of legal and equitable remedies. Samuel L. Bray, *The Supreme Court and the New Equity*, 68 Vand. L. Rev. 997 (2015). He notes that equitable remedies can be exceptional, in the sense of requiring some special justification, without being rare or infrequent, in the sense that that special justification is hard to show. And he thinks that something like this captures the Court's view of the matter. He offers a sympathetic description of what the Court has done rather than a sustained argument for why the Court was right to do it, but he seems to broadly approve, and to excuse acknowledged mistakes at the detail level. He concludes:

> One might look at the spectrum of the opinion writers in these cases and draw the conclusion that the tradition of equity must be hale and hearty. On the other hand, the very need to invoke a tradition can be a sign that it is losing its force. No one knows for sure which one is true here. For now, though, the Chancellor is back in the saddle, and his foot is back in the stirrup.

Page 437. At the end of note 7, add:
    7. Developments in the lower courts. . . .
    Professor Ardia has collected 56 cases enjoining defamation, 31 of them since
2000. David S. Ardia, *Freedom of Speech, Defamation, and Injunctions*, 55 Wm. &
Mary L. Rev. 1 (2013). Nearly half of these cases involve speech on the internet,
often posted by individuals with few assets from which a damage judgment might be
collected. Professor Ardia argues that the law should permit these injunctions in
limited circumstances; his most important proposed limitations are that the injunction
be confined to statements that have been fully litigated and found to be false and to
statements that are about private matters and irrelevant to any public issue.

B. Preliminary or Permanent Relief

1. The Substantive Standards for Preliminary Relief

Page 444. At the end of note 3, add:
    3. The four-part test. . . .
    On further reflection, the Ninth Circuit has concluded that the sliding scale
survives *Winter*, and that a preliminary injunction can issue on a showing of serious
questions going to the merits and a balance of hardships that tips sharply in favor of
plaintiffs. Alliance for the Wild Rockies v. Cottrell, 632 F.3d 1127 (9th Cir. 2011).
The Seventh Circuit has adhered to its sliding scale approach in a series of cases, and
to its rule that plaintiff need only show only a "better than negligible" chance of
success on the merits (or in some formulations, "at least" a negligible chance of
success) to trigger the sliding scale. D.U. v. Rhoades, 825 F.3d 331, 338 (7th Cir.
2016).
    A survey focused on preliminary injunctions, only in environmental cases,
reports several findings. Sarah J. Morath, *A Mild Winter: The Status of
Environmental Preliminary Injunctions*, 37 Seattle U.L. Rev. 155 (2013). The
Second, Third, Fourth, Seventh, Eighth, Ninth, and Tenth Circuits have considered
the effect of *Winter* "either implicitly or explicitly;" only the Fourth "has expressly
held that *Winter* invalidates its earlier standard." Second, there has been no
significant change in the rate at which preliminary injunctions are granted in
environmental cases. The success rate dropped from about 48 percent to about 46
percent, which is little change at most and may be a random blip. Third, Professor
Morath found 41 such cases in the three years after *Winter*, and 33 in the three years
before *Winter*, so environmentalists did not maintain their success rate by filing fewer
cases. Yet she also reports that environmental lawyers who represent plaintiffs view
Winter as a serious problem.

Page 445. After note 5, add:
    5.1. *Chafin.* A unanimous Court quoted *Nken* for "the four traditional stay
factors" in Chafin v. Chafin, 568 U.S. 165 (2013). The context was the return of
children to foreign countries in international custody disputes. "[A]pplication of the
traditional stay factors ensures that each case will receive the individualized treatment
necessary for appropriate consideration of the child's best interests." *Id.* at 179.

5.2. *Teva.* In Teva Pharmaceuticals USA, Inc. v. Sandoz, Inc., 134 S. Ct. 1621 (2014), Teva asked Chief Justice Roberts, as Circuit Justice, to stay and recall the mandate of the Federal Circuit. The intended effect of this motion was to reinstate a preliminary injunction against patent infringement, issued by the district court and vacated by the Federal Circuit. The Supreme Court had already granted cert on the underlying issue, and the Chief said that Teva had shown a "fair prospect" of success on the merits. But Teva could recover damages for patent infringement, so it had not shown irreparable injury.

Teva said that the Federal Circuit routinely finds irreparable injury when one drug company threatens to bring out a generic version of a drug that infringes a valid patent. But the Federal Circuit does not appear to have much credibility with the Supreme Court on remedies issues, and Teva did not effectively explain why such harm is irreparable. The most straightforward explanation would be that such damages are difficult to calculate: how much of plaintiff's loss of market share and how much of its reduced prices were because of the infringement, and how long will those losses persist even if plaintiff eventually gets a permanent injunction for the remaining life of the patent? See *Bosch*, described in supplement to page 427. Sandoz said the damages could be calculated here because the remaining life of the patent was short, and Teva did not successfully refute that. This would have been a preliminary injunction before Teva had fully proved its case, which should raise the standard of proof and helps explain the result, but Roberts made nothing of that.

5.3. *Glossip.* In Glossip v. Gross, 135 S. Ct. 2726 (2015), condemned prisoners sought a preliminary injunction prohibiting use of the sedative midazolam in their executions. The Court quoted the sentence from *Winter* that plaintiff "must establish" the four elements of the four-part test, and it held that plaintiffs had not established that they were "likely" to succeed on the merits. On the majority's view of the facts and law, plaintiffs had not come close to meeting their burden of proof, so the opinion casts no light on the question of just how likely success must be.

5.4. The travel ban — balancing again. "Crafting a preliminary injunction is an exercise of discretion and judgment, often dependent as much on the equities of a given case as the substance of the legal issues it presents." The Court cited two pages of *Winter* for this proposition — the page where it announced the four elements to be established, and the page where it talked about balancing the equities and the hardship to the Navy. The Court continued: "The purpose of such interim equitable relief is not to conclusively determine the rights of the parties, but to balance the equities as the litigation moves forward." Trump v. International Refugee Assistance Project, 137 S. Ct. 2080, 2087 (2017). The Court did not march through *Winter*'s four elements.

This was in President Trump's travel-ban cases; there were two preliminary injunctions, from separate courts, in two consolidated cases. The Court was not deciding the appeals from those preliminary injunctions; it was deciding Trump's request to stay those injunctions pending a decision on the merits. The injunctions forbade enforcement of an executive order that temporarily prohibited persons from six countries from entering the United States. The Court left the injunctions in place with respect to persons who have a relationship with a United States person or entity. This included persons with relatives in the United States, with a job offer in the

United States, admitted as students to a school in the United States, invited to lecture in the United States, and presumably similar relationships, but not persons invited by refugee organizations seeking to create a right of entry. The injunctions were stayed, meaning that the travel ban was reinstated, with respect to persons without such a relationship. The Court did not put this in terms of *Winter*'s four elements, but the clear implicit rationale is that the travel ban imposed much more hardship on persons with such a relationship than on persons without.

There is similar talk of "what is necessary, what is fair, and what is workable" in North Carolina v. Covington, 137 S. Ct. 1624, 1625 (2017), further described in supplement to page 496.

2. The Procedure for Obtaining Preliminary Relief

Page 460. After note 5, add:
6. Legislation. The Defend Trade Secrets Act of 2016 explicitly authorizes ex parte applications to seize property "necessary to prevent the propagation or dissemination" of a trade secret. 18 U.S.C.A. §1836(b)(2) (Supp. 2017). There are multiple procedural safeguards, including the inadequacy of remedies under Rule 65, "immediate and irreparable injury" if the seizure is not ordered, a balance of equities favoring plaintiff, likely success in proving trade secret and misappropriation, a bond (which does not limit liability for wrongful seizure), and a finding that the person against whom the order is directed "would destroy, move, hide, or otherwise make such matter inaccessible to the court, if the applicant were to proceed on notice to such person." The order is to be denied if the plaintiff publicizes the application.

There is a similar provision for trademark cases, 15 U.S.C. §1116(d) (2012), which appears to have been there for a while before I noticed it.

7. Capable of repetition, yet evading review. *Carroll* relied on a well-settled exception to the usual rule of refusing to decide cases that have become moot. If a dispute is capable of repetition *between the same two parties*, yet so short lived that it tends to evade judicial review, the case can still be decided on appeal because the underlying controversy between the parties continues. The rule was reaffirmed without dissent in Kingdomware Technologies, Inc. v. United States, 136 S. Ct. 1969 (2016), and in Turner v. Rogers, 564 U.S. 431 (2011).

Page 468. At the end of note 9, add:
9. Stays and injunctions pending appeal. . . .
An injunction from an individual justice "demands a significantly higher justification" than a stay of an injunction granted by one of the lower courts. Lux v. Rodrigues, 561 U.S. 1306, 1307 (2010) (Roberts, C.J.), quoting Ohio Citizens for Responsible Energy, Inc. v. Nuclear Regulatory Commission, 479 U.S. 1312, 1313 (1986) (Scalia, J.). I first noticed this distinction being made by the more conservative justices, but Justice Sotomayor made essentially the same point in Hobby Lobby Stores, Inc. v. Sebelius, 133 S. Ct. 641 (2012).

Page 469. At the end of note 11, add:
   11. Appeals that suddenly turn final. . . .
   In Munaf v. Geren, 553 U.S. 674, 691-692 (2008), the Court invoked an older line of cases to similar effect. Most of these cases say that if it is clear on appeal from the preliminary injunction that plaintiff has not stated a claim on which relief can be granted, the appellate court can grant final judgment for defendant and order the complaint dismissed. But the Court also cited one famous constitutional case in which both the district court and the Supreme Court issued opinions that appear to finally resolve the legal issue against the defendant, effectively ending the litigation, even though the only order actually issued and affirmed was a preliminary injunction. Youngstown Sheet & Tube Co. v. Sawyer, 343 U.S. 579, 584-585 (1952).

C. Prospective or Retrospective Relief

1. Suits Against Officers in Their Official Capacities

Page 478. After note 8, add:
   9. Suits by state agencies. A state agency may sue officials of its state in federal court under Ex parte Young. Virginia Office of Protection and Advocacy v. Stewart, 563 U.S. 247 (2011). The possibly unprecedented case arose because Congress offered the states money to create independent agencies to investigate abuse and neglect of persons who are mentally ill or developmentally disabled. These agencies must be free of political control and authorized to litigate without oversight by the Attorney General or other state officials. It is this unusual legislation that created the possibility that one state agency might sue to enforce a federal right against the head of another state agency. Most states created private agencies to perform these functions, but Virginia and seven others created independent state agencies.
   Justice Scalia's opinion for the Court said that whatever other federalism issues might be lurking in the case, they had nothing to do with sovereign immunity or the limits of Ex parte Young. He repeated his simple two-part formulation from *Verizon Maryland*. Justices Kennedy and Thomas joined in the opinion of the Court but filed a concurring opinion that once again took a cautious view of Ex parte Young. Chief Justice Roberts, joined by Justice Alito, dissented, rejecting the *Verizon Maryland* test and arguing that it was an unconstitutional affront to the dignity of the state to have this intramural dispute resolved in federal court. Justice Kagan did not participate.

Page 481. At the end of note 6, add:
   6. The fiction of Ex parte Young and the distinction between official-capacity suits and personal-capacity suits. . . .
   The Court had to explain it again in Lewis v. Clarke, 137 S. Ct. 1285 (2017). An employee of an Indian tribe, driving on tribal business, collided with plaintiffs on I-95 in Connecticut. Plaintiffs sued the employee for damages in his personal capacity; he was not protected by the tribe's sovereign immunity. The tribe was obligated by its own rules to indemnify him, but that voluntary undertaking could not create sovereign immunity where it did not otherwise exist. The decision was

unanimous. Justices Thomas and Ginsburg noted their continuing objection to tribal sovereign immunity; see note 18 in supplement to page 484.

Page 482. After note 10, add:

10.1. Subdividing the Family and Medical Leave Act. The Family and Medical Leave Act, 29 U.S.C. §2612(a)(1) (2012), guarantees employees up to twelve weeks of unpaid leave to care for a family member, or to deal with an exigency resulting from a family member's military service, or because the employee himself is sick. The Supreme Court held that the provision for the employee's own illness is not Fourteenth Amendment legislation. Coleman v. Court of Appeals, 566 U.S. 30 (2012). The Court upheld the family-leave provisions in *Hibbs* on the ground that women disproportionately bear the burden of caring for families. But the four-justice plurality in *Coleman* said that that rationale does not apply to the sick-leave provision, because both men and women get sick.

Four dissenters argued that the sick-leave provision was also included to protect women, and that it had originated in an effort to provide gender-neutral protection for pregnant women and those who had just given birth. Congress also feared that a family-leave provision would increase sex discrimination at the hiring stage, because employers might anticipate that it would be disproportionately used by women. Requiring sick leave as well would reduce that incentive, because sick leave would be used more or less equally by both sexes.

Justice Scalia concurred in the judgment. Finding the debate between the two groups of four irresolvable and irrelevant, he proposed to tighten the standard for what counts as Fourteenth Amendment legislation.

Page 483. After note 11, add:

11.1. *Sossamon.* In Sossamon v. Texas, 563 U.S. 277 (2011), the Court held that a statute authorizing "appropriate relief against a government" was not sufficient to authorize damage suits against states. The result is hardly surprising, but Justices Sotomayor and Breyer dissented, and the Eleventh Circuit had gone the other way. The statute was the Religious Land Use and Institutionalized Persons Act, 42 U.S.C. §2000cc *et seq.* (2012).

Page 483. At the end of note 13, add:

13. Sister states. . . .

A Nevada jury awarded Hyatt $389 million in compensatory and punitive damages, for multiple intentional torts, based on Hyatt's evidence of egregious misconduct by California tax auditors. The Nevada Supreme Court threw out most of this judgment, but it affirmed $1 million awarded for fraud, and it remanded for a new trial on intentional infliction of emotional distress. It held that California was entitled to Nevada's immunity from punitive damages, but not to Nevada's $50,000 statutory cap on compensatory damages against the state. It reasoned that "legislative control, administrative oversight, and public accountability" protected Nevada citizens from Nevada agencies, but that Nevada could exercise no such control over California agencies. Franchise Tax Board v. Hyatt, 335 P.3d 125, 147 (Nev. 2015), quoting Faulkner v. University of Tennessee, 627 So.2d 362 (Ala. 1992).

The Supreme Court reversed. 136 S. Ct. 1277 (2016). It split four-four on whether Nevada v. Hall should be overruled, leaving that precedent in place. But it held that Nevada violated the Full Faith and Credit Clause by refusing to apply the immunity law of either California or Nevada. The special rule of unlimited liability for compensatory damages, not derived from the law of either state, reflected a "policy of hostility to the public Acts" of a sister state. *Id.* at 1282-1283. Chief Justice Roberts and Justice Thomas dissented, concluding that the state court had applied the law of Nevada, as it was entitled to do, and had adequately explained why Nevada law distinguished in-state and out-of-state agencies. Justice Alito concurred in the judgment, but not the opinion, without explanation.

Page 483. After note 15, add:
15.1. Municipalities. Municipalities are not sovereign and are not protected by the Eleventh Amendment. They can be sued in their own name in federal court, and their officials can be sued. But under the principal federal source of state and local liability, 42 U.S.C. §1983 (2012), municipalities cannot be sued for the wrongdoing of their agents or employees. They can be sued only for their official policies or customs. Monell v. New York City Department of Social Services, 436 U.S. 658 (1978). Federal suits against municipalities are further explored in note 4 at page 525 and supplement.

Page 484. After the second paragraph of note 16, add:
16. Waivers of immunity....
This circuit split can be described in more general terms as follows: when a state removes to federal court, does it waive its immunity in all circumstances, or only when it would not also have been immune in state court? Some circuits have added other variations. For an updated account of the split, see Stroud v McIntosh, 722 F.3d 1294, 1300-1301 (11th Cir. 2013).

Page 484. After note 17, add:
18. Indian tribes. Indian tribes are "domestic dependent nations," subject to the plenary power of Congress but sovereign as against the rest of the world. They have sovereign immunity in their own courts and in state and federal courts. This immunity extends even to commercial activities off the reservation, until and unless Congress acts to limit that immunity. The Court reaffirmed this rule in Michigan v. Bay Mills Indian Community, 134 S. Ct. 2024 (2014). As the case name implies, tribes have immunity even as against states. But the Court emphasized that states can regulate tribal activity off the reservation, and enforce their laws with Ex parte Young suits, or even criminal prosecutions, against tribal leaders.

Justice Kagan wrote the opinion for herself, Chief Justice Roberts, and Justices Kennedy, Breyer, and Sotomayor. Justice Thomas's dissent for himself and Justices Scalia, Ginsburg, and Alito questioned the whole concept of tribal sovereign immunity in any application, and wholly rejected its application to commercial activities off the reservation. He included a section describing all the terrible things that can be done by an entity with sovereign immunity. Justice Ginsburg joined that dissent and added her view that the immunity of states is equally "beyond the pale." *Id.* at 2055.

19. Government contractors. Government contractors have been held to be immune for damages caused by carrying out the government's instructions. Yearsley v. W.A. Ross Construction Co., 309 U.S. 18 (1940). But the Court unanimously held that contractors are not immune for illegal actions not directed by the government, even though committed in the course of performing the government contract. Campbell-Ewald Co. v. Gomez, 136 S. Ct. 663, 672-674 (2016).

20. State law. Justice Souter once reported that every state allows declaratory and injunctive relief in state court against state officials, citing cases from 49 states; he somehow missed Indiana. Idaho v. Coeur d'Alene Tribe, 521 U.S. 261, 317 n.15 (1997) (dissenting). His discussion concerned federal claims in state court, and it is conceivable that some of the cited cases are limited to that context.

Georgia just held that sovereign immunity bars suits to enforce the state constitution against state officers in their official capacity. Lathrop v. Deal, 2017 WL 2625463 (Ga. June 19, 2017). But they can still be sued for injunctions or declaratory judgments in their individual capacity — what note 6 calls personal capacity; the two phrases are interchangeable in this context. An elaborate opinion that reviews Georgia sovereign immunity law from the founding forward appears to have produced only a change to an unconventional nomenclature. The apparent reason for the opinion is that defendant officials were going for the home run. They claimed that sovereign immunity barred official-capacity suits, and that official immunity barred individual-capacity suits, so that no one could ever sue the state or any state official to enforce state law, not even prospectively.

It remains to be seen if these individual-capacity suits in Georgia will work just like official-capacity suits elsewhere. The court noted the possibility that individual-capacity judgments would not be binding on successors in office. But without deciding that question, it noted that any appellate decisions would be precedent binding on successors in office. *Id.* at *20 n.32.

2. Suits Against Officers in Their Personal Capacities

Page 491. After note 2, add:

2.1. Working for the government but not as an employee. A private attorney, retained by the city to lead an investigation of a firefighter suspected of abusing sick leave, is entitled to qualified immunity. Filarsky v. Delia, 566 U.S. 377 (2012). The Court thought that the reasons for immunity apply to anyone conducting government business, whether full-time or part-time and whether as an employee or an independent contractor. The Court distinguished Wyatt v. Cole on the ground that the defendant there was pursuing only private interests. The Court characterized Richardson v. McKnight as a narrow holding based on the view that the private employer's profit motive tended to ensure that its employees would not be unduly timid in performing their duties.

Page 492. After note 5, add:

5.1. Better pleading. The Second Circuit held that another set of plaintiffs had plausibly pleaded violations of clearly established law by Ashcroft, Mueller, the Commissioner of the Immigration and Nationalization Service, and the wardens of the Administrative Special Housing Unit. Turkmen v. Hasty, 789 F.3d 218 (2d Cir. 2015), *rev'd on other grounds as* Ziglar v. Abbasi, 137 S. Ct. 1843 (2017). The Supreme Court dismissed most of the complaint on the ground that there is no cause of action for damages for constitutional violations in this context; that holding is summarized in supplement to page 536.

One count alleged a violation of 42 U.S.C. §1985(3) (2012), which expressly authorizes damages for conspiracy to deny any person the equal protection of the laws. The Court dismissed this count on qualified immunity grounds. Plaintiffs alleged a conspiracy to imprison them, because of their race, religion, or ethnicity, beyond the point at which there was probable cause to believe they had committed an offense. The Court did not say that the law against such an imprisonment was not clearly established. Rather, it said that it is not clearly established that a conspiracy among employees of the same government department is a conspiracy. Both this case and Hernandez v. Mesa, summarized below in note 8.f, suggest that not just the primary rule governing the officer's conduct, but all collateral issues that might affect the lawsuit, must be clearly settled.

Justice Thomas joined the opinion to make a majority. But he said that the whole body of law on qualified immunity is illegitimate judicial policy making, made up out of whole cloth in Harlow v. Fitzgerald. He said the legitimate basis for immunity is the common law in 1871, which Congress is presumed to have intended to apply to suits under §1983, and that the clearly-established-law standard has no basis in that common law.

Page 493. At the end of note 8.a., add:
  a. Specificity. . . .
  i. In Ashcroft v. al-Kidd, 563 U.S. 731 (2011), the government arrested the plaintiff as a material witness, allegedly with no intention of calling him as a witness, because it suspected him of supporting terrorism but had no evidence sufficient to get an arrest warrant. The Court again emphasized specificity, holding that it was not clearly settled that pretextual use of material-witness warrants is unconstitutional, and it was irrelevant that the Ninth Circuit thought that the unconstitutionality of the practice could be deduced from clearly established general principles. In an opinion for the five conservatives, Justice Scalia said: "We do not require a case directly on point, but existing precedent must have placed the statutory or constitutional question beyond debate." *Id.* at 741. The Court also said that dictum in one district court opinion was not sufficient to clearly establish anything, even if the defendant in the later case was referenced by name in the dictum in the earlier case.

The Court was unanimous that the relevant law had not been clearly settled. Four Justices said that what the government had done was not unconstitutional, at least not on the plaintiff's theory. Justices Kennedy, Ginsburg, Breyer, and Sotomayor said the government's actions may well have been unconstitutional on other theories that remained open on remand. Justice Kagan did not participate.

ii. In Ryburn v. Huff, 565 U..S. 469 (2012), the Court unanimously and summarily reversed a finding of no immunity. In a fact-intensive opinion, the Court held that reasonable police officers could have believed there was an imminent threat of violence that justified them in entering plaintiffs' house without a search warrant.

iii. The Court again emphasized specificity in Mullenix v. Luna, 136 S. Ct. 305 (2015). Plaintiff's decedent fled from police officers, traveling at high speeds on an Interstate highway. Officers at three different locations deployed spike strips to puncture the tires of the fleeing vehicle. An officer has to remain in position to operate the spike strips, leaving them down for all vehicles except the suspect's, and on occasion, officers operating spike strips have been injured or killed.

Officer Mullenix thought he had a better idea. He took his rifle and stood on the overpass where the first spike strip was deployed, planning to shoot out some essential part of the fleeing vehicle as it approached the overpass. The officers involved had all been trained in the operation of spike strips; none had been trained in shooting at the engine block of a car traveling at high speeds. The officer's supervisor told him by radio to wait and see if the spike strip worked, but he fired six shots at the fleeing vehicle. None hit any critical part of the vehicle, but four hit the driver in the torso, killing him.

The Fifth Circuit held that the shooting violated the clearly settled rule that officers could use deadly force against a fleeing suspect only if that suspect posed a sufficiently "substantial and immediate threat" to the safety of others. Whether the decedent had posed such a threat was a disputed question of fact, so the district court had properly denied summary judgment for the officer.

The Supreme Court summarily reversed. Both spike strips and shooting carried risks, and no case clearly settled that it was unreasonable to choose shooting over spike strips. The Court said four times that the illegality of the officer's specific actions had to be "beyond debate," and it said that qualified immunity protects "all but the plainly incompetent or those who knowingly violate the law." 136 S. Ct. at 308. It did not decide whether the Constitution had been violated. Justice Sotomayor dissented.

iv. The Court unanimously found qualified immunity for a fatal shooting in another bungled police action in White v. Pauley, 137 S. Ct. 548 (2017), but it remanded for further consideration of other officers and other factual theories in the case. The case is too fact intensive to serve as much of a precedent. But the Court said again that the illegality of the officer's conduct must be "beyond debate," and it commented on its frequent reversals of courts of appeals on qualified immunity issues. These reversals had been necessary because "qualified immunity is important to 'society as a whole,'" and because the "immunity from suit" is "effectively lost if a case is erroneously permitted to go to trial." *Id.* at 551, quoting Pearson v. Callahan, 555 U.S. 223, 231 (2009).

Page 494. At the end of note 8.d., add:
d. Division in the lower courts. . . .
At least three times now the Court has said that it is assuming without deciding "that a controlling circuit precedent could constitute clearly established federal law in these circumstances." City and County of San Francisco v. Sheehan, 135 S. Ct. 1765.

1776 (2015); Carroll v. Carman, 135 S. Ct. 348, 350 (2014); Reichle v. Howards, 566 U.S. 658, 665-666 (2012). It is not clear what "circumstances" the Court viewed as relevant. A fourth case used a slightly different formulation, assuming that circuit precedent can clearly establish a right "despite disagreement in the courts of appeals." Taylor v. Barkes, 135 S. Ct. 2042, 2045 (2015). The facts in *Sheehan* and *Carroll* arguably involved such disagreement.

Sheehan and *Taylor* both appeared to go further: "to the extent that a 'robust consensus of cases of persuasive authority' could itself clearly establish the federal right," there was no such consensus in those cases. 135 S. Ct. at 2044; 135 S. Ct. at 1778, quoting Ashcroft v. Al-Kidd, summarized in this supplement to page 493. The Court seems to be edging towards a suggestion that only Supreme Court cases count. Or maybe it is drafting around disagreement on that point.

The Court summarily reversed a refusal to grant qualified immunity in Stanton v. Sims, 134 S. Ct. 3 (2013). A police officer in hot pursuit of a fleeing felon can enter a home without a warrant; the Ninth Circuit thought it clearly settled that he could not enter in hot pursuit of someone suspected only of a misdemeanor. The Supreme Court said that the two cases the Ninth Circuit had relied on were readily distinguishable; that the state supreme courts were deeply divided on the question; and that the state courts in California, where the case arose, were on the officer's side.

In Lane v. Franks, 134 S. Ct. 2369 (2014), the Supreme Court unanimously found a constitutional violation where the Eleventh Circuit had found none. It is unconstitutional to fire a government employee for truthfully testifying under subpoena in a criminal trial. The facts were even worse than that statement of the rule suggests; the plaintiff had discovered ongoing financial fraud in the office he was appointed to head, and he fired the principal culprit, who was also a state legislator. The legislator-thief was convicted and the guy who cleaned up the mess was fired, allegedly for firing the thief.

But the Court also unanimously found that the law had not been clearly settled. The Court did not say what seems most obvious: that if the Eleventh Circuit ruled one way, there must not have been clearly established law the other way in the Eleventh Circuit. The Court appeared to treat the Eleventh Circuit's merits decision as irrelevant, presumably because it had not been decided when the defendant acted. The Eleventh Circuit had relied on a similar Eleventh Circuit decision from 1998. Plaintiff relied on two earlier cases, one of which had been distinguished in the 1998 decision, and on two cases from other circuits; none of that was enough to render the circuit decision most closely in point unsettled.

And the Court left something unsettled for the future: it reserved judgment on whether its decision would apply to employees who frequently testify as part of their regular job duties, such as police officers and crime-lab technicians.

e. New decisions that unsettle settled law. In Reichle v. Howards, 566 U.S. 658 (2012), plaintiff sued two Secret Service agents for arresting him while on a rope line greeting Vice President Cheney. He was charged with "harassment," but the charges were dismissed. Plaintiff offered evidence, sufficient to present a triable issue of fact, that he was arrested in retaliation for criticizing the Iraq war while in the line. But the court of appeals also found that the agents had probable cause to arrest him for making a false statement when they interviewed him.

It was clearly settled in the Tenth Circuit that law enforcement officers are liable if they make an arrest in retaliation for an exercise of the arrestee's free speech rights, even if they have probable cause for the arrest. But in Hartman v. Moore, 547 U.S. 250 (2006), the Supreme Court held that there is no liability for a retaliatory prosecution if there was probable cause to prosecute.

The Tenth Circuit held that *Hartman*'s decision on retaliatory *prosecution* did not change the law of retaliatory *arrest* in the Tenth Circuit. The Supreme Court reversed, noting that retaliatory arrests and prosecutions had traditionally been treated similarly and that a reasonable officer might have thought *Hartman* applied, or would apply, to retaliatory arrests. So the law was no longer clearly settled when plaintiff was arrested.

Hartman was decided on April 26, 2006; plaintiff in *Reichle* was arrested on June 16, 2006. So the odds are good that the agents knew nothing about *Hartman* when they made the arrest. No matter; it was decided before they acted, so they got the benefit of it.

f. Places outside the law? The Court remanded for consideration of qualified immunity in a case where an officer shot and killed a 15-year-old boy who, allegedly, was doing nothing threatening. Hernandez v. Mesa, 137 S. Ct. 2003 (2017). The officer and the government claimed that the boy had been part of a group of boys that was throwing rocks; the complaint, taken as true on a motion to dismiss, alleged that he was not part of the rock throwing. Surely it is clearly settled that officers cannot shoot and kill without provocation. But the officer was in the United States, patrolling the border; the boy was in Mexico, and the officer and the government argued that it was not clearly settled that constitutional rights applied to the boy in Mexico or that foreign nationals outside the United States have any right not to be shot and killed without reason. That may not be how they would characterize it, but that was the bottom line of their argument, and the Court appeared to take it seriously. An earlier decision held that the Fourth Amendment did not apply to a search conducted in Mexico by U.S. and Mexican authorities. United States v. Verdugo-Urquidez, 494 U.S. 259 (1990).

The Court did say that the officer could not rely on the fact that the boy had no previous contacts with the United States, an arguably relevant fact under *Verdugo-Urquidez*, because the officer could not have known that when he fired.

Page 495. After note 9, add:

9.1. The sequence of decision in the Supreme Court.

a. *Camreta.* When a court of appeals holds that a defendant official has violated the law, but dismisses the claim on qualified immunity grounds because the law was not clearly established, the defendant official can seek review in the Supreme Court, and the Court can review the constitutional holding. Camreta v. Greene, 563 U.S. 692 (2011). Justice Kagan's opinion for the Court said that the official may have a continuing stake in the case if he remains in the same office and his conduct of that office is effectively restrained by a holding that what he did was illegal. And the plaintiff may have a continuing stake if she is at risk of being subjected to the same illegal behavior again.

On the plaintiff's continuing stake, the Court seemed to apply a looser standard than that of City of Los Angeles v. Lyons. While a child, plaintiff had been interviewed at school, without a warrant and without a parent present, in an investigation of alleged sexual abuse; the Ninth Circuit held that this was an unconstitutional seizure of her person. She presumably could not have sued for an injunction, because she was not at sufficient risk of being similarly treated again. Perhaps the risk of repetition sufficient to avoid mootness is a lower threshold than the risk of repetition sufficient to create standing to sue. If not, this new rule will not authorize Supreme Court review in the cases where it is most necessary to reach the constitutional issue. The Court did not fully explore how much stake plaintiff must retain, because here it was clear that she retained none: she had grown up, was about to graduate from high school, had moved out of the Ninth Circuit, and had no intention of returning.

The Court vacated as moot not the Ninth Circuit's judgment, but that portion of its opinion discussing the merits of the constitutional question. The usual rule is that the Court reviews judgments, not opinions, so this disposition highlights the anomalous nature of these cases.

Justices Kennedy and Thomas dissented, arguing for the normal standards of jurisdiction and justiciability in qualified immunity cases. But they hinted that perhaps the solution should be to allow plaintiffs to recover nominal damages and no attorneys' fees. There is a full argument for the nominal-damages solution in James E. Pfander, *Resolving the Qualified Immunity Dilemma: Constitutional Tort Claims for Nominal Damages*, 111 Colum. L. Rev. 1601 (2011).

Justice Scalia, concurring, said he would be happy to consider barring the lower courts from reaching the constitutional question when they dismissed on immunity grounds, but these defendants had not asked for that relief.

b. al-Kidd. *Camreta* offered a major discussion of the issue. Ashcroft v. al-Kidd, 563 U.S. 731 (2011), just did it. And the posture was a little different. The court of appeals had denied a motion to dismiss, holding that the former Attorney General's conduct had been unconstitutional and that the law had been clearly established when he acted. The Court reversed on both grounds. First it held that the alleged conduct had not been unconstitutional, at least on plaintiff's theory. Then it held that even if the conduct had been unconstitutional, the law would not have been clearly established.

c. The 2014 cases. In Plumhoff v. Rickard, 134 S. Ct. 2012 (2014), the Court decided the merits first, holding that defendants had not violated the Constitution and were entitled to summary judgment, and then decided that no law to the contrary had been clearly established when they acted. Plaintiff claimed that police officers had used excessive force in shooting to end a high-speech chase; both the driver and his passenger were killed. The Court said that deciding the merits first "is especially valuable with respect to questions that do not frequently arise in cases in which a qualified immunity defense is unavailable," quoting *Pearson*. There were no dissents.

In Lane v. Franks, further described in this supplement to page 494, the Court decided the merits first, and then the immunity issue, without explanation. Maybe that sequence seemed obvious. The cert petition presented both questions, and there was a circuit split on the merits question, which highlights the need to answer the merits question and suggests that the law was not clearly established either way.

In Wood v. Moss, 134 S. Ct. 2056 (2014), the Court decided only the immunity issue, without explanation. The case began with two groups of demonstrators, one supporting President Bush and one protesting his policies, on opposite sides of a street where the presidential motorcade would pass. When the President unexpectedly stopped for dinner in a nearby restaurant, the anti-Bush demonstrators moved down the street to face the restaurant. It was undisputed that there were sound security reasons for moving them away from the restaurant. But instead of returning them to their original location, the Secret Service moved them two blocks in the opposite direction, to a point out of sight and sound of the presidential motorcade when it resumed its original route. The Court unanimously held that no decision put Secret Service agents on notice of an obligation to give pro- and anti-Bush demonstrators equal access to the motorcade route.

And in Tolan v. Cotton, 134 S. Ct. 1861 (2014), the Court summarily reversed a grant of summary judgment on qualified immunity grounds to a police officer who shot the plaintiff on his parents' front porch. The officer had been criminally prosecuted but acquitted, and the testimony about the reasons for the shooting was sharply conflicting. The Court said that the lower courts had improperly resolved these factual disputes on summary judgment, and while the Supreme Court could not normally correct such errors, this one "reflects a clear misapprehension of summary judgment standards in light of our precedents." *Id.* at 1868.

9.2. Empirical studies. Professors Nielson and Walker surveyed all published and unpublished court of appeals cases on Westlaw from 2009 to 2012 that cited *Pearson* and either decided a qualified immunity issue or decided the constitutional merits of a claim in which qualified immunity was offered as a defense. Aaron L. Nielson & Christopher J. Walker, *The New Qualified Immunity*, 89 So. Cal. L. Rev. 1 (2015). There were 844 cases and 1,460 separately identifiable constitutional claims. In about 45 percent of the claims, courts found the law not clearly established but went on to decide the merits of the constitutional claim. In about 28 percent, they found the law not clearly established and declined to decide the merits of the claim. And in about 27 percent of the claims, they found a violation of clearly established constitutional law.

When they went on to the merits after finding the law not clearly established, they found a constitutional violation only eight percent of the time. It was hard to tease out strategic behavior by litigants and courts, but they found some evidence that it may be going on. They argue that courts should be required to state reasons for reaching or not reaching the constitutional merits after deciding that the law was not clearly established. The article also collects and summarizes earlier empirical studies. Helpful graphs are available in the hard copy and on HeinOnline, but not on Westlaw.

Page 495. At the end of note 10, add:
    10. Interlocutory appeals. . . .

    If a qualified immunity motion is denied because immunity depends on disputed issues of fact, interlocutory appeal is not available. Johnson v. Jones, 515 U.S. 304 (1995). And normal rules of appellate procedure apply to any appeal after final judgment. Ortiz v. Jordan, 562 U.S. 180 (2011). So if defendant moves for summary judgment on qualified immunity, the court denies the motion, and defendant does not take an immediate appeal — either because he chooses not to or because he cannot under *Johnson* — and the trial court eventually enters a final judgment for plaintiffs (typically after a trial), the only appeal is from the final judgment, and that appeal is subject to the usual rules on preservation of error.

    There is nothing surprising about this holding, but some courts of appeals had been ruling otherwise. They had been reviewing the summary judgment motion after final judgment, and sometimes throwing out an error-free trial result on the ground that the trial should never have been held because the trial court should have granted the motion for summary judgment.

Page 496. After note 1, add:
    1.1. Another rationale for immunity rules. For a masterful overview and critique of the Court's body of immunity rules, see John C. Jeffries, Jr., *The Liability Rule for Constitutional Torts*, 99 Va. L. Rev. 207 (2013), further discussed in this supplement to page 530. He offers a different argument for a (reformed) version of qualified immunity: Strict liability for damages for all constitutional violations would severely inhibit the development of constitutional law. If every extension of constitutional doctrine led to damage liability, even for violations that occurred before the extension was announced, courts would be reluctant to expand constitutional rights or adapt them to new situations. It therefore makes sense to limit damage liability to cases where defendants had reasonable notice of the constitutional rule they violated. But he thinks that the current emphasis on a factually similar precedent, especially as qualified immunity is applied in some of the courts of appeals, goes far beyond what is required for reasonable notice.

    The Court has taken a remarkable number of these cases in recent years, investing great effort in determining what law was clearly settled at various points in the past instead of, or in addition to, determining what the law actually is for the future.

Page 496. After the third paragraph of note 2, add:
    2. The law before the 1990s. . . .

    In North Carolina v. Covington, a three-judge district court found that North Carolina's state legislative districts were racially gerrymandered. There was an appeal to the Supreme Court within the Court's mandatory jurisdiction, and the Court summarily affirmed with no opinion. 2017 WL 2407469 (U.S. June 5, 2017).

    The district court also ordered that the terms of all incumbent legislators be shortened from two years to one, and that special elections be held to fill the vacancies for the remaining year. The Supreme Court summarily vacated that order, in a brief per curiam opinion, because the district court "failed to meaningfully weigh any equitable considerations." 137 S. Ct. 1624, 1625 (2017). A court must take account of "what is necessary, what is fair, and what is workable." *Id.*, quoting New York v. Cathedral Academy, 434 U.S. 125, 129 (1977), and in the context of deciding whether to order a special election, "there is much for a court to weigh." Ordering a special election in every racial gerrymandering case would be "clearly at odds with our demand for careful case-specific analysis." *Id.* at 1626.

CHAPTER SIX

REMEDIES AND SEPARATION OF POWERS

A. More on Governmental Immunities

1. Consented Suits Against the Government

Page 513. At the end of note 6, add:
6. Hurricane Katrina. . . .
The government did appeal, and the losing plaintiffs from outside the Lower Ninth Ward and St. Bernard Parish also appealed. The court of appeals initially affirmed on all claims. In re Katrina Canal Breaches Litigation, 673 F.3d 381 (5th Cir. 2012). With respect to the discretionary function exception, the court accepted the district court's view that the Corps had not made a public-policy judgment, but rather, had misapplied "objective scientific principles." *Id.* at 391. The decision was unanimous.

On petition for rehearing, the same panel unanimously changed its mind. 696 F.3d 436 (5th Cir. 2012). The court on rehearing said that the government "need not have actually considered any policy implications; instead, the decision must only be 'susceptible to policy analysis.'" *Id.* at 451, quoting Spotts v. United States, 613 F.3d 559, 572 (5th Cir. 2010). The court now seemed to doubt that the key mistake had really been a scientific misjudgment, but it did not reject any of the district court's findings of fact.

Relying on the factual findings from this litigation under the Tort Claims Act, and making additional findings of her own, a judge of the Court of Federal Claims has held the Corps of Engineers liable for taking the property of St. Bernard Parish and Lower Ninth Ward property owners who were subjected to increased and recurrent flooding by the Mississippi River Gulf Outlet (MRGO). Saint Bernard Parish Government v. United States, 121 Fed. Cl. 687 (2015). The Katrina flooding was of course the worst, but the court found that flooding from several more recent hurricanes and smaller storms had also been aggravated by the MRGO. The court has since tried eleven test cases and awarded substantial damages, and certified a class of the remaining property owners. 126 Fed. Cl. 707 (2016). The court entered a final judgment in the eleven test cases, so that the government can appeal. The government permanently closed the MRGO in 2009.

7. Nashville. The Sixth Circuit applied the discretionary function exception in a case arising out of a disastrous flood in Nashville. A.O. Smith Corp. v. United States, 774 F.3d 359 (6th Cir. 2014). Plaintiffs alleged that the reservoir above Nashville was nearly full, and that the Corps of Engineers had three-days warning from the Weather Service, which forecast more than six inches of rain. That forecast was later raised to 8.6 inches. Plaintiffs alleged that the Corps failed to release water before the storm or early in the storm and failed to warn people downstream when it was forced to release vast quantities of water after the reservoir completely filled. They alleged that the Corps's Water Manager left the office for six hours early in the crisis, and again overnight, and that employees seeking authority to release water could not get answers. The court affirmed a dismissal of the complaint, holding that all these alleged decisions were "susceptible to policy analysis." *Id.* at 365, 366, 370, quoting United States v. Gaubert, 499 U.S. 315, 325 (1991). *Gaubert* also said that government officials have no discretion when their conduct is "controlled by mandatory statutes or regulations." 499 U.S. at 328. Much of the Nashville opinion is devoted to showing that the relevant officials violated no such mandatory regulations. Before they could litigate negligence, plaintiffs apparently had to prove a regulatory violation.

8. Bernard Madoff. Victims of Bernard Madoff's massive Ponzi scheme sued the United States, alleging that the scheme would have been exposed much sooner if the Securities and Exchange Commission had exercised even a minimal level of competence. Baer v. United States, 722 F.3d 168 (3d Cir. 2013); Molchatsky v. United States, 713 F.3d 159 (2d Cir. 2013). But both courts said that how to go about investigating fraud is a discretionary function.

Page 514. After note 2, add:

2.1. The intentional-tort exception. The intentional-tort exception figured in two recent Supreme Court cases.

a. Sexual assault by prison guards. The Tort Claims Act:

> **shall not apply** to . . . (h) Any claim arising out of assault, battery, false imprisonment, false arrest, malicious prosecution, abuse of process, libel, slander, misrepresentation, deceit, or interference with contract rights: *Provided*, That, with regard to acts or omissions of investigative or law enforcement officers of the United States Government, the [Tort Claims Act] **shall apply** to any claim arising . . . out of assault, battery, false imprisonment, false arrest, abuse of process, or malicious prosecution.

28 U.S.C. §2680(h) (2012) (boldface emphasis added). The law-enforcement proviso was enacted in response to Bivens v. Six Unknown Agents, excerpted at page 530 of the main volume, which implied a cause of action for damages for an unconstitutional search by federal agents. Some of the lower courts read additional requirements into the proviso, limiting the waiver of immunity to specific contexts, usually involving investigation or arrest.

The Court unanimously rejected all those cases in Milbrook v. United States, 133 S. Ct. 1441 (2013), where a prisoner alleged that he was sexually assaulted by a guard. The Court said that these rules narrowing the waiver of immunity had no basis in the statutory text. In fact, they had so little basis that the Solicitor General confessed error and agreed that immunity had been waived. The Court had to appoint an amicus to defend the lower courts' rule.

b. Unconsented medical treatment. It is far more common for the government to be tenacious in asserting its immunity. An example is Levin v. United States, 568 U.S. 503 (2013). Levin was a veteran being treated in a Navy hospital. He alleged that he became alarmed at conditions in the operating room and withdrew his consent to surgery, and that the surgeon proceeded anyway. Both sides agreed that the surgery went badly. Levin sued for battery, one of the intentional torts covered by the intentional-tort exception, and in this medical context, not covered by the law-enforcement proviso.

The case turned on the provisions of the Medical Malpractice Immunity Act, 10 U.S.C. §1089 (2012), often called the Gonzalez Act. Section 1089(a) makes the Tort Claims Act the exclusive remedy for any medical malpractice by personnel of the armed forces, the Department of Defense, or the CIA. Section 1089(e) says: "For purposes of this section, the provisions of section 2680(h) [the intentional-tort exception] of title 28 shall not apply" to any claim for a negligent or wrongful act in the course of medical treatment. The Court unanimously held that the surgeon is immune and the United States is substituted as defendant under §1089(a), the intentional-tort exception does not apply under §1089(e), and the case should proceed to the merits. The three statutory sections may seem complicated when compressed to a paragraph, but working through them seems very straightforward. Yet the government had persuaded both lower courts that §1089(e) did not unambiguously waive immunity for battery; it merely made clear that the government's immunity from intentional tort claims did not mean that the surgeon was liable instead.

The Gonzalez Act is one of a number of statutes immunizing particular federal employees in particular contexts and substituting the United States as the defendant. This approach was generalized in the Westfall Act, described in the next note in the main volume. But as *Levin* illustrates, the older and more specific provisions remain on the books.

2.2 "Shall not apply." Section 2680, which lists the exceptions to the Tort Claims Act, begins by saying, "The provisions of this chapter and of section 1346(b) of this title shall not apply to —" and then lists all the exceptions. The Court has held that this means not merely that the waiver of immunity shall not apply, but that nothing in the chapter (§§ 2671 to 2680) applies to claims within the exceptions. Simmons v. Himmelreich, 136 S. Ct. 1843 (2016).

Himmelreich sued the United States, alleging that the negligence of its employees caused him to be severely beaten by a fellow prisoner. The case was dismissed under the discretionary function exception. Himmelreich separately filed a constitutional tort suit against individual employees. Normally, a judgment in an action under the Tort Claims Act "shall constitute a complete bar to any action by the claimant, by reason of the same subject matter, against the employee of the government whose act or omission gave rise to the claim." 28 U.S.C. § 2676 (2012). But that provision "shall not apply" to any case falling within one of the exceptions. So a judgment dismissing the claim against the United States because the claim falls within one of the exceptions does not bar a subsequent action against the employees.

Page 516. At the end of note 4.a, add:
   a. Claims based on federal law. . . .
   In United States v. Bormes, 568 U.S. 6 (2012), the Court unanimously reaffirmed a line of cases holding that "[w]here a specific statutory scheme provides the accoutrements of a judicial action, the metes and bounds of the liability Congress intended to create can only be divined from the text of the statute itself." *Id.* at 19. And therefore, the substantive statute must waive sovereign immunity; the waiver in the Tucker Act is irrelevant.

There is an obvious potential for a Catch-22 here. If the substantive statute does not create a cause of action, the Tucker Act is no help, because it does not create a cause of action either. And if the substantive statute does create a cause of action — at least if it creates it in any detail — the Tucker Act is no help, because it cannot supplement or expand the substantive statute.

In *Bormes*, the Fair Credit Reporting Act created a cause of action for damages against "any person" who violated its terms, and defined "person" to include "any . . . government or governmental subdivision or agency." 15 U.S.C. §1681a(b) (2012). The Court remanded for consideration of whether this language was sufficient to waive sovereign immunity.

Page 517. At the end of note 6, add:
6. Sue-and-be-sued clauses. . . .
A federal sue-and-be-sued clause does not necessarily confer federal jurisdiction. If the clause says the entity may sue or be sued in any state or federal court, as some do, that is enough to authorize suit in federal court and to confer jurisdiction over that suit. But if it says the entity may sue or be sued "in any court of competent jurisdiction," the sue-and-be-sued clause is agnostic on which courts are competent; any cases must fall within some other grant of federal jurisdiction. The issue arose most recently when a former homeowner sued the Federal National Mortgage Association (better known as Fannie Mae) in state court over an allegedly unlawful foreclosure, and Fannie Mae unsuccessfully tried to remove the case to federal court. Lightfoot v. Cendant Mortgage Corp., 137 S. Ct. 553 (2017).

2. Suits Against Officers — Absolute Immunity

Page 524. After note 2, add:
2.l. Putting the liability on the officer. The Court recently emphasized that an officer in Malley's situation will usually be protected by qualified immunity, and that it is the rare case where a reasonable officer should recognize the invalidity of a judicially approved warrant. Messerschmidt v. Millender, 565 U.S. 535 (2012). The dissenters in *Messerschmidt* thought the officer had used a report of a specific assault, committed with a specific weapon, to authorize a general search of the suspect's residence for any evidence of gang affiliation or other weapons violations. The majority spun a theory of how a reasonable officer might have thought it was all related; without holding the warrant valid, they did conclude that a reasonable officer might have thought it valid.

The Eighth Circuit imposed liability only on the police officer in Snider v. City of Cape Girardeau, 752 F.3d 1149 (8th Cir. 2014). Plaintiff cut up an American flag and threw the pieces in the street as an act of political protest. The officer sought an arrest warrant for a violation of Missouri's flag-desecration statute; the prosecutor submitted the request to a judge; and the judge issued the warrant. A reporter called the prosecutor to ask if he had ever heard of Texas v. Johnson, 491 U.S. 397 (1989), which upheld the right to burn a flag. The prosecutor read the case and dismissed the prosecution; plaintiff was released after eight hours in jail.

The officer had never heard of Texas v. Johnson either, but the law had been clearly established for twenty years, so there was no qualified immunity. The city was not liable because the arrest did not result from any city policy; see the last paragraph of note 4 on page 525 of the main volume. Plaintiff did not seek damages from the judge or prosecutor, each of whom presumably had absolute immunity. The court awarded $7,000 in compensatory damages against the officer. Probably the city indemnified him, but we don't know that. The court also awarded $61,000 in attorneys' fees jointly and severally against the officer and Missouri, which had intervened in a futile effort to defend the constitutionality of its statute. States are not immune from awards of attorneys' fees.

Page 524. After note 3, add:

3.1. Misconduct before grand juries. The Court unanimously held that an investigator in the prosecutor's office has absolute immunity for his allegedly perjured testimony to the grand jury. Rehberg v. Paulk, 566 U.S. 356 (2012). He was the only witness before the grand jury, so plaintiff argued that he was the complaining witness and within the rule of *Kalina*. The Court held him immune, and within the rule of witnesses at trial. Unlike the prosecutor in *Kalina*, and unlike the complaining witness at common law, defendant here was just a witness, without the power to decide whether to initiate a prosecution. The opinion offers a succinct overview of absolute immunity in general and of witness immunity in particular.

But the Second Circuit has held prosecutors liable for presenting false evidence to a grand jury. Morse v. Fusto, 804 F.3d 538 (2d Cir. 2015), *cert. denied*, 137 S. Ct. 126 (2016). The prosecutors presented a spreadsheet said to summarize a dentist's fraudulent billings to Medicaid; the chart was riddled with errors and exaggerations and the jury found that the prosecutors knew that. The dentist was indicted, and later acquitted, but his practice was destroyed. The court said that the prosecutors' work before the grand jury was investigative, and that it was clearly established that prosecutors cannot present false evidence.

The jury awarded $6.7 million compensatory and $1 million punitive, which the trial judge reduced to $4.6 million and $100,000. The compensatory reduction was in the award for emotional distress and pain and suffering, reduced from $2.5 million to $100,000. The award of $4.2 million for lost earnings was not reduced. 2013 WL 4647603 (E.D.N.Y. 2013). These are huge sums for an Assistant United States Attorney; presumably they will be paid by the United States. Eliminating or reducing immunity would leave prosecutors at risk of such huge judgments. But that would be because prosecutorial misconduct inflicts huge losses. Those losses are real, whether or not a factfinder ever puts a number on them or anyone ever has to compensate them.

Page 525. At the end of note 4, add:

4. Other remedies for prosecutorial misconduct. . . .

In 2010, the City of Long Beach settled with Goldstein for "nearly $8 million." Andrew Blankstein, *Long Beach to Pay Man $8 Million*, L.A. Times 3 (Aug. 12, 2010). And his claim against Los Angeles County appears to have settled for an undisclosed sum. The docket shows settlement conferences followed by an unexplained dismissal with prejudice on plaintiff's motion. Goldstein v. City of Long Beach, No. 2:04-cv-09692 (C.D. Cal. 2014).

4.l. Another egregious example. In Connick v. Thompson, 563 U.S. 51 (2011), Thompson served eighteen years, fourteen of them on death row, for an armed robbery and murder he did not commit. The case focused primarily — exclusively in the majority's view of the case — on the prosecutor's failure to turn over a blood sample that exonerated Thompson of the armed robbery. When that misconduct was revealed, the state courts vacated the murder conviction, because the armed robbery conviction had made it impossible, as a strategic matter, for Thompson to testify in his own defense at the murder trial. On a new trial, the jury acquitted of murder in 35 minutes.

Thompson then sued for damages, and a jury awarded $14 million. Thompson's theory was that the prosecutor's office, as a governmental agency, was liable for a policy of failing to train prosecutors about their obligation to disclose exculpatory evidence. So the applicable rules were not the prosecutor's absolute immunity in his personal capacity, but the rules on municipal liability. Earlier cases established that a municipality could be liable for a policy of deliberate indifference to constitutional rights, including a policy of failure to train. Proof of such a policy usually requires a pattern of similar violations, but the Court has left open the possibility that such a policy could be proved by one violation that was sufficiently obvious or egregious.

The Supreme Court reversed the damage award. It found no unconstitutional policy of inadequate training, because it said that Thompson had not relied on a pattern of failing to disclose, and because the one violation involving the blood sample did not by itself show such a policy. Justice Ginsburg, dissenting for herself and Justices Breyer, Sotomayor, and Kagan, found many other examples of evidence that should have been disclosed, and a culture of deliberate indifference to the obligation to disclose such evidence.

4.2. More on municipal liability. The Court has unanimously held that *Monell* applies to suits for injunctions or declaratory judgments as well as to suits for damages. That is, plaintiff can get an injunction against a municipality under §1983 only if a policy or custom of the municipality violates federal law. Los Angeles County v. Humphries, 562 U.S. 29 (2010).

Page 530. After note 4, add:

5. An overview. John Jeffries finds the Court's immunity doctrines in constitutional cases incoherent:

> There is no liability rule for constitutional torts. There are, rather, several different liability rules, ranging from absolute immunity at one extreme to absolute liability at the other. . . . Most defendants — including federal, state, and local officers — are neither absolutely immune nor strictly liable. Instead, they are protected by qualified immunity, a fault-based standard approximating negligence as to illegality.
>
> This fracturing of constitutional torts into disparate liability rules does not reflect any plausible conception of policy. Although the Court occasionally makes functional arguments about one or another corner of this

landscape, it has never attempted to justify the overall structure in those terms. Nor could it. The proliferation of inconsistent policies and arbitrary distinctions renders constitutional tort law functionally unintelligible. Blame may be cast on the shadow (though certainly not the terms) of the Eleventh Amendment, on the incorporation into constitutional tort doctrine of bits and pieces of the common law, and on accidents of timing and personnel: when and under what circumstances did particular issues come to the Court? However sympathetic one may be [to the difficulties caused by such factors,] the fact remains that constitutional tort doctrine is incoherent. It is so shot through with inconsistency and contradiction as to obscure almost beyond recognition the underlying stratum of good sense.

John C. Jeffries, Jr., *The Liability Rule for Constitutional Torts*, 99 Va. L. Rev. 207, 207-208 (2013).

He would sharply limit absolute immunity to the bounds of its core justifications. Simplifying somewhat, those bounds would be legislative work on generally applicable legislation that can be challenged in litigation with the executive branch, prosecutorial misconduct in the courtroom and constrained by the adversary process, and judicial decisions subject in fact to correction on appeal. He would eliminate any distinction between state and local government, preferably by interpreting §1983 to override sovereign immunity in constitutional cases. He would reform and generalize qualified immunity: governments and government officials should be liable in damages when they reasonably should have known that their conduct was unconstitutional. He collects cases of obvious unconstitutionality where defendants were held immune because there was no case with sufficient factual similarity to satisfy current judicial understandings of the clearly-established-law test; he would impose liability in such cases.

He does not discuss *Goldstein* or *Thompson*, but he does discuss the lack of deterrence for violations of the duty to disclose exculpatory evidence. And he collects studies finding rampant violations of that duty. *Id.* at 227 n.68.

B. Creating Causes of Action

Page 535. After note 2, add:

2.1. Employees in private prisons. Relying heavily on Wilkie v. Robbins, the Court has held that no *Bivens* action lies against employees of a private corporation that operates a prison under contract with the government. Minneci v. Pollard, 565 U.S. 118 (2011). Defendants allegedly withheld medical care and in other ways aggravated injuries plaintiff suffered in an accident in the prison. The Court found that state-law tort remedies, which are generally unavailable against federal employees, would be available against employees of a private corporation and would be adequate. These remedies "may sometimes prove less generous" than a *Bivens* remedy, but "in general," they would "provide roughly similar incentives for potential defendants to comply with the Eighth Amendment while also providing roughly similar compensation to victims of violations." *Id.* at 625. The Court reserved the possibility of a case in which state remedies were not comparable in this way. Justice Ginsburg dissented.

Page 536. At the end of note 7, add:
    7. State law. . . .
The Georgia Supreme Court has created some confusion on suits for injunctions and declaratory judgments, but perhaps not changed the bottom line. See the summary of Lathrop v. Deal in supplement to page 484.

Page 536. After note 8, add:
    9. Creeping ever closer to repudiation? Justice Thomas appeared to get most of what he wanted in Ziglar v. Abbasi, 137 S. Ct. 1843 (2017). The Court held that there is no *Bivens* remedy for well-pleaded claims that in the wake of the September 11 attacks, Arabs and Muslims were imprisoned in harsh conditions on the basis of their religion or ethnicity even after they had been cleared of any connection to terrorism. The Court said that any claim that differs in any significant way from the claims in *Bivens*, *Davis*, or *Green* has to be assessed for any special factor that might counsel hesitation. And this assessment has to begin from the premise that expanding *Bivens* is disfavored. *Bivens, Davis*, and *Green* were decided in the day when the Court implied causes of action to enforce statutes; that day is long past. The cases refusing to allow *Bivens* claims are not a series of cases with special factors counseling hesitation; they are now the general rule.

There was also a well-pleaded claim that the guards abused these prisoners, and that the warden knew about it and allowed it to continue. The Court remanded that claim to the Second Circuit to decide in the first instance whether there were special factors counseling hesitation. Justice Thomas concurred in the result to make a majority to dispose of the case, but he would have preferred outright reversal and an opinion confining *Bivens* to the precise circumstances of *Bivens*, *Davis*, or *Green*.

Justice Breyer, joined by Justice Ginsburg, dissented on all issues. He said that this was not a new context; *Green* had also been a suit about prison conditions. Congress had not created any other remedy, and it was far too late for an injunction. And the national security context was not a sufficient factor counseling hesitation. The alleged violations had continued long after the immediate aftermath of September 11, and there were ample other safeguards protecting defendant officials — stringent pleading requirements after *Iqbal*, qualified immunity, the courts' power to limit discovery, and the substantive law, which recognizes that measures that would be unconstitutional in normal times might be constitutional in emergencies. And he thought it would be indefensible for state officials to be liable for their constitutional torts but federal officials not.

Justices Kagan and Sotomayor were recused. The case had been pending while Kagan was Solicitor General, and Sotomayor had presumably voted on en banc petitions in earlier appeals in the Second Circuit. Justice Gorsuch was appointed too late to participate.

The Court appeared to reaffirm *Bivens* in its original Fourth Amendment context. It reaffirmed judicial power to order compliance with the Constitution in the future. And it did not formally say that there could never be another *Bivens* cause of action beyond those recognized in *Bivens*, *Davis*, and *Green*. But lower court judges may draw that inference.

10. **Another remand.** The Court remanded another *Bivens* claim for further consideration in light of *Abbasi*. Hernandez v. Mesa, 137 S. Ct. 2003 (2017), more fully described in supplement to page 494. The defendant officer shot across the border and killed a 15-year-old boy in Mexico. Shooting and killing without justification is a more extreme seizure of the person, and a more extreme Fourth Amendment violation, than in *Bivens* itself. The boy's parents also claimed that he had a Fifth Amendment substantive due process right not to be shot for no reason. But the officer and the government claimed that the Constitution does not apply in Mexico, so the boy had no right not to be shot and killed. That argument led the Court to treat both the Fourth and Fifth Amendment claims as novel in the *Bivens* context, so that a new *Bivens* claim would have to be justified.

Page 542. At the end of note 4 (inside the parentheses), add:
    4. **Title VI of the Civil Rights Act of 1964.** . . .
The Supreme Court has unanimously and summarily reversed in a case where the lower courts granted summary judgment to defendants because plaintiffs pleaded their case under the Fourteenth Amendment and not under § 1983; the lower courts had also denied leave to amend. Johnson v. City of Shelby, 135 S. Ct. 346 (2014).

Page 543. After note 6, add:
    6.1. **The same idea in other contexts.** More generally, the Court will confine plaintiffs to a cause of action and remedy created by Congress if it believes that Congress meant the statutory remedy to be exclusive, and if the statutory remedy is specified in reasonable detail, the Court will generally infer that it is meant to be exclusive. A recent example is Elgin v. Department of the Treasury, 567 U.S. 1 (2012). Plaintiffs sought to enjoin enforcement of a law that bars from government employment any male who failed to register for the stand-by draft. The Court held that the administrative remedies under the Civil Service Reform Act, 5 U.S.C. §1101 *et seq.* (2012), were exclusive — even though the agency could not consider the constitutional claim. The Federal Circuit would be able to consider the constitutional claim when it reviewed the agency's action.

    There is a similar holding in Sandoz Inc. v. Amgen Inc., 137 S. Ct. 1664 (2017), interpreting a specialized patent statute for drugs derived from living organisms and far too complex to be worth summarizing here. The point for our purposes is that a complex federal statute authorized a declaratory judgment for the violation plaintiff alleged, but did not mention injunctions. The Court held that the declaratory judgment was the exclusive federal remedy. It left open on remand the possibility that there might be a state-law remedy if the federal violation amounted to unfair competition under state law.

Page 543. After note 7, add:
    7.1. **Narrowing express rights of action.** The European Union and twenty-six of its member states sued RJR Nabisco, alleging violations of RICO, the Racketeer Influenced and Corrupt Organizations Act. RJR allegedly laundered drug money as

part of the means to smuggle untaxed cigarettes into EU countries, and gave material aid to terrorism by selling cigarettes to Iraq in violation of international sanctions. Of course RJR denied the allegations.

The Court presumes that federal statutes do not apply outside the United States unless Congress says so. But it unanimously agreed that Congress had said so with respect to money laundering and aid to terrorism, each of which is a predicate offense for RICO liability. RJR Nabisco, Inc. v. European Community, 136 S. Ct. 2090 (2016). And RICO expressly creates a private right of action for "any person injured in his business or property by reason of a violation of" the section with extraterritorial application. 18 U.S.C. §1964(c) (2012). But the Court held, four to three, that Congress has to separately indicate its intention that the private cause of action be available extraterritorially. Because Congress had not separately so indicated, and because the plaintiffs sought to recover for injuries suffered abroad, the case must be dismissed. "Any person" was not clear enough to mean persons suffering injury abroad. Congress may need to sprinkle clear statements through statutes, one for every element that might be questioned.

Justice Ginsburg for the dissenters said that the section providing the private right of action incorporated the substantive provision that it referenced, including that provision's express provisions for extraterritorial application. She also said that much of this alleged conspiracy was carried out in the United States, so that the presumption against extraterritoriality had little effect. Justice Sotomayor was recused, because she had written an opinion in a much earlier phase of the case. It seems quite likely, although we can never be sure, that the vote would have been four-four, and that the judgment below upholding the private cause of action allowed to stand, if she could have voted. Recusals matter. Of course it also seems likely that the vote would have been five-four for RJR if she had participated and if Justice Scalia had lived.

7.2. The Supremacy Clause. The Supreme Court reached an unsurprising result, in a puzzling but potentially significant set of opinions, in Armstrong v. Exceptional Child Center, Inc., 135 S. Ct. 1378 (2015). Section 30A of the Medicaid Act, 42 U.S.C. §1396a(a)(30)(A) (2012), sets standards that states must apply in setting the rates they pay to medical providers who treat low-income patients covered by Medicaid. The standards are broad and somewhat in tension. Rates must enlist enough providers to deliver care comparable to that available in the general population; they must also safeguard against unnecessary treatment and be consistent with efficiency, economy, and quality of care. Plaintiffs alleged that Idaho's rates were too low to comply with this standard, and the Ninth Circuit held that there was an implied cause of action under the Supremacy Clause to enjoin Idaho's violation of federal law. 567 F. App'x 496 (9th Cir. 2014).

The Court reversed. It said that the Supremacy Clause did not create a cause of action. And it said that the Medicaid Act did not create a cause of action, because §30A lacked rights-creating language, let alone language clearly creating a right to sue. The Court acknowledged that federal courts had long enjoined violations of federal law, including state laws preempted by federal law. It said that this practice "is the creation of courts of equity, and reflects a long history of judicial review of illegal executive action, tracing back to England." 135 S. Ct. at 1384. Such an equitable claim was precluded in this case by a fair reading of the Medicaid Act; that Act explicitly created another remedy (a cutoff of federal funds), and the broad and vague standard in §30A was judicially unadministrable.

The Court plainly treated these theories as *three* separate and independent theories. That is, it treated the claim in equity as distinct from an implied cause of action under either the Supremacy Clause or the statute. And it did not explain. This seems inconsistent with *Sandoval*, which treated a suit in equity to enjoin enforcement of an alleged state violation of federal law as presenting a question of whether there was an express or implied cause of action to enforce the federal statute allegedly violated.

Justice Sotomayor dissented, joined by Justices Kennedy, Ginsburg, and Kagan. She thought the equitable claim to enjoin violations of law was so well established that Congress "should generally be presumed to contemplate such enforcement unless it affirmatively manifests a contrary intent." *Id.* at 1392. She found no such affirmative expression in the Medicaid Act. She said that an equitable claim for an injunction is *not* a claim for an implied cause of action, which could lead to a variety of remedies, including damages, that Congress must intentionally create. And she treated *Sandoval* as an implied-cause-of-action case, without explanation.

Sandoval's apparent extension of the implied-cause-of-action cases to lawsuits seeking only an injunction may be implicitly limited to its facts by *Armstrong*. The *Sandoval* opinion said nothing about the historic availability of injunctions; it simply subjected such a claim to the implied-cause-of-action jurisprudence. Plaintiffs in *Sandoval* sought only an injunction, but their brief made nothing of that fact; they simply argued it out under the implied-cause-of-action cases. *Armstrong* does talk about the historic availability of injunctions, and treats a claim for an injunction as distinct from the implied-cause-of-action jurisprudence. But it does so without explanation.

Justice Breyer provided the fifth vote. He joined the parts of the Court's opinion that rejected a cause of action under the Supremacy Clause and that found the historic claim in equity overridden by a fair reading of §30A. He wrote separately on whether there was an implied right of action under §30A, emphasizing not only that the statutory standard was vague, but also that it involved rate setting, which was far more appropriate for administrative agencies than for courts.

D. The Right to Jury Trial

Page 569. After note 1, add:

1.1 Reconsidering *Great-West*. Relying on dictum in Sereboff v. Mid Atlantic Medical Services, Inc., 547 U.S. 356 (2006), six of eight circuits to consider the issue had allowed claims to general assets, claims apparently barred by *Great-West*. But the Court reaffirmed *Great-West* in Board of Trustees v. Montanile, 136 S. Ct. 651 (2016), more fully described in supplement to page 101.

1.2. *CIGNA*. There is another elaborate discussion of ERISA remedies in CIGNA Corp. v. Amara, 563 U.S. 421 (2011). For any change in retirement plans, the plan administrator is required to disclose the changes to the employees in comprehensible form in a plan summary. When CIGNA made substantial changes to its plan, its disclosures assured the employees that CIGNA was saving no money from these changes and that no employee would be worse off because of them. In fact, the company was saving $10 million a year, and most employees were made worse off in multiple ways. The company could have imposed these changes without consent after full disclosure, but that presumably would have caused employee unrest.

The lower courts held that they could enforce the retirement plan as it would have been if it had conformed to the disclosures, and that they could do this under 29 U.S.C. §1132(a)(1)(B), which authorizes suits by beneficiaries to enforce plans. But the Supreme Court held that this section authorized enforcement only of the plan as written, and that the disclosures were not part of the plan.

The district court had also noted the possibility of "other appropriate equitable relief" under §1132(a)(3). The Supreme Court remanded for further consideration of this theory, with a substantial analysis suggesting that what the district court had done "closely resembles three other traditional equitable remedies." *Id.* at 440.

First, it might be reformation of the plan. Reformation, taken up in section 7.C, judicially amends documents to conform to the parties' mutual understanding of what the documents said or to what one side fraudulently represented that they said.

Second, it might be estoppel, which prevents a party from denying now what he earlier represented as true. This book treats estoppel as a remedial defense in section 11.C; the Court also, and plausibly, treated it as an equitable remedy.

And third, the district court's order of back benefits to employees who had already retired might be a "surcharge" of the trustee of the retirement plan, the traditional equitable label for actions to recover money or property due under a trust. Here the trust analogy again appeared to be dispositive.

And while detrimental reliance was an element of estoppel, it was not an element of reformation or surcharge. So the plan could be reformed, and the trustee surcharged under the plan as reformed, without a showing that the employees could have done anything different if they had received proper disclosures. Whether those remedies were appropriate on the facts of the case was left for the district court on remand, but the Supreme Court's view seemed pretty clear. Justices Scalia and Thomas thought the entire analysis of §1132(a)(3) was an advisory opinion that should not have been issued.

Less helpfully, the Court also repeated the dictum that "injunctions, mandamus, and restitution" are typical forms of equitable relief. And it mysteriously referred to the relief provided in §1132(a)(1)(B) as an "exception" to the general rule that "the remedies available to those courts of equity were traditionally considered equitable remedies." 563 U.S. at 440. Of course all remedies in equity were equitable; that is tautological. And the right to sue for trust benefits, codified in §1132(a)(1)(B), was an equitable remedy available in equity. The exception to which the Court apparently referred was quite narrow: if it were time for the trust to terminate, so that undistributed assets were payable directly to a beneficiary and not to be held in continuing trust, the beneficiary had the option of suing at law for a simple money judgment, or in equity to surcharge the trustee. *Restatement (Third) of Trusts* §95 & cmts. a, b; *id.* §100 (Am. Law Inst. 2012). The legal option, obviously, was a legal remedy; the equitable option, also obviously, remained an equitable remedy.

1.3. Implementing *CIGNA*. On remand in *CIGNA*, the lower courts reformed the plan for fraud and mistake, and ordered benefits paid under the plan as reformed. Amara v. CIGNA Corp., 775 F.3d 510 (2d Cir. 2014). At least eight circuits have recognized estoppel claims in the wake of *CIGNA*, often in cases involving individual claimants who were promised benefits they never got. These cases are collected in Guerra-Delgado v. Popular, Inc., 774 F.3d 776 (1st Cir. 2014). The First Circuit did not follow the trend. It will recognize an estoppel claim, if ever, only when the written plan is ambiguous, and so far, it has not found an ambiguous plan. The Ninth Circuit has also limited *CIGNA* to narrow circumstances.

Page 572. After note 4, add:

5. Greater content for public rights? "The apparently settled rule" in note 3 came unsettled, and the restriction to public rights got substantial new life, in Stern v. Marshall, 564 U.S. 462 (2011). This was the latest installment in the long-running litigation by and on behalf of Anna Nicole Smith to recover her share of the estate of the fabulously wealthy husband she married when she was 26 and he was 89.

She filed for bankruptcy, and her deceased husband's son filed a defamation claim against her in the bankruptcy court. Smith filed a counterclaim for tortious interference with the gift her husband had allegedly intended to make to her. The question in the Supreme Court was whether her counterclaim could be adjudicated in the bankruptcy court. The Court said no.

Langenkamp and *Katchen* were explained not as cases of a counterclaim against a creditor who filed a claim in the bankruptcy court, but as cases of a counterclaim that was based on bankruptcy law and that could be adjudicated in the course of adjudicating the creditor's claim. Smith's state-law tort claim was not based on bankruptcy law. And although it was sufficiently related to her stepson's claim that the lower courts had held it to be a compulsory counterclaim, it presented significant issues of law and fact not presented by the stepson's claim. (Try not to be confused by the fact that the stepson was nearly thirty years older than his stepmother.)

Recognizing that its discussions of "the public rights exception" had "not been entirely consistent," the Court held that Smith's common law tort claim was not a claim of public right. "[W]hat makes a right 'public' rather than private is that the right is integrally related to particular federal government action." *Id.* at 490-491. The Court considered several other factors mentioned in earlier public-right cases, and said that Smith's claim did not satisfy any of them. It also emphasized that bankruptcy courts are courts (although not Article III courts), and that they decide a broad range of issues, so they are unlike administrative agencies with special expertise. So the administrative-agency cases might be different from the bankruptcy cases.

Justice Scalia, concurring, thought the long list of factors from earlier cases was wholly unworkable. He would have held, quoting his concurring opinion in *Granfianciera*, that "a matter of public rights . . . must at a minimum arise between the government and others." *Id.* at 503.

Justice Breyer, dissenting for himself and Justices Ginsburg, Sotomayor, and Kagan, read *Langenkamp* and *Katchen* as your editor read them in note 3, and as Congress apparently read them when it authorized bankruptcy court jurisdiction over all counterclaims. 28 U.S.C. §157(b)(2)(C) (2012). Justice Breyer thought the majority's opinion was entirely too formalistic, and that it relied too much on older cases and gave little weight to more recent cases. He would have held that even private disputes can be committed to non-Article-III tribunals sitting without juries if there is no threat to the independence of the judiciary. Letting bankruptcy courts adjudicate counterclaims was constitutional, even as applied to common-law tort claims like the one at issue here, because of a list of practical considerations that bore little resemblance to the majority's list of factors.

6. Patent validity. Patents are granted in a non-adversary administrative process. Under longstanding law, a party challenging the validity of a patent had to sue in court and overcome a strong presumption of validity. In 2011, under the curious label "inter partes review" (literally, among-the-parties review), Congress provided that some of the basic grounds for challenging patents could be asserted in an administrative adversary proceeding before the Patent and Trademark Appeal Board. 35 U.S.C. §311 (2012). The Court has agreed to decide whether this process "violates the Constitution by extinguishing private property rights through a non-Article III forum without a jury." Oil States Energy Services, LLC v. Greene's Energy Group, LLC, 2017 WL 2507340 (U.S. June 12, 2017). The petition for certiorari relied on *Stern* and *Granfianciera* and several nineteenth-century cases. The response relied on *Atlas* and *Pernell* and argued that a patent is a "quintessential public right."

CHAPTER SEVEN

PREVENTING HARM WITHOUT COERCION:
DECLARATORY REMEDIES

A. Declaratory Judgments

1. The General Case

Page 584. After note 3, add:

3.1. Reviewing administrative agencies. The Administrative Procedure Act provides that courts can review final actions of administrative agencies, but only when "there is no other adequate remedy in a court." 5 U.S.C. §704 (2012). This is an obvious analogue of the irreparable injury rule, and the *Young* dilemma applies. The Court recently held that excavating wetlands without an environmental permit, waiting for an enforcement action, and then defending on the ground that no permit was required because the wetlands at issue are not "waters of the United States" is not an adequate remedy where draconian penalties would apply if the court decided that a permit was required. U.S. Army Corps of Engineers v. Hawkes Co., 136 S. Ct. 1807 (2016). The puzzle is why the government even tried to argue otherwise.

The Court held that applying for the permit and then seeking judicial review if the permit were denied was also an inadequate remedy, because applying for the permit would require expensive environmental studies, litigation costs, and long delays. The cost and delay of litigation generally does not count as irreparable injury when the plaintiff is trying to skip some required procedural step. But in *Hawkes*, the Corps had determined that the wetlands at issue were waters of the United States, and the Court had held that this determination was final agency action, ripe for review. Without much discussion, the Court unanimously treated the cost and delays of litigation as relevant to the adequacy of waiting for a later and completely separate final agency action on granting or denying the permit.

Page 586. After note 10, add:

11. Burden of proof. The declaratory judgment action reverses the usual alignment of the parties. The potential plaintiff in a suit for damages becomes the defendant in the declaratory judgment action; the declaratory plaintiff fears becoming the defendant in that suit for damages. Plaintiffs usually bear the burden of persuasion. But the declaratory judgment action could not achieve its purpose if the declaratory plaintiff bore the burden of disproving the feared damage claim that the damages plaintiff would normally have to prove.

The Supreme Court has unanimously held that an alleged patent infringer, who sues for a declaratory judgment that he is not infringing, does not bear the burden of proving non-infringement. The burden of proving infringement remains on the patent holder, where it would be if the patent holder had sued the alleged infringer for infringement. Medtronic, Inc. v. Mirowski Family Ventures, LLC, 134 S. Ct. 843 (2014). The Court emphasized that the Declaratory Judgment Act is procedural, but the burden of proof is substantive. The point is not confined to patent cases; it should apply to declaratory judgments generally.

The issue arose because the Federal Circuit held otherwise, at least in cases where the declaratory plaintiff was not at immediate risk of an infringement suit because he was operating under a license as in *Medimmune*, or (presumably) refraining from the conduct alleged to infringe until after the dispute was resolved. The Federal Circuit claimed at least some support for its result in state-law insurance cases.

12. Mootness. A declaratory judgment claim can become moot in the same ways that an injunction claim can become moot. In Already, LLC v. Nike, Inc., 568 U.S. 85 (2013), the Court applied the voluntary cessation rule from injunction cases to a declaratory judgment claim. *Already* is more fully described in this supplement to page 284.

Page 587. After note 2, add:
2.l. Spider Man. Marvel Entertainment bought the patent to a Spider Man toy, and agreed to pay a three percent royalty with no ending date. When the patent expired after twenty years, Marvel sued for a declaratory judgment that it had no further liability to pay royalties on the contract. The Supreme Court entertained the declaratory claim without comment, and on the merits, ruled for Marvel. Kimble v Marvel Entertainment, LLC, 135 S. Ct. 2401 (2015). Marvel had removed Kimble's contract suit to federal court based on diversity of citizenship, and then counterclaimed for a declaratory judgment. And Marvel, the declaratory plaintiff, was not asserting a contract claim, but rather a federal right under the Patent Act. So the declaratory judgment claim could have been in federal court even without diversity.

2. The Special Case of Interfering with State Enforcement Proceedings

Page 594. After note 3, add:
3.1. Litigation with a state agency, but not directed to enforcement. The second sentence at the top of 594 says that "[t]he *Younger* doctrine bars almost any form of federal relief that would directly or indirectly interfere with a pending state proceeding to which the state or one of its agencies, officials, or subdivisions is a party." That turns out to be overbroad. There can be parallel state and federal litigation between a state or one of its agencies and a private party, and the federal action can proceed so long as the state litigation is not an enforcement proceeding.

Put the other way around, the Court says that *Younger* applies in only three circumstances: 1) where the federal claim would interfere with "ongoing state criminal prosecutions;" 2) where the federal claim would interfere with "certain 'civil enforcement proceedings;'" and 3) where the federal claim would interfere with orders "uniquely in furtherance of the state courts' ability to perform their judicial functions.'" Sprint Communications, Inc. v. Jacobs, 134 S. Ct. 584, 591 (2013), quoting New Orleans Public Service, Inc. v. Council of City of New Orleans, 491 U.S. 350, 368 (1989).

Sprint involved a complicated dispute between Sprint and a local Iowa phone company. The Iowa Utilities Board resolved Sprint's state and federal claims, on the merits and against Sprint, and over the objection that the Federal Communications Commission had exclusive jurisdiction of the federal claim. Sprint then filed suit in federal court to enjoin enforcement of the Board's order. See Verizon Maryland, Inc. v. Public Service Commission, 535 U.S. 635 (2002), summarized at page 478 of the main volume, illustrating this remedy and unanimously rejecting a sovereign-immunity defense. Sprint also filed a petition for review of the Board's order in state court, presenting its state-law claims and also, in an "abundance of caution," in case its federal lawsuit was dismissed, presenting its federal claim to the state court.

The Board argued that it was seeking to enforce its order, and that the federal suit interfered both with its administrative proceedings and with the state court's review of those proceedings. But the Supreme Court treated this as ordinary parallel civil litigation. It emphasized that the civil-enforcement proceedings to which it had applied *Younger* were generally initiated by the state, that they involved alleged misconduct by the private litigant, and that they were often quasi-criminal. This case involved none of those things. The administrative proceeding and both the state and federal lawsuits were civil proceedings initiated by Sprint, complaining about activities of the local phone company.

Page 595. After note 1, add:

1.1. The myth of mildness. *Steffel* says that the declaratory judgment is "a much milder form of relief than an injunction," and Professor Bray thinks that claim is worth refuting, because a fair number of people have taken that statement seriously. Samuel L. Bray, *The Myth of the Mild Declaratory Judgment*, 63 Duke L.J. 1091 (2014). He demolishes the idea that declaratory judgments are any less effective, any less likely to be obeyed, or any less binding than an injunction.

He argues that the real difference between the two remedies is that the injunction gives the court far more "managerial" capacity. The declaratory judgment gives a binding answer to a legal question and leaves implementation of that answer to the parties. The injunction tells defendant what she must do; those instructions must be specific and if necessary they can be very specific; this specification can be modified in response to changed circumstances; and the contempt power is available if needed. He also argues, less successfully in my view, that there is a difference in the ripeness requirement, and that declaratory judgments really are available in situations where an injunction would not be.

Page 597. After note 4, add:

4.1. The latest word on ripeness. The Court devoted a full opinion to ripeness in Susan B. Anthony List v. Driehaus, 134 S. Ct. 2334 (2014). The facts are worth exploring, and a bit complicated. But the bottom line here is that plaintiff has standing to challenge the constitutionality of a statute if he faces 'a credible threat" of future prosecution. And the Court took a realistic view of the risk to plaintiffs, despite several unusual steps between them and prosecution. Plaintiffs sought both declaratory and injunctive relief, and nothing in the Court's opinion suggests any distinction between the two.

An Ohio statute prohibited false statements in political campaigns, if the false statement was made knowingly, or in some cases, with reckless disregard of the truth.

Any person could file an administrative complaint with the Ohio Elections Commission; if a complaint was filed in the last ninety days before a general election, the Commission was required to hold a probable cause hearing within two days, and if it found probable cause, to hold a hearing on the merits within ten days. The parties were entitled to discovery, and the Commission had subpoena power. If the Commission found a violation by clear and convincing evidence, it was required to refer the case to a county prosecutor for criminal prosecution as a first-degree misdemeanor; the potential penalty for a first offense was six months in jail and a $5,000 fine. The Commission was handling thirty or forty cases a year; the Court did not say how many criminal prosecutions followed, if any.

One plaintiff had issued press releases claiming that Congressman Driehaus had voted for government-funded abortions; Driehaus said this statement was false. The dispute turned on whether the Affordable Care Act provided government funds for abortions. Driehaus filed a complaint; the Commission found probable cause; the parties agreed to postpone the merits hearing until after the election. Driehaus lost the election and withdrew his complaint. One plaintiff said it desired to make the same charge against other incumbents in future election cycles, but it feared renewed prosecution. This plaintiff also said that it had attempted to buy a billboard publicizing its charge against Driehaus, but that the billboard company, after receiving a threat of prosecution from Driehaus, cancelled the contract. The other plaintiff said that it had wanted to make the same charge against Driehaus, and wanted to make similar charges in the future, but that it had been deterred by the Commission proceedings against the first plaintiff.

The court of appeals found no ripe threat of future prosecution. 525 F. App'x 415 (6th Cir. 2013). Plaintiffs did not allege that they intended to knowingly or recklessly make false statements, and Driehaus had joined the Peace Corps and gone to Africa; he would not be running again.

The Supreme Court unanimously reversed, in an opinion by Justice Thomas. Plaintiffs had alleged that they intended to "engage in a course of conduct arguably affected with a constitutional interest." 134 S. Ct. 2342, quoting Babbitt v. United Farm Workers, 442 U.S. 289, 298 (1979). This appears to mean only that plaintiffs claim constitutional protection for their intended conduct; it is not clear if the Court meant anything more than that by quoting *Babbitt*'s vague formulation. Plaintiff's course of conduct was arguably prohibited by the challenged statute. It mattered not that plaintiffs believed their statements to be true; the Commission had already found probable cause to believe that they were false. Plaintiffs wanted to talk about the Affordable Care Act, not just about Driehaus.

And there was a credible threat of future prosecution, as illustrated most obviously by the history of past enforcement, by the finding of probable cause, and by the fact that any person could file a complaint. Even the administrative process before the Commission could seriously disrupt a campaign, but the Court did not have to decide whether that threat alone was sufficient to support a ripeness finding. That threat combined with the more attenuated threat of criminal prosecution was certainly sufficient.

On remand, the Sixth Circuit held the Ohio statute unconstitutional. Susan B. Anthony List v. Driehaus, 814 F.3d 466 (6th Cir. 2016). The Commission was also a defendant, so there was someone to defend the statute.

Page 603. At the end of note 2, add:
   2. *Rooker-Feldman*. . . .
The Court repeated its narrow understanding of *Rooker-Feldman* in Skinner v. Switzer, 562 U.S. 521 (2011), a case in which a convicted criminal defendant sued to force DNA testing of key evidence in the case.

B. Quiet Title and the Like

Page 610. After note 13.c, add:
   d. Plaintiff not claiming an interest in the property. The Supreme Court has held that a suit seeking to divest the United States of title to land is not a quiet title suit if the plaintiff does not himself claim an interest in the land. Match-E-Be-Nash-She-Wish Band of Pottawatomi Indians v. Patchak, 567 U.S. 209 (2012). This odd question was created by an intersection of Indian law and sovereign immunity law.

The United States acquired a parcel of land in trust for the tribe, which planned to build a casino on the lot. A neighbor opposed to the casino for the usual anti-development reasons (aesthetics, traffic, etc.) sued to reverse the transaction, disputing the government's authority on the theory that the tribe had not been a federally recognized tribe when Congress passed the statute authorizing such purchases. He relied on the waiver of sovereign immunity in the Administrative Procedure Act (main volume at 516), but that waiver does not apply if any other waiver of immunity implicitly excludes the plaintiff's claim. The Quiet Title Act, 28 U.S.C. §2409 (2012), waives immunity to quiet title suits against the United States, but that waiver does not apply to Indian trust lands. So if Patchak's suit was a quiet title action, immunity was not waived; if it was something else, immunity was waived.

All agreed that Patchak was seeking to divest the government of title, but he claimed no right, title, or interest in himself, and the Court held that this was not a quiet title suit. Justice Sotomayor dissented.

C. Reformation

Page 615. After note 9, add:
   10. A Supreme Court example. The Court appeared to authorize reformation of a retirement plan, on the basis of deceptive disclosures about the plan in plan summaries issued to employees, in CIGNA v. Amara, 563 U.S. 421 (2011). The case is described in this supplement to page 569.
   11. And maybe another. Kansas v. Nebraska, 135 S. Ct. 1042 (2015), more fully described in this supplement to page 686, involved a dispute over the waters of the Republican River There was an interstate compact from 1943, a Supreme Court interpretation of the compact in 2000, and a settlement agreement in 2002. The settlement agreement had a technical appendix specifying how Nebraska's water

usage would be calculated. It turned out that in dry years, the calculation method did not work as intended, and the error was large. The Supreme Court modified the calculation method to correct the error.

The Court used forms of the word "modify" nine times, and forms of the word "reform" four times, to describe what it was doing. The Court relied on its power to equitably apportion the water even as it interpreted and enforced the states' agreement. It talked more as though it were modifying the earlier judgment than reforming a contract. And it emphasized that it was making a technical correction to achieve the principal goals of the agreement.

The four dissenters argued that the rules for reformation were not satisfied. The problems with the calculation method resulted from neglecting an important fact about the world, not from any error in drafting. The Court could not reform the contract to make it fair and equitable, or even to make the technical detail better conform to the larger purpose set out in in the agreement. And in this seemingly technical dispute, the four dissenters were Roberts, Scalia, Thomas, and Alito.

CHAPTER EIGHT

BENEFIT TO DEFENDANT AS THE MEASURE OF RELIEF: RESTITUTION

A. Restitution from Innocent Defendants — and Some Who Are Treated As Innocent

1. Introducing Restitution — Mistake

Page 621. At the end of note 2, add:
2. Innocent and not so innocent. . . .
Cashing the check would once have been a conversion, but no more. Uniform Commercial Code §3-420(a) repeals Blue Cross's right to sue for conversion, on the theory that Blue Cross has an adequate remedy against its bank, which paid the checks on what turned out to be forged endorsements. But that remedy is lost if Blue Cross's own negligence substantially contributed to the making of the forged signature. UCC §3-406(a). That negligence defense would present a jury question as between Blue Cross and its bank. Whoever wound up bearing the loss, whether Blue Cross or the bank, would have the restitution remedy against the Sauers. Here Blue Cross apparently chose to go after the Sauers, some of whom appeared to be solvent, rather than pick a dubious fight with its bank. Assuming that the part of the judgment awarded only against the younger Sauer turned out to be uncollectible, and if the statute of limitations had not run out, Blue Cross could still try to pursue its bank for that part of the loss.

Page 622. At the end of note 5, add:
5. The *Restatement (Third)*. . . .
Despite a firm belief and firm intention that the section numbers were final, a few of them have been shuffled. In the final published version, what had been §26 became §30, and what had been §§27-30 each moved up one, becoming §§26-29. The change was made for good reasons, and I will note the new numbers where the main volume refers to any of the affected sections.

Page 623. At the end of note 8, add:
8. Measuring restitution. . . .
On remand, Owner failed to prove that he had also paid the taxes on the property. Owner's liability for restitution was limited to 12 years, on the theory that he might have figured out what was happening if he had investigated a mysterious extra tax bill that he received in 1993. This extra tax bill was in fact wholly unrelated to the property at issue; this part of the holding looks suspiciously like an attempt to split the difference. The court awarded Neighbor an equitable lien on the property to secure the judgment. Buckett v. Jante, 787 N.W.2d 60 (Wis. Ct. App. 2010). Equitable liens are taken up at page 726 of the main volume.

Page 626. At the end of note 3, add:
    3. Specific grounds. . . .
Section 29 became §28 in the final published version.

Page 633. At the end of note 3, add:
    3. Joint ownership of property. . . .
Section 27 became §26 in the final published version.

B. Recovering More Than Plaintiff Lost

1. Disgorging the Profits of Conscious Wrongdoers

Page 654. At the end of note 9.b, add:
    b. The *Restatement (Third)*. . . .
    Section 51 of the *Restatement* is a critical section for our purposes, and its subsections were further subdivided after the main volume went to press. The references to §51(3) in notes 9.b and 9.c. should be 51(4); the reference to §51(4)(a) should be §51(5)(a).

Page 654. At the end of note 9.c, add:
    c. "Disgorgement." . . .
    The Securities and Exchange Commission enforces "disgorgement" remedies in fraud cases, but it has persuaded courts of appeals to require much more than disgorgement of profits. Defendants are sometimes denied credit for their expenses, and co-conspirators can be required to disgorge money they never received but that some other conspirator did. The Court said that this remedy imposes a penalty, a characterization that mattered for statute of limitations purposes. Kokesh v. Securities and Exchange Commission, 137 S. Ct. 1635 (2017). But the Court reserved judgment on whether the courts of appeals had correctly interpreted disgorgement in this context, and it repeatedly quoted the *Restatement.*, including a comment that disgorgement becomes punitive when defendant is denied appropriate deductions for marginal costs. *Restatement (Third)* §51 cmt. *h.* So the holding that disgorgement is punitive appears to be confined to the SEC cases, and not to apply to disgorgement in private litigation.
    The same day, the Court rejected joint and several liability for forfeiture of the proceeds of crime. Honeycutt v. United States, 137 S. Ct. 1626 (2017). Defendant could not be required to "forfeit" proceeds he never received but which went to a co-conspirator. The SEC operates under a different statute, but this decision, combined with the reservation of the issue in *Kokesh*, would seem to invite renewed challenges to what the SEC calls "disgorgement."

Page 656. After note 1, add:
    1.1. Antitrust. A district court has held, in what it said was a case of first impression, that the United States can recover profits earned through a violation of the Sherman Antitrust Act, 15 U.S.C. §1 *et seq.* (2012). United States v. Keyspan Corp., 763 F. Supp. 2d 633 (S.D.N.Y. 2011). The court was approving a consent

decree, and it does not appear that the defendant opposed approval, but nonetheless, the court wrote a substantial opinion. Perhaps disgorgement claims have not been used in antitrust because they were unfamiliar and not expressly authorized in statutory text, or perhaps they are rarely attractive under an Act that provides for trebling of compensatory damages.

Page 656. At the end of note 2, add:
2. Conscious wrongdoers and defaulting fiduciaries. . . .
The first reference to §51(3) in note 2 is correct; the second should be to §51(4). Section 51(3) in its final form spells out that conscious wrongdoing means "knowledge of the underlying wrong" or "a known risk that the conduct in question violates the rights of the claimant." Reference to §69 is no longer required.

Page 661. At the end of note 1, add:
1. Accounting for profits. . . .
The reference to §51(3) at the end of note 1 should be §51(4).
1.1. Law and equity again. Historically, defendant's profits could be recovered at law in quasi-contract, as in *Olwell*, or in equity in an accounting for profits. The Supreme Court has generally treated recovery of defendant's profits in intellectual property cases as equitable, without much modern attention to the question. Faced with a case where the characterization mattered, the Court had this to say:

> Like other restitutional remedies, recovery of profits "is not easily characterized as legal or equitable," for it is an "amalgamation of rights and remedies drawn from both systems." *Restatement (Third)* §4, cmt. b. Given the "protean character" of the profits-recovery remedy, see *id.*, cmt. c, we regard as appropriate its treatment as "equitable" in this case.

Petrella v. Metro-Goldwyn-Mayer, Inc., 134 S. Ct. 1962, 1967 n.1 (2014). This avoids arguments about history and may be as sensible a solution as any. The issue was the availability of laches, an equitable defense based on plaintiff's unreasonable delay in filing suit. *Petrella* is more fully described in supplement to page 964.
This is the first time I have encountered the word "restitutional." "Restitutionary" outnumbers "restitutional" more than 13 to 1 in state and federal cases and law review articles on Westlaw.

Page 662. After note 6.c, add:
c.1. Design patents. Disgorgement of defendant's profits survives with respect to design patents, which cover "ornamental" features of a product. 35 U.S.C. §171 (2012). One who infringes a design patent "shall be liable to the owner to the extent of his total profit." 35 U.S.C. §289 (2012). The lower courts interpreted "total profit" to mean total profit from the product, without apportionment, and not total profit attributable to the patented design. This interpretation was not textually compelled; the next sentence, which preserves other remedies, says that plaintiff "shall not twice recover the profit *made from the infringement*." The italicized language implies causation, and therefore apportionment, and the two sentences could be read together.

But the no-apportionment rule gets ambiguous support from legislative history from 1887. That legislation was inspired by a case about a carpet pattern, where the design appears to have been the product's only distinctive feature.

The Federal Circuit emphatically reaffirmed this rule in Apple Inc. v. Samsung Electronics Co., 786 F.3d 983 (Fed. Cir. 2015). The Federal Circuit said that whether the rule makes any sense is a policy issue for Congress. Samsung said that Apple had not shown that *any* of Samsung's smartphone sales were caused by the infringing design features.

The Supreme Court reversed, unanimously and quickly. Samsung Electronics Co. v. Apple Inc., 137 S. Ct. 429 (2016). The Court did not address causation; Samsung had abandoned that argument. But Samsung argued, and the Court held, that the statute authorized an award of the total profit from the "article of manufacture" to which the design was applied, and that the relevant article of manufacture could be either the final product sold to consumers or a component of that final product. And such a component need not be sold separately. It remanded to the Federal Circuit to identify the relevant article of manufacture in this case.

The Federal Circuit remanded to the trial court. 679 F. App'x 1012 (Fed. Cir. 2017). Samsung was demanding a new trial on Apple's design-patent profits; Apple was arguing that Samsung had never identified any possible article of manufacture except the phone itself. Maybe it should not have abandoned the causation argument, but there were also questions whether it had preserved that.

Page 663. At the end of note d, add:
    d. Trade secrets. . . .
There is now a federal remedy for misappropriation of trade secrets, in addition to existing state remedies. The monetary remedies precisely track those in the Uniform Act, including the misuse of the word "damage" to describe recovery for unjust enrichment. 18 U.S.C.A. §1836(b)(3)(B) (Supp. 2017).

Page 664. After note 5.d, add:
    e. The Federal Circuit. There is a good explanation of the Federal Circuit's approach to reasonable royalty in Aqua Shield v. Inter Pool Cover Team, 774 F.3d 766, 770-773 (Fed. Cir. 2014). It is based on a "hypothetical negotiation" to reconstruct what royalty the parties would have agreed to. A key input into that negotiation would have been the infringer's anticipated profits from use of the invention, based on what was known at the time. The infringer's actual profits "may be relevant, but only in an indirect and limited way — as some evidence bearing on a directly relevant inquiry into anticipated profits."

This hypothetical negotiation simply adapts to the patent context the law's general definition of value as what a willing buyer would pay and a willing seller would accept, each having reasonable knowledge of the facts and neither under any compulsion to buy or sell. See main volume at 22. In the patent context, the seller had the monopoly conferred by the patent, and depending on how badly the infringer needed to use that invention, the infringer might have been under some compulsion to buy. But in patents as elsewhere, the court's task is to estimate what the parties would have agreed to.

2. Measuring the Profits

Page 671. At the end of note 8, add:
8. **The bought-and-paid-for standard. . . .**
The block quote in note 8 now appears in §51(5)(c), not §51(4)(c).

Page 678. At the end of note 8, add:
8. *The Restatement (Third).* . . .
The references to §51(4) and §51(4)(d) in notes 6 and 8 should be to §51(5) and §51(5)(d). The reference to "subsection (3)" in the quotation in note 8 should be a reference to "subsection (4)."

3. Breach of Contract

a. Disgorging the Profits from Opportunistic Breach

Page 686. After note 7.d, add:
8. **Did the Supreme Court just adopt §39 of the *Restatement (Third)*?** Kansas v. Nebraska, 135 S. Ct. 1042 (2015), awarded partial disgorgement for a reckless breach of contract. A settlement agreement divided the waters of the Republican River between the two states. Nebraska was the upstream state, with physical power to take more than its share of the water. And it did. The Court's special master did not find that Nebraska deliberately took more than its share, but he found that Nebraska was reckless, regulating water use in a way that it knew created a substantial risk that it would take more than its share.

And it turned out that water for irrigation is substantially more valuable in Nebraska than in Kansas (for reasons that the Court did not explain). The special master found that Kansas's damages were $3.7 million and that Nebraska's gains were likely several times that. He recommended awarding Kansas's damages plus partial disgorgement of $1.8 million. It is not clear how he arrived at the $1.8 million figure, but the Court approved it.

Relying on the *Restatement* as well as other sources, the Court held that Nebraska had been sufficiently culpable to justify disgorgement, that its breach had been profitable, and that if it were liable only for compensatory damages, it would have incentives to deliberately breach. But it rejected Kansas's demand for disgorgement of all Nebraska's profits, emphasizing its equitable discretion and Nebraska's diligent compliance in recent years. Partial disgorgement had been sufficient to achieve the purpose of obtaining Nebraska's compliance.

Over the last generation, the Court has tended to the view that equitable remedies should be tied to the position the parties would have occupied but for the wrong. But this opinion clearly comes down on the side of equitable discretion. In part the Court emphasized that disputes between two sovereign states are special and that its obligation to be fair and equitable predominated. And of course this was a case in which the Court exercised discretion to award *less* than full relief, not more. Compare United States v. Virginia, 518 U.S. 515 (1996), where the Court relied on the rightful-position principle to insist that plaintiff get a complete remedy, not a partial remedy.

Justices Scalia, Thomas, and Alito dissented. They thought disgorgement was inappropriate in contract cases, but that if it were to be awarded, it should be based on a calculation of defendant's profits and not a discretionary compromise with no visible rationale for the number selected. Justice Thomas cited a comment by the special master suggesting that the disgorgement award might have been a disguised award of attorneys' fees, which would not otherwise be authorized.

b. Rescission

Page 692. After note 5, add:

6. Rescission and damages? A plaintiff claiming restitution may have incidental or consequential damages that are not compensated by recovery of what he gave to defendant. For example, a buyer may have paid shipping costs in addition to the price. When the sale is rescinded and the purchase price returned, he still has lost the shipping costs. Or he may have spent money trying to repair the goods before rescinding, or the defective goods may have damaged his other property. Sellers and parties to other kinds of contracts may suffer similar losses. Finally, the party who rescinds loses his expected profit from the contract. Courts have generally allowed recovery of nonduplicative damages, but they have split on lost profits. The cases are reviewed in 1 Palmer, *Restitution* §3.9. With respect to contracts for the sale of goods, UCC §2-721 provides that rescission does not bar recovery of damages; there is no exception for lost profits.

A recent article argues on economic grounds that it should not be difficult to rescind, but that any recovery following rescission should be limited to restitution of what plaintiff transferred to defendant. Richard R.W. Brooks & Alexander Stremitzer, *Remedies On and Off Contract*, 120 Yale L.J. 690 (2011). They think that the right to rescind provides inexpensive and efficient incentives to higher-quality performance. They are ambivalent about whether rescission plus reliance damages erodes those benefits, but emphatic that rescission plus expectancy damages undoes them.

C. Restitutionary Rights in Specific Property

1. Constructive Trusts

Page 709. At the end of note 8, add:

8. *Omegas* in other circuits. . . .

The holding in *Omegas* depends on the argument that when Congress recodified the law of bankruptcy in 1978, it implicitly repealed the then-existing law of constructive trusts in bankruptcy by failing to explicitly codify it. Supporting and opposing this premise leads to a series of detailed arguments about the meaning of various sections of the Bankruptcy Code and their relationship to underlying principles of law and equity. Those arguments are summarized in notes 9-12. Some professors will want you to read those notes and think about them; some will be happy for you to stop at note 8 and not get into the Bankruptcy Code. Your own professor should tell you which camp she's in.

2.   Tracing the Property

Page 723. At the end of note 4, add:

4. Disproportion . . .
That is, it has never happened in a restitution case. But there are at least two cases of drug dealers using their illegal drug income to buy a winning lottery ticket. People v. $35,315.00 United States Currency, 64 N.E.3d 754 (Ill. App. Ct. 2016); United States v. Betancourt, 422 F.3d 240 (5th Cir. 2005). The lottery winnings in Betancourt were $5.4 million! Identifiable proceeds of crime are generally returned to the rightful owner or forfeited to the prosecuting jurisdiction, and with drug dealer defendants, neither court was troubled by any argument about disproportionality.

Page 723. At the end of note 5.a, add:
a. The original Ponzi scheme. . . .
The rule of Cunningham v. Brown is applied, and explained in a short and simple opinion, in In re Foster, 275 F.3d 924 (10th Cir. 2001). You get tracing, a clear explanation of lowest intermediate balance, and no tracing fictions as between multiple victims, all in just over two pages.

Page 724. At the end of note 5.b, add:
b. Bernard Madoff. . . .
The court of appeals affirmed on the essential disputed point — that the rights and liability of Madoff's customers should be based on their cash investment net of withdrawals, and not on the last fictitious statement of their supposed holdings. 654 F.3d 229 (2d Cir. 2011).

Page 725. At the end of note 6.a, add:
a. Life insurance and divorce. . . .
These cases, and similar state statutes (some protecting the first spouse, some the second), are often preempted by federal law. Preemption can arise when federal benefits are at issue; more generally, ERISA (the Employee Retirement Income Security Act) can preempt with respect to insurance with private employers. The most recent example, which cites some of the others, is Hillman v. Maretta, 133 S. Ct. 1943 (2013). In Egelhoff v. Egelhoff, 532 U.S. 141, 152 (2001), the Court reserved judgment on whether ERISA preempts state-law rules that bar killers from inheriting from their victim, briefly noted in note 1 at 655 of the main volume. The Court hinted that these rules might be so old and well established that they could survive.

3.   Equitable Liens and Subrogation

Page 730. At the end of note 4, add:
4. An aside: the substantive theory in *Robinson*. . . .
Section 28 became §27 in the final published version.

Page 733. In Mort v. United States, delete the section of the opinion headed "Background," and substitute the following:

BACKGROUND

[This case arose out of a series of loan transactions secured by real property in Nevada. Simplifying slightly:

Dec. 12, 1990: DeLee Trust borrows $30,000 from the Kerns; gives mortgage on property.

Aug. 24, 1992: IRS files tax lien on the property for $33,000 in income tax due from the Trust.

Nov. 13, 1992: Trust borrows $38,000 from the Belmonts; gives mortgage on property. Uses loan proceeds to pay off Kerns and to pay off a state tax lien.

Fidelity National Title fails to discover federal tax lien and insures title for the Belmonts' interest in the property

Dec. 21, 1992: Belmonts sell their note, mortgage, and rights under the title policy to the Morts for $38,000.

Aug. 12, 1993: IRS seizes the property pursuant to its tax lien.

So to summarize, the four liens on the property were filed in this order:

Kern
IRS
Belmont
Mort]

The Morts then filed a complaint in the United States District Court for the District of Nevada seeking injunctive relief and a declaratory judgment that their trust deed interest was superior to the federal tax lien [because they were subrogated to the Kern mortgage, which had priority over the IRS tax lien.] The district court dismissed the Morts' complaint without prejudice, concluding that the Morts could not bring their claim for equitable subrogation without first pursuing their legal remedies against the title insurer. 874 F. Supp. 283 (D. Nev. 1994). . . .

Page 737. After note 5, add:

5.1. A case going the other way. The Delaware court refused to allow subrogation on similar facts in Eastern Savings Bank, FSB v. CACH, LLC, 124 A.3d 585 (Del. 2015). Eastern refinanced mortgages on the home of a couple named Johnson; CACH filed a judgment lien on the same home. Eastern made its loan on December 19; CACH recorded its lien in the real estate records on December 21; Eastern's mortgage was recorded on December 29. So CACH had priority unless Eastern was subrogated to the mortgages it refinanced, which had been recorded long before.

The court said that Eastern had an adequate legal remedy in suing the title company, which should have found the CACH lien before it disbursed Eastern's funds. The court's opinion shows limited familiarity with the law of subrogation; preserving an equity court mostly for purposes of corporate law does not necessarily preserve knowledge of the rest of equity. Justice Seitz, dissenting, explained how subrogation is supposed to work.

Page 739. At the end of note 7, add:
7. Subrogation for "volunteers." . . .
On facts that were a simpler version of *Mort*, a federal court applying Michigan law refused subrogation. Bednarowski & Michaels Development, LLC v. Wallace, 293 F. Supp. 2d 728 (E.D. Mich. 2003). A taxpayer's property was subject to a mortgage when the IRS filed a tax lien. Plaintiff paid off the mortgage as part of a transaction to buy two-thirds of the property; plaintiff financed the deal with his own mortgage lender. The court said that plaintiff and his lender were both volunteers and took subject to the tax lien. The result is that the IRS gets paid without regard to the mortgage that was ahead of it, and (depending on the size of the tax lien) plaintiff and his lender may lose their entire investment. Isn't the IRS unjustly enriched at the expense of plaintiff and his lender? The volunteer rule strikes again.

D. Defenses and the Rights of Third Parties

1. Bona Fide Purchasers

Page 745. At the end of note 5.a., add:
a. Common law and equity. . . .
There is a similar holding in Federal Trade Commission v. Network Services Depot, Inc., 617 F.3d 1127 (9th Cir. 2010). The court emphasized that once an attorney is on notice that the money used to pay his fees might be proceeds of wrongdoing, it is not enough to merely ask the client and take his word for it.

CHAPTER NINE

ANCILLARY REMEDIES: ENFORCING THE JUDGMENT

A. Enforcing Coercive Orders: The Contempt Power

1. The Three Kinds of Contempt

Page 767. After note 2.c., add:

2.1. Attacking the distinction between civil and criminal. John Robertson beat his girlfriend in two separate incidents in 1999. After the first incident, she obtained a civil protective order, i.e., an injunction ordering him not to assault her, harass her, communicate with her, or come near her. The United States Attorney for the District of Columbia, a direct representative of the federal government, prosecuted Robertson for aggravated assault in the first incident; that case ended in a guilty plea and an agreement not to prosecute the second incident. The girlfriend, represented by the Corporation Counsel of the District, a representative of the local government, then initiated a criminal contempt prosecution for the second incident. In a decision clearly at odds with *Dixon*, the D.C. Court of Appeals held that the criminal contempt proceeding was an essentially private proceeding that did not violate the plea agreement. In re Robertson, 940 A.2d 1050 (D.C. 2008).

The Supreme Court granted cert to hear this case, then dismissed the writ as improvidently granted. Robertson v. United States ex rel. Watson, 560 U.S. 272 (2010). The Chief Justice, joined by Justices Scalia, Kennedy, and Sotomayor, filed a lengthy and passionate dissent arguing that the judgment below fundamentally misunderstood the law of criminal contempt.

Plaintiff's alternate theory in the case, and perhaps the reason why the writ was dismissed, was the dual-sovereignty doctrine. Separate prosecutions for the same offense by a state and the federal government do not violate the Double Jeopardy Clause, on the ground that each prosecution is brought by a separate sovereign who is not bound by the actions of the other. However plausible or implausible that rule is with respect to the states, it seems quite implausible to suppose that the District of Columbia could be a separate sovereign and not be bound by the actions of the federal government. The District is a federal instrumentality subject to the plenary authority of Congress, and its powers of local self-government are delegated by Congress. More recently, the Court held that Puerto Rico is not a separate sovereign for this purpose. Puerto Rico v. Sanchez Valle, 136 S. Ct. 1863 (2016).

The status of the District is an aside for our purposes, but the other issue is central: The D.C. court's private-proceeding theory strikes at the heart of the distinction between criminal and civil contempt.

Page 768. After note 6, add:

7. A high-profile example: Sheriff Joe Arpaio. In long-running litigation against Maricopa County, Arizona (metropolitan Phoenix) and its long-time sheriff, Joe Arpaio, the federal district court ordered defendants not to enforce federal civil immigration laws and not to detain persons they believed to be in the country without authorization but whom they had no basis to detain for violations of state law. The court later found, on a civil standard of proof, that Sheriff Arpaio made no effort to comply with the injunction and that his officers, acting under pre-existing policy, routinely violated it. Plaintiffs and the county agreed to a $500,000 fund, created by the county, to be administered in compensatory civil contempt to compensate persons who were detained in violation of the injunction. Melendres v. Arpaio, 2016 WL 3996453 (D. Ariz. July 26, 2016).

The court also referred Arpaio to the United States Attorney to be prosecuted for criminal contempt, and asked that another judge, randomly selected, be assigned to hear the criminal contempt case. Melendres v. Arpaio, 2016 WL 4414755 (D. Ariz. Aug. 19, 2016). The United States, which had intervened in the case as an additional plaintiff, filed criminal contempt charges in October. Fernanda Santos, *Sheriff Joe Arpaio, Accused of Targeting Latinos, Is Charged with Contempt*, N.Y. Times (Oct. 17, 2016). In November, he lost his re-election bid after twenty-four years in office. Fernanda Santos, *Sheriff Joe Arpaio Loses Bid for 7th Term in Arizona*, N.Y. Times (Nov. 9, 2016). Arpaio claims that he was held in contempt for doing what the Trump Administration now demands that all local governments do. The contempt charge was tried to the court in early July and is awaiting decision; the prosecutors have been accused of not trying very hard. *Did Feds Phone in Arpaio Prosecution*, Arizona Republic (July 14, 2017).

This is one of many cases involving Arpaio over the years. A Phoenix newspaper reported in 2015 that "cases involving him or his office have cost taxpayers $142 million in legal expenses, settlements and court awards." Michael Kiefer, *Sheriff Joe Arpaio Has Always Done It His Way*, Arizona Republic (Sept. 11, 2015).

2. How Much Risk of Abuse to Overcome How Much Defiance?

b. Anticipatory Contempt

Page 790. After note 7.c, add:

7.1. Recent examples.

a. The issue arose again in Brown v. City of Upper Arlington, 637 F.3d 668 (6th Cir. 2011). Plaintiff got a temporary restraining order in state court to prevent the city from cutting down a large tree, located on city property but in front of plaintiff's home. The city removed the case to federal court. When the TRO expired at the end of its allotted time, the federal judge said: "I would expect that between now and the time the Court issues its decision," if the City decides to take action it will notify the court and plaintiff's counsel immediately. *Id.* at 670. "The City agreed." *Id.* And the City literally kept its word.

On October 29, the court rejected plaintiff's federal claims on the merits and dismissed the case with leave to refile the state-law claims in state court. Plaintiff's lawyer immediately notified the City's lawyer that he would refile in state court no later than October 31. On the morning of October 30, the City cut down the tree. The trial judge held the City in contempt and ordered it to replace the tree and pay plaintiff's attorneys' fees.

The court of appeals reversed. The court treated it as obvious that no order had been violated, and plaintiff seemed to concede that "none of these conventional grounds" for contempt applies. *Id.* at 672. Plaintiff relied principally on Chambers v. NASCO, which the court distinguished on the ground that if the City had interfered with the jurisdiction of any court, it was that of the state courts, not the federal district court.

Neither *Griffin* nor §401 was cited, and of all the cases debated in *Griffin*, only *Merrimack* was cited. The court distinguished *Merrimack* on the ground that the Supreme Court was punishing contempt of the lower court's injunction, which was still in effect and not vacated by a mere opinion before the issuance of the mandate.

b. The Massachusetts court threw out an award of $240,000 in attorneys' fees, imposed as a sanction against a lawyer who derailed a settlement in a complex multi-party dispute by sending letters to 106 creditors who were not yet parties, stating that he could get full recoveries for them. Wong v. Luu, 34 N.E.3d 35 (Mass. 2015). The lawyer had violated no order, statute, rule, or contractual obligation; he had not been held in contempt. Massachusetts judges have inherent power to impose sanctions on conduct that interferes with the "fair administration of justice," but the court said that settlements are not necessary to the fair administration of justice.

4. The Rights of Third Parties

Page 813. At the end of note 2, add:
2. Persons in active concert. . . .
There is a careful analysis of *Alemite* and *Merriam* in National Spiritual Assembly of the Bahá'ís Under the Hereditary Guardianship, Inc. v. National Spiritual Assembly of the Bahá'ís, Inc., 628 F.3d 837 (7th Cir. 2010), emphasizing the remand in *Merriam* to consider the possibility that the brother there was a key employee who had been so involved in the original litigation "that it can fairly be said that he has had his day in court in relation to the validity of the injunction." *Bahá'ís*, 628 F.3d at 852, quoting *Merriam*, 639 F.2d at 36.

The *Bahá'ís* court also rather clearly believed it settled that successors in interest are subject to contempt for violating an injunction against their predecessor in interest. That question is the subject of the next note in the main volume.

6. Drafting Decrees

Page 821. At the end of note 3, add:
3. Two opportunities for defendants. . . .
Defendants can raise specificity issues on direct appeal following a default judgment. City of New York v. Mickalis Pawn Shop LLC, 645 F.3d 114, 143 (2d Cir. 2011), citing cases from the Second and Seventh Circuits. The opinion is also a nice review of how not to draft an injunction. "An injunction is overbroad when it seeks to restrain the defendants from engaging in legal conduct, or from engaging in illegal conduct that was not fairly the subject of litigation." *Id.* at 145. In addition to violating these restrictions, the injunction ordered defendants to "adopt those practices that in the opinion of the Special Master serve to prevent" various harms the

injunction sought to prevent, and it enjoined "failure to cooperate with the Special Master." *Id.* The court held that these delegations of authority violated Rule 65(d). The City defended the injunction principally on the ground that twenty other defendants had agreed to substantially identical injunctions in settlements.

Page 825. After note 9, add:

10. The Supreme Court muffs the details. In Trump v. International Refugee Assistance Project, 137 S. Ct. 2080 (2017), more fully described in supplement to page 445, the Supreme Court stayed in part the injunctions entered by two district courts against enforcement of President Trump's executive order barring immigration from six Muslim countries. The Court's opinion concluded:

> The Government's application to stay the injunction with respect to §§ 6(a) and (b) is accordingly granted in part. Section 6(a) may not be enforced against an individual seeking admission as a refugee who can credibly claim a bona fide relationship with a person or entity in the United States. Nor may § 6(b); that is, such a person may not be excluded pursuant to § 6(b), even if the 50,000–person cap has been reached or exceeded. As applied to all other individuals, the provisions may take effect.

> **3**

> Accordingly, the petitions for certiorari are granted, and the stay applications are granted in part.
>
> *It is so ordered.*

Probably the Court thought this was clear enough. It gave some discursive examples of the kinds of relationships it had in mind. But it did not actually draft a revised injunction to be entered on remand, or edit the language of the district courts' injunctions to show what remained in effect and what was stayed. And of course it did not enter an injunction of its own; that would have posed the risk of contempt hearings in the Supreme Court. So there was no order anywhere that complied with Rule 65 and also with the Court's opinion.

Not surprisingly, a dispute broke out immediately. The government interpreted "relationship" very narrowly, claiming for example that grandparents have no relevant relationship with grandchildren in the United States, and instructing rank and file officials that doubts should be resolved against persons seeking admission — despite the "credibly claim" language in the opinion. After some procedural sparring, the District Court in Hawaii issued a modified injunction protecting a broader set of relatives and also refugees with "a formal assurance" of reception and placement services. 2017 WL 2989048 (D. Hawaii July 13, 2017). The government is attempting a direct appeal to the Supreme Court, which is likely to be dismissed for want of jurisdiction. But the government has offered the Court theories for reaching the merits if it really wants to.

B. Collecting Money Judgments

1. Execution, Garnishment, and the Like

Page 836. After note 4, add:

4.1. Inherited IRAs. If the owner of an Individual Retirement Account dies with money left in the IRA, she can leave it to her heirs as an inherited IRA. The heirs (the rules are different for a surviving spouse) are free to withdraw all the money immediately if they choose; they owe tax on the withdrawal but no tax penalty. They are required to begin taking mandatory minimum withdrawals, whatever their age. The Supreme Court unanimously held that these rules show that funds in an inherited IRA are not held for anyone's retirement, and thus are not "retirement funds" and not exempt from creditors in bankruptcy. Clark v. Rameker, 134 S. Ct. 2242 (2014).

The case involved a joint bankruptcy for a married couple. The wife had inherited a $450,000 IRA from her mother, and the account still held about $300,000 at the time of bankruptcy. That money is now available to the creditors. The effect of the decision may just be that well-advised middle-class debtors spend all the money in an inherited IRA before they file for bankruptcy.

Page 837. At the end of note 7, add:

7. Forfeiture? . . .

The Supreme Court has held that bankruptcy courts have no power to override exemptions in this way. Law v. Siegel, 134 S. Ct. 1188 (2014). The reasoning was straightforward; the Bankruptcy Code spells out exemptions, and grounds for forfeiting exemptions, in great detail, and courts have no inherent power to add to the list.

The facts of Law v. Siegel were spectacular. The bankrupt debtor listed two mortgages on his house, one to a bank and one to "Lili Lin." Lili Lin said she had known the debtor but had never loaned him money, and that he had repeatedly tried to involve her in sham transactions related to the mortgage. But then another Lili Lin began to file documents with the court. This Lili Lin said she lived in China and spoke no English, but that she had loaned the money and was entitled to enforce the mortgage. After five years of litigation, the bankruptcy court concluded that no Lili Lin in China had filed anything, either in the mortgage records or in the court, and that probably all of Lili Lin's pleadings and briefing had been filed by the debtor. Had the scheme succeeded, the debtor would have retrieved all the money payable to Lili Lin — $147,000 according to the debtor.

The trustee in bankruptcy spent more than $500,000 in attorneys' fees combatting the nonexistent Lili Lin. The debtor's only asset was $75,000 of the equity in his house, the amount that was exempt under California law. The Court said the trustee could not recover from that exempt equity. But it said the bankruptcy court could sanction the debtor for litigation misconduct, and because the misconduct occurred after the bankruptcy petition, the sanctions would not be dischargeable in the bankruptcy. Whether it is worthwhile for the trustee to spend more money pursuing that remedy, in hopes of collecting out of the debtor's post-bankruptcy income, is a very different question.

Page 841. At the end of note 4, add:
    4. The risk to exemptions. . . .
    The Second Circuit approved certification of a class action alleging a conspiracy to buy consumer debt, submit false affidavits that process had been served, and obtain default judgments in every case. Sykes v. Mel S. Harris & Associates, 780 F.3d 70 (2d Cir. 2015). More recently, the district court approved a $60 million settlement in the case. 2016 WL 3030156 (S.D.N.Y. May 24, 2016). Mel S. Harris is a law firm; other defendants are a process-serving company and a publicly traded finance and asset-management company that allegedly bought the debt and obtained the judgments.

Page 841. After note 5, add:
    6. A regulatory response. The United States now pays most federal benefits electronically, and the electronic label on most benefits that federal law exempts from garnishment now begins with XX: for example, XXSOC SEC. Banks are now required to search for that code and to protect from garnishment either the amount of any exempt benefit deposited within the sixty days preceding the search, or the balance in the account on the day of the search, whichever is less. They are required to search the records within two days of receiving a garnishment order. The labeling of deposits is explained in Garnishment of Accounts Containing Federal Benefit Payments, 76 Fed. Reg. 9939, 9941 (Feb. 23, 2011); the bank regulation is Garnishment of Accounts Containing Federal Benefit Payments, 31 C.F.R. §212.1 *et seq.* (2016).
    7. The reach of garnishment. New York has held that garnishment of assets in the hands of a New York bank does not reach foreign branches, or implicitly, out-of-state branches, of that bank. Motorola Credit Corp. v. Standard Chartered Bank, 21 N.E.3d 223 (N.Y. 2014). The court thought that such liability risked subjecting banks to inconsistent regulation and orders, and that it was impractical for a bank to search all its branches worldwide. It dubiously distinguished, instead of overruling, a recent decision in which the point had not been argued. Koehler v. Bank of Bermuda Ltd., 911 N.E.2d 825 (N.Y. 2009). The dissenter thought the rule obsolete in light of modern computers, and that any risks of inconsistent regulation or double liability could be addressed case by case.
    The underlying judgment was entered in 2003 ($2.1 billion compensatory) and 2006 ($1 billion punitive). Defendants have vigorously, and apparently successfully, resisted all collection efforts. They are subject to arrest orders in the United States and the United Kingdom and have been convicted of bank fraud in Turkey, but they appear to have kept their substantial assets safe. The underlying judgment is described in the main volume at page 232.

Page 844. After note 8, add:
    8.1. Suing on barred claims. The Supreme Court has held that it is not false, deceptive, misleading, unfair, or unconscionable for a creditor to file a claim in bankruptcy on a debt that the creditor knows is uncollectible because the statute of limitations has run out. Midland Funding, LLC v. Johnson, 137 S. Ct. 1407 (2017).

The statute of limitations is an affirmative defense, and the debtor or his trustee in bankruptcy must identify the barred claim and assert the defense.

Justice Sotomayor's opinion for the three dissenters provides context. Debt-collection firms buy up barred claims for pennies on the dollar. Then they would file suit on the stale debt in small-claims court, correctly anticipating that most consumer debtors would default, giving the firm an enforceable judgment in place of a barred claim. Midland's parent company filed 245,000 lawsuits in 2009. The lower federal courts largely stopped this practice by holding that it violated the Fair Debt Collection Practices Act, because it was unfair and misleading. That exposed the creditors to liability for actual and statutory damages and attorneys' fees. So then the firms shifted to filing these claims in chapter 13 bankruptcies, where the debtor makes partial payments on her debt.

The majority assumed without deciding that the cases on the practice of filing barred claims in small-claims court were correctly decided. But it said that bankruptcy was different, because the debtor had taken the initiative to file the proceeding and because the trustee, who could also object, was more sophisticated. Sotomayor responded that all the actors in the bankruptcy system said this wasn't true — that the bankruptcy courts were flooded with barred claims, the trustees were overworked, and that many barred claims were approved because no one noticed or objected. The majority was also troubled by the prospect of debtors filing separate suits under the FDCPA after the claim was allowed or disallowed in bankruptcy.

8.2. Never mind. In Henson v. Santander Consumer USA Inc., 137 S. Ct. 1718 (2017), the Court held that the Act does not apply to anyone who owns the debt it is collecting. The holding is not implausible as a matter of statutory interpretation. But it means that the entire debt-collection industry can exempt itself from the Act by simply buying the defaulted debt rather than undertaking to collect it for a fee. Much of the industry consists of companies that buy defaulted debt, but the prevailing understanding of the statute, also textually plausible, had been that companies were exempt only if they bought the debt before default.

Some states have similar laws that apply to creditors exempt from the federal law; some do not. In states where original lenders are relatively free to harass debtors, bankruptcy filings are somewhat higher, but default rates are not much different. That is, the right to harass some debtors more intensely does not appear to extract much in the way of additional payments, but it does drive some debtors to file for bankruptcy.

8.3. Empirical studies. An emerging set of empirical studies examines state-court collection litigation, out-of-court collection by hounding debtors to pay, and "informal bankruptcy," in which debtors stop paying but do not file for bankruptcy.

Consumer-debt collection suits are examined in Richard M. Hynes, *Broke But Not Bankrupt: Consumer Debt Collection in State Courts*, 60 Fla. L. Rev. 1 (2008). The study focuses mostly on Virginia, with comparisons to earlier, less detailed data from other states. Virginia is at one end of the continuum of state variation, with a very high litigation rate.

The searchable electronic data compiled by the courts are incomplete, and the sample sizes in the review of individual case files appear to be small, so numbers reported from this study should be taken as approximate. But Professor Hynes was able to conclude with reasonable confidence that there was more than one civil lawsuit for every ten Virginians in 2005, that more than 60 percent of these cases were consumer-debt collection actions, and that nearly 25 percent more were landlords suing to evict tenants. Nearly all the debt-collection cases ended in default judgments. The median judgment in a debt action was only $685. There were about 175,000 garnishment actions, or about one for every four debt collection actions.

Only a very small fraction of these consumer defendants file for bankruptcy; there were 33,000 consumer bankruptcies in Virginia in 2011. Amanda E. Dawsey, Richard M. Hynes, & Lawrence M. Ausubel, *Non-Judicial Debt Collection and the Consumer's Choice Among Repayment, Bankruptcy, and Informal Bankruptcy*, 87 Am. Bankr. L.J. 1 (2013). And it appears that even in creditor-friendly Virginia, creditors sue on only a small fraction of bad debts. Data from mandatory reporting by payday lenders indicate that at least that class of creditors sues on only a little more than ten percent of the debts it writes off. But even when they do not sue, creditors try to collect by repeatedly calling and writing the debtor, sometimes within the bounds of laws against harassing or deceptive tactics, and sometimes not.

The picture that emerges is of a dual system. Middle-class debtors file for bankruptcy when their situation gets bad enough. They can raise the cash to pay the lawyer; they are more likely to have stable addresses and employment, so their creditors can find them; and they are more likely to have assets to protect. Lower-income debtors do not file for bankruptcy. They can't afford it, and they are harder to find and harder to collect from. When they can't pay, they can try to ignore or wait out their creditors, and take their lumps from any effective collection steps the creditor invokes against them. And very few debtors were sued by more than one creditor.

According to court records, only 23 percent of these judgments were satisfied within five years, and by then, most creditors had abandoned collection efforts. The actual collection rate may be higher. The courts depend on the parties to report payments, but these judgment debtors are unsophisticated and the penalty on judgment creditors who fail to report payments is only $50, to be collected only if the judgment debtor takes effective steps to complain.

The litigation rate is high in Virginia because Virginia is creditor friendly. Filing fees are low, and garnishment is permitted. Because filing is cheap, and most debtors default, the expected value of a collection suit may be positive even if the odds of collection are small. Exemptions are also generally low, but one sheriff told Professor Hynes that he could not remember ever levying execution on a consumer's tangible assets.

There is evidence that consumer-debt collection is a very large fraction of all litigation in many states. But litigation rates vary remarkably, from more than 17,000 per 100,000 population in Maryland to 323 per 100,000 in Hawaii. Some of these differences are artifacts of how the data are compiled, but many of these differences are real. Some states, such as Texas, have such generous exemptions that the prospect of collecting a judgment against a consumer is close to zero. Some states, such as California, appear to have deliberately limited creditor access to small-claims court. Both Texas and California have very low civil-litigation rates. But Virginia may be reasonably representative of states where filing is cheap and wage garnishment is available.

Page 845. At the end of note 10, add:
    10. "Asset-protection jurisdictions." ...
    The court of appeals affirmed the coercive contempt order. 396 F. App'x 635 (11th Cir. 2010). Now what? Maybe the Cook Islands banks have a way for an imprisoned contemnor to say he really means it when he asks for the money. Or maybe not. If they really don't, does Solow have to be released because is it now impossible for him to comply with the court's order? The court clearly was not buying that, in part because it found his testimony not credible. If he stays in jail, and the money stays in the Cook Islands, will he eventually have to be released on the ground that coercion has failed? See the issue of perpetual coercion, in the main volume at 775.

Page 845. After note 11, add:
    12. **Arrest warrants?** The press reports widespread use of arrest warrants to collect debt. Jessica Silver-Greenberg, *Welcome to Debtors' Prison, 2011 Edition,* Wall St. J. (Mar. 17, 2011). But the reporter appears to be confused about the basis for these warrants, just as many of the debtors subject to them are probably confused. Courts may order debtors to appear in court for post-judgment proceedings; they may order debtors to respond to post-judgment discovery; or they may order debtors to turn over specific assets known to be in their possession or control. A debtor who fails to obey such a direct order may be jailed for contempt — and he may mistakenly believe that he is in jail for not paying the debt. But American courts do not order ordinary debtors to pay and then jail them when they cannot or will not do so.

Page 847. After note 5, add:
    5.1. **School finance in Washington.** The Washington constitution provides that "It is the paramount duty of the state to make ample provision for the education of all children residing within its borders, without distinction or preference on account of race, color, caste, or sex." Art. IX, §1. In Seattle School District No. 1 v. State, 585 P.2d 71 (Wash. 1978), the court held that this clause states an enforceable duty and is not a mere rhetorical preamble. It affirmed a declaratory judgment that the state had failed in this duty, which required "sufficient funds derived through dependable and regular tax sources to permit school districts to carry out a basic program of education." *Id.* at 77, 96. The court left it to the legislature to define "basic education" and to develop a plan for ample funding, and it did not retain jurisdiction to supervise this process.
    In McCleary v. State, 269 P.3d 227 (Wash. 2012), the court held that the state still had not complied with its constitutional duty, "consistently providing school districts with a level of resources that falls short of the actual costs of the basic education program." *Id.* at 261. It continued to defer to the legislature on means, but this time it retained jurisdiction "to help ensure progress in the State's plan to fully implement education reforms by 2018." *Id.* What followed appears in a series of unpublished orders, and filings by the parties, available at http://www.courts.wa.gov/appellate_trial_courts/SupremeCourt/?fa=supremecourt.McCleary_Education.
    In July 2012, the court directed the state to file a report at the end of each legislative session through 2018, summarizing the legislature's actions to implement

school-finance legislation enacted in 2009 and to achieve compliance with the state constitution. The court would review these reports with a focus on "real and measurable progress" toward full compliance by 2018.

In December 2012, the court found the first report inadequate. School funding had actually been cut since the 2009 legislation and was now below levels previously held unconstitutional. The court set out more detailed specifications for future reports. In January 2014, the court found that the 2013 report showed modest progress, but by the state's own analysis, it was not on track to comply by 2018. The court ordered the state to submit by April 30 "a complete plan for fully implementing its program of basic education for each school year between now and the 2017-18 school year."

In September 2014, the court held the state in contempt of court. The legislature had not enacted "additional time lines in 2014 to implement the program of basic education," and the state's April 30 report did not contain the complete year-by-year plan that had been ordered. No sanctions were imposed. If the state had not complied at the end of the 2015 legislative session, the court would "reconvene to impose sanctions and other remedial measures as necessary."

The 2015 legislature failed to pass a budget until its third special session; the governor signed it twenty minutes before the end of the fiscal year, when spending authority would have expired. Joseph O'Sullivan, *Budget Bill's Done, but Legislature Still Isn't*, Seattle Times (July 1, 2015). On August 13, the court found the budget's funding for education inadequate in multiple ways, and imposed a fine of $100,000 per day on the state "until it adopts a concrete plan for complying with article IX, section 1 by the 2018 school year. The penalty shall be payable daily to be held in a segregated account for the benefit of basic education."

The 2016 legislature passed what it said was a plan for full compliance, which the court characterized as more a promise than a plan. On October 6, it ordered that the daily fines continue, and that the state report again within thirty days after the 2017 legislature adopted a budget. It also reminded the state that the fines were to be *paid* daily, not merely accrued in the state's accounts. It took no action on the plaintiffs' request that it coerce compliance either by enjoining all state expenditures on public schools or by holding unconstitutional all state tax exemptions (some six hundred of them).

Near the end of their third special session, and near the expiration of all spending authority at midnight on June 30, legislative leaders announced agreement on a budget that would add $1.8 billion of state spending on public schools, increase the state property tax, and limit local property taxes. The deal still had to be passed through committees and floor votes in both houses. Melissa Santos, *Budget Deal Must Be Signed into Law by Midnight to Prevent Government Shutdown*, Tacoma News Tribune (June 30, 2017). By the time it passed, after further negotiations, it was said to add $7.3 billion in school funding. Neal Morton, *$7.3 Billion School Funding Plan*, Seattle Times (July 1, 2017).

5.2. School finance in Kansas. A similar showdown is going on in Kansas, where the state supreme court has been trying since 2003 to enforce constitutionally adequate and not unreasonably unequal funding for education. In 2010, Sam Brownback was elected governor on a promise of large tax cuts, which the legislature enacted. The promised surge in economic activity and tax revenue did not appear, and the state suffered budget shortfalls. Per capita state funding for schools declined between 2011 and 2016.

In February 2016, the court said that if the state had not enacted a constitutionally adequate school funding system by June 30, it would enjoin operation of the unconstitutional system, forcing a shutdown of the public schools. Gannon v. State, 368 P.3d 1024 (Kan. 2016). The Senate passed a bill, SB 439, to authorize impeachment of judges for "attempting to usurp the power of the legislative or executive branch of government." But that bill died in the House.

The legislature passed a funding bill. On May 27, the court found that it cured some inequities but left others in place, and that the inadequate provisions were not severable from the adequate provisions. 372 P.3d 1181 (Kan. 2016). But the legislature had expressed its intent to fully comply, so the court stayed remedial orders, but again threatened to shut down the schools if an adequate bill were not passed by June 30. Governor Brownback called a special session, and the legislature enacted $38 million in additional funding for poorer school districts. Julie Bosman, *Kansas Lawmakers Pass Bill in Bid to Stop Court from Closing Schools*, N.Y. Times (June 24, 2016). The parties stipulated that the bill achieved compliance with the equity portion of the court's order. The court then entered an order stating that "the legislature has currently satisfied the court's orders . . . concerning equity," and that "no judicial remedy is necessary at this time." It ordered further briefing and argument on the issues of educational adequacy.

In March 2017, the court found the funding inadequate, and again gave the legislature to June 30 to fix the problem. Gannon v. State, 390 P.3d 461 (Kan. 2017). The opinion briefly reviews other school-finance orders in state supreme courts around the country. On June 6 the lopsidedly Republican legislature overrode the governor's veto of SB 30, which raises the state income tax. This decision may have been less about the pressure from the court than a response to voters angry about cuts in government services, including schools. The prospect of more revenue presumably helped enable the passage of SB 19, which will add $488 million to school funding over two years. Hunter Woodall & Bryan Lowry, *Brownback Signs New Kansas School Finance Formula*, Kansas City Star (June 15, 2017). It remains to be seen whether the state supreme court will find this adequate. The court seemed skeptical at an hour of oral argument on July 18. Hunter Woodall, *School Districts Call for More Funding as State Defends Spending to Kansas Supreme Court*, Kansas City Star (July 18, 2017).

5.3. School finance in Texas. The Texas Supreme Court finally threw in the towel, after thirty years of judicial efforts to reform school finance in Texas. Morath v. The Texas Taxpayer and Student Fairness Coalition, 490 S.W.3d 826 (Tex. 2016). In this latest effort, more than half the state's school districts were plaintiffs, the record exceeded 200,000 pages, and the trial court entered 1,508 findings of fact and 118 conclusions of law. The state supreme court found much wrong with the school finance system, and rhetorically appealed to the state to do better. "But our function is limited to reviewing the constitutionality of the system under an extremely deferential standard." *Id.* at 868. And on that standard, the system passed. The extreme difficulty of implementing any remedy surely contributed to the selection of this "extremely deferential standard."

Page 847. After note 6, add:

7. **Foreign governments: Argentina.** Collecting money from resistant or scofflaw foreign governments can be even more difficult. Argentina has repeatedly issued bonds to borrow money in the international markets, and it has repeatedly defaulted on the bonds. In 2001, it suspended payment on some $80 billion of foreign debt, and later enacted legislation prohibiting payment and closing its courts to the holders of those bonds. In 2005 and 2010, it issued replacement bonds to bondholders willing to accept a new promise to pay about 25 percent of the original amount.

Argentina's bonds, like most sovereign bonds issued in the international markets, contained broad waivers of sovereign immunity. Some investors refused to accept the 2005 and 2010 exchange offers and sued on the original bonds in the Southern District of New York. They got judgments for the amounts originally owed, with interest, but collecting has been a different matter.

The Supreme Court upheld postjudgment discovery directed to banks doing business with Argentina and aimed at finding Argentina's assets held anywhere in the world. Republic of Argentina v. NML Capital, Ltd., 134 S. Ct. 2250 (2014). The Court said that the Foreign Sovereign Immunities Act, 28 U.S.C. §1602 *et seq.* (2012), provides no immunity from such discovery; it did not rely on Argentina's waiver of immunity. The Court said that immunity was the only issue before it.

But the Court also appeared to approve the scope of the requested discovery. The Court thought that sorting out which assets were subject to execution and which were not, under the varied laws of all the places where assets might be found, could come after discovery. Argentine government assets held for commercial purposes in the United States would be subject to execution; assets held for governmental purposes would not be subject to execution, despite Argentina's attempt to waive that immunity. Justice Ginsburg would have limited discovery to commercial assets, treating that limitation as an international norm; she worried about the United States becoming an information clearing house for creditors of defaulting governments. The majority thought that such a limitation would force plaintiffs to identify the exempt or nonexempt status of assets before knowing what assets existed.

Some of the defaulted bonds also had a clause guaranteeing equal treatment with holders of other Argentine bonds. The Second Circuit interpreted this clause to include the reissued bonds, and it affirmed a grant of specific performance of this obligation. NML Capital, Ltd. v. Republic of Argentina, 699 F.3d 246 (2d Cir. 2012). So if Argentina makes a payment on the replacement bonds, it must pay the same percentage of the *unreduced* amount of the original bonds to the holders of those bonds. The court said that legal remedies were inadequate, because Argentina would simply refuse to pay a money judgment, and its courts would refuse to enforce it.

But how to enforce the specific performance decree? Argentina makes payments to bondholders through banks, and most of those banks do business in New York. The court held that many of those banks were in active concert with Argentina, and subject to its obligation to make proportionate payments to holders of the original and replacement bonds. NML Capital, Ltd. v. Republic of Argentina, 727 F.3d 230 (2d

Cir. 2013). Questions about which banks were in active concert with Argentina, and which were subject to jurisdiction in New York, were left to later efforts to enforce the injunction against individual banks.

Argentina at first attempted to continue paying the replacement bonds through a New York bank, but the bank refused to make the payment. New York banks are unwilling to subject themselves to contempt sanctions on behalf of Argentina. Then Argentina attempted to issue new replacement bonds, governed by Argentine law and payable through Argentine banks. The district court held Argentina in contempt of court, but held any contempt sanctions in abeyance. NML Capital, Ltd. v. Republic of Argentina, No. 1:10-cv-4101 (S.D.N.Y. Sept. 29, 2014), ECF No. 385.

In December 2015, a newly elected President took office in Argentina. He began serious settlement discussions, with the assistance of a court-appointed special master acting as mediator and with the judge keeping the pressure on. Negotiations were difficult, but Argentina and the holdouts settled for amounts reported as 70 to 75 percent of the total amounts claimed.

In April 2016, the Second Circuit affirmed an order vacating the injunction, conditioned on Argentina repealing the laws that prevented enforcement of the bonds and on the terms of any settlement being offered to all the holdout plaintiffs. Aurelius Capital Master, Ltd. v. Republic of Argentina, 644 F. App'x 98 (2d Cir. 2016), noting the settlements to date and Argentina's apparent good faith as substantial changes in fact. Argentina's legislature had already repealed the laws, conditioned on the court vacating the injunction.

Days later, Argentina sold $16.5 billion of new bonds, without apparent difficulty and with high demand. Its checkered financial history was reflected in interest rates about 1.5 percent higher than the average for emerging market debt. Much of the proceeds were used to fund the settlements with the earlier bondholders. The details here come from the court's opinion and from press accounts. Alexandra Stevenson, *How Argentina Settled a Billion-Dollar Debt Dispute with Hedge Funds*, N.Y. Times (April 25, 2016); Julie Wernau and Carolyn Cui, *Argentina Returns to Global Debt Markets with $16.5 Billion Bond Sale*, Wall St. J. (April 19, 2016).

Many bond issues have clauses that authorize settlements based on partial payment if a supermajority of bondholders approves. These clauses seek to avoid the problem of holdouts who insist on the original deal, and if they ever actually collect, get paid much more than everyone else. But voting is typically within each bond issue, and there is some concern in the financial community that hedge funds could buy up enough of the bonds in a single issue to again acquire a veto over any settlement.

8. Foreign governments: Iran. Iran is subject to judgments on behalf of more than a thousand victims of terrorist acts sponsored by Iran. All of these judgments were entered by default; plaintiffs were required to proffer sufficient evidence to support the judgment, but that evidence was uncontested. Iran did not have sovereign immunity, because there is a terrorism exception in the Foreign Sovereign Immunity Act. 28 U.S.C. §1605A(a)(1) (2012).

The plaintiffs attempted to collect in part by seeking a turnover order for $1.75 billion of bonds held by the Central Bank of Iran, allegedly in New York. The bank offered many defenses, including that the bonds were really in Luxembourg and anyway, did not belong to the bank or to the government of Iran. While litigation of those issues was pending, Congress passed a statute authorizing execution, on behalf of any victim of personal injury or death caused by Iran-sponsored terrorism, on "the financial assets that are identified in and are the subject of proceedings in" the pending litigation, identified by case name and docket number. 22 U.S.C. §8772 (2012).

The Supreme Court upheld this legislation as a prospective amendment of the law applicable to the dispute. Bank Markazi v. Peterson, 136 S. Ct. 1310 (2016). Compare Miller v. French in the main volume at 357. Chief Justice Roberts and Justice Sotomayor dissented, arguing that the statute simply told the courts how to decide a specific case and thus violated the separation of powers.

In another of these cases, the Court agreed to decide whether plaintiffs with a judgment against Iran can execute on ancient Persian artifacts, owned by the government of Iran but on loan to Chicago museums since the 1930s. Rubin v. Islamic Republic of Iran, 830 F.3d 470 (7th Cir. 2016), cert. granted, 2017 WL 2742896 (U.S. June 27, 2017). The case turns on the scope of a terrorism exception to the execution provisions of the Foreign Sovereign Immunities Act.

2. Coercive Collection of Money

Page 853. After note 3, add:

3.1. Due process. A defendant at risk of incarceration in a civil contempt proceeding to collect child support is not entitled to court-appointed counsel. But he is entitled to other procedural safeguards. Turner v. Rogers, 564 U.S. 431 (2011). The Court suggested notice to defendant that ability to pay is a crucial issue, a form to elicit financial information, an opportunity at a hearing to respond to questions about his financial status, and an express finding by the court that defendant has the ability to pay. The Court said that other safeguards would be acceptable if they provided as much protection as these four safeguards provide in combination.

Justices Thomas, Scalia, and Alito, and Chief Justice Roberts, would not have reached any question other than the right to counsel, and Thomas and Scalia seemed to think that the Court's procedural safeguards were a bad idea. They emphasized that deadbeat dads often have hidden income that is revealed only by the threat of going to jail. Turner had held eight jobs in three years, which made it difficult for wage withholding orders to keep up, and he had sold drugs for two years while paying no child support. Id. at 460 n.6 (Thomas, J., dissenting). Both the majority and the dissent emphasized that the plaintiff in the case was a single mom who was also poor and unrepresented by counsel. The Court reserved the question of cases in which plaintiff was a government agency.

Page 857. After note 1, add:

1.1. A dead letter? Bearden appears to be widely flouted; there are widespread reports of jailing defendants for failure to pay fines and fees, and more recently, class actions challenging the practice. See, e.g., Neil L. Sobol, Charging the Poor: Criminal Justice Debt and Modern-Day Debtors' Prisons, 75 Md. L. Rev. 486 (2016); UCLA Institute for Research on Labor and Employment, Get to Work or Go *to Jail: Workplace Rights Under Threat* (2016), available at http://www.labor.ucla.edu/publication/get-to-work-or-go-to-jail/ [https://perma.cc/5WF7-48N7]. The UCLA study also reports widespread incarceration for contempt among low-income and minority fathers unable to pay child support.

Page 857. At the end of note 2, add:
   2. Informal collection through criminal laws. . . .
   ACCS declared bankruptcy in 2009. Del Campo v. American Corrective Counseling Services, Inc., 2011 WL 1099879 (N.D. Cal. Mar. 24, 2011). The case continued against individual defendants, and the trial court granted summary judgment on liability for plaintiffs, finding multiple violations of the Fair Debt Collection Practices Act, 15 U.S.C. §1692 *et seq.* (2012). Defendants charged unauthorized fees, misrepresented themselves as the prosecutor, misrepresented the prosecutor's intention to prosecute, and failed to make required disclosures. Order Granting in Part and Denying in Part the Parties' Cross Motions for Summary Judgment, No. 3:01-cv-21151 (N.D. Cal. June 3, 2010), ECF No. 877.
   Meanwhile, Congress has authorized the practice with additional safeguards. 15 U.S.C. §1692p (2012). The private company must make certain disclosures, principally about the right to dispute the bad check, but apparently need not disclose that it is not really the prosecutor. And some categories of checks are excluded from such programs, including post-dated checks to payday lenders and checks that bounced because the bank debited an account without notice to the depositor.
   The Standing Committee on Ethics and Professional Responsibility of the American Bar Association has said that such programs are still widespread, and that it is unethical for prosecutors to participate unless a lawyer from the prosecutor's office has reviewed the case file to determine whether a crime has been committed and prosecution is warranted, or reviewed the dunning letter to ensure that it complies with the Rules of Professional Conduct. Formal Opinion 469, http://www.americanbar.org/content/dam/aba/administrative/professional_responsibility/aba_formal_opinion_469.authcheckdam.pdf [https://perma.cc/G3XT-L4W4] (2014). The Committee said that prosecutors who authorize such letters without individualized review violate Model Rules 8.4(c), which prohibits "conduct involving dishonesty, fraud, deceit or misrepresentation," and Model Rule 5.5(a) on "assisting another" in the unauthorized practice of law. These issues are distinct from the more general issue considered in note 3 — whether it is ethical for an attorney who does nothing deceptive to use the criminal process in aid of efforts to collect an obligation.
   2.1. Outside counsel for the state. The Supreme Court unanimously approved a superficially similar but actually quite different practice in Sheriff v. Gillie, 136 S. Ct. 1594 (2016). Ohio hires outside counsel to collect debts owed to state agencies. These outside lawyers use the Attorney General's letterhead, but identify themselves as debt collectors, sign as "special counsel" or "outside counsel," and give the private law firm's contact information in a signature block and in instructions on responding to the letter. And none of the collection letters at issue in the Supreme Court threatened criminal prosecution. The Court held that this use of the Attorney General's letterhead was not misleading under the Fair Debt Collection Practices Act.

3. Preserving Assets Before Judgment

Page 868. After note 3, add:

4. The English experience. *Mareva* injunctions are now called "freezing injunctions" after a procedural reform. E-mail exchanges with English solicitors, and a recent article on the practice, suggest that the English bar views the current law as appropriately flexible and as reasonably balanced between the legitimate interests of plaintiffs and defendants. The targets are most commonly foreign entities or businesses that are already defunct; an operating business is often allowed to continue to transfer assets in ordinary course of business, including for legal fees. For a broad assessment, see the opening paragraph of Paul McGrath, *The Freezing Order: A Constantly Evolving Jurisdiction*, 31 Civ. Just. Q. No. 1, at 12 (2012).

CHAPTER TEN

MORE ANCILLARY REMEDIES:
ATTORNEYS' FEES AND THE COSTS OF LITIGATION

A. Fee-Shifting Statutes

Page 882. At the end of note 1, add:
  1. Attorneys' fees and the rightful position. . . .
  The Court recently emphasized that only a "specific and explicit" provision in a statute or contract can override the American rule, quoting several earlier cases. Baker Botts L.L.P. v. ASARCO LLC, 135 S. Ct. 2158 (2015). The Court appeared to say that most fee-shifting statutes easily meet this test. The provision at issue, as applied to the expense of litigating a fee petition in bankruptcy, did not.

Page 883. At the end of note 1.b., add:
  b. The Equal Access to Justice Act. . . .
  Despite the limitation to cases where government's position is not substantially justified, fees are awarded in nearly half of all social security cases and a majority of veterans' benefit cases. The great bulk of awards under the Act are modest amounts for claims under these two programs. Astrue v. Ratliff, 560 U.S. 586, 600 nn.1-2 (2010) (Sotomayor, J., concurring).

  In Windsor v. United States, 133 S. Ct. 2675 (2013), the government continued to enforce the Defense of Marriage Act, refusing to recognize same-sex marriages, even though it argued that the law was unconstitutional. The First Circuit has held that this litigation strategy was substantially justified, refusing to award fees in a parallel litigation presenting the same issues. McLaughlin v. Hagel, 767 F.3d 113 (1st Cir. 2014). Had the government simply started recognizing marriages, it would have violated and failed to enforce the law on the basis of "a novel legal theory while simultaneously precluding judicial review of that novel theory." *Id.* at 117-118.

Page 883. After note 1.c., add:
  d. Something new in Texas. A Texas statute offers a new variation. Tex. Govt. Code §22.004(g) (West Supp. 2016) directs the state supreme court to "adopt rules to provide for the dismissal of causes of action that have no basis in law or fact on motion and without evidence." Tex. Civ. Prac. & Remedies Code §30.021 (West 2015) provides that whenever a court grants or denies a motion to dismiss under these newly mandated rules, it "shall award costs and reasonable and necessary attorney's fees to the prevailing party."

  How can the court determine without evidence that a claim has no basis in fact? The state supreme court responded with Tex. R. Civ. Proc. 91a. It says, among other things, that "A cause of action has no basis in fact if no reasonable person could believe the facts pleaded."

Page 884. At the end of note 2, add:
   2. The bad-faith litigation exception. . . .
   In *Chambers*, the Court affirmed an award of all of plaintiff's attorneys' fees, where defendant had engaged in a pervasive course of bad-faith litigation. But in Goodyear Tire & Rubber Co. v. Haeger, 137 S. Ct. 1178 (2017), the Court said that the normal award should be only those fees that were the but-for consequence of the other side's violations. It applied this rule even though it did not question the lower courts' view that Goodyear's misconduct was "egregious." Goodyear withheld test results showing that the tire at issue overheated when driven at highway speeds; plaintiffs had requested all test results "early and often." Other cases had gone to trial even though those test results were produced, so the Court could not infer that the case would have immediately settled, or that all litigation expenses after the first request for test results flowed from the dishonest responses.
   Justice Kagan's unanimous opinion said that this rule followed, "pretty much by definition," from the nature of compensation. Anything more would be punishment and would require criminal-procedure style protections, citing contempt-of-court cases that appeared in chapter 9 — United Mine Workers v. Bagwell and United Mine Workers v. United States. The Court also relied on a similar holding with respect to fee awards in frivolous cases. Fox v. Vice, described in supplement to page 890. On remand, the Ninth Circuit further remanded the case to the district court. 2017 WL 2621251 (9th Cir. June 8, 2017).

Page 885. After the first paragraph of note 9, add:
   9. Procedure. . . .
   The Court unanimously held that *Budinich* is fully applicable to claims for fees based on a contract. Ray Haluch Gravel Co. v. Central Pension Fund, 134 S. Ct. 773 (2014). Plaintiff unsuccessfully argued that a contractual fee award was part of the merits because the liability was on the contract; the Court emphasized the desirability of a uniform rule. The contract at issue was a collective-bargaining agreement, governed by federal common law; the case probably also applies to ordinary contract litigation in federal court under the diversity jurisdiction. Of course most claims for contractual fee awards will arise in state court and be governed by state law.

Page 885. At the end of note 2, add:
   2. Statutes interpreted to provide for one-way fee shifting. . . .
   The Court applied *Christiansburg* to 42 U.S.C. § 1988 (2012). Hughes v. Rowe, 449 U.S. 5 (1980). Section 1988 is the statute at issue in *Rivera*, and the statute that makes fee awards available in most civil rights and civil liberties actions against state and local governments. The Supreme Court of Idaho refused to follow *Hughes*, on the ground that it was a decision about judicial discretion. "Although the Supreme Court may have the authority to limit the discretion of lower federal courts, it does not have the authority to limit the discretion of state courts where such limitation is not contained in the statute." James v. City of Boise, 351 P.3d 1171, 1192 (Idaho 2015). The Supreme Court summarily and unanimously reversed, quoting Justice Story's opinion in Martin v. Hunter's Lessee, 14 U.S. (1 Wheat.) 304 (1816), which first

explained why Supreme Court interpretations of federal law must necessarily be binding in state courts. James v. City of Boise, 136 S. Ct. 685 (2016).

Page 888. At the end of note 9.a, add:
a. The Copyright Act. . . .

More recently, the Court held that "the objective reasonableness" of the losing party's position is "an important factor" but "not the controlling one." Kirtsaeng v. John Wiley & Sons, Inc., 136 S. Ct. 1979, 1988 (2016). A court deciding whether to award fees must consider all the relevant circumstances. These were not specified, but the Court gave two examples: litigation misconduct in the course of litigating an otherwise reasonable claim or defense, and the need to deter repeated infringement or repeated and overaggressive claims, even if in the particular case the repeat offender's position was reasonable.

The cert petition in the case describes a wide range of positions in the courts of appeals, with none of them acting on *Fogerty*'s attention to the financial resources of the litigants. The most influential passage from *Fogerty* appears to have been the Court's quotation of "several nonexclusive factors" from the Third Circuit: "frivolousness, motivation, objective unreasonableness (both in the factual and in the legal components of the case) and the need in particular circumstances to advance considerations of compensation and deterrence." Fogerty v. Fantasy, Inc., 510 U.S. 517, 534 n.19 (1994), quoting Lieb v. Topstone Industries, Inc., 788 F.2d 151, 156 (3d Cir. 1986).

9.a.1. The Patent Act. The Patent Act provides that "[t]he court in exceptional cases may award reasonable attorney fees to the prevailing party." 35 U.S.C. §285 (2012). The Court held that "an 'exceptional' case is simply one that stands out from others with respect to the substantive strength of a party's litigating position (considering both the governing law and the facts of the case) or the unreasonable manner in which the case was litigated." Octane Fitness, LLC v. Icon Health & Fitness, Inc., 134 S. Ct. 1749, 1756 (2014). This determination is committed to the discretion of the trial court based on the totality of the circumstances. And trial court determinations on this issue are reviewable only for abuse of discretion. Highmark Inc. v. Allcare Health Management System, Inc., 134 S. Ct. 1744 (2014).

The Court described the copyright provision construed in *Fogarty* as "similar," 134 S. Ct. at 1756 n.6, although that provision reads like the fee provision in most civil rights laws and does not use the word "exceptional." The Patent Act provision had originally read the same way; the word "exceptional" was added in 1952, and the Court said the amendment was intended to clarify the original intent, not to actually change anything. So *Kirtsaeng*'s emphasis on the totality of the circumstances may influence the patent cases as well.

Page 890. After note 1, add:
1.1 Partially prevailing defendants. In Fox v. Vice, 563 U.S. 826 (2011), the Court faced the problem of defendants entitled to fees because some, but not all, of plaintiff's claims were frivolous. The Court unanimously announced a but-for standard: defendant can recover those fees that would not have been incurred but for the frivolous claims. So if frivolous and non-frivolous claims are factually related,

defendants can recover no fees for work that would have been done even if the frivolous claim had not been filed.

Page 891. At the end of note 2, add:
    2. The requirement of relief on the merits. . . .
    The Fourth Circuit bizarrely held that plaintiffs were not prevailing parties where they got an injunction ordering defendants to comply with the law in the future, but no damages for the past. Lefemine v. Wideman, 672 F.3d 292, 302-303 (4th Cir. 2012). The idea seemed to be that the injunction gave them only what they were already entitled to under the First Amendment. But all injunctions (with the arguable exception of the prophylactic terms of prophylactic injunctions) enforce pre-existing rights that defendant had been violating. The Supreme Court unanimously and summarily reversed. 568 U.S. 1 (2012).
    2.1. Prevailing defendants. A defendant can prevail on grounds other than the merits. CRST Van Expedited, Inc. v. Equal Employment Opportunity Commission, 136 S. Ct. 1642 (2016). The EEOC sued CRST on behalf of some 250 female employees, alleging sexual harassment. The district court dismissed the pattern-and-practice claim on the merits, and dismissed all the individual claims on a variety of other grounds — statute of limitations, failure to investigate and attempt settlement as the statute requires, and as a sanction for discovery abuse. The court of appeals revived only two individual claims.
    The Court thought it obvious that CRST was a prevailing party. It did not question the *Christiansburg* rule, main volume at 885 note 2, that prevailing defendants are entitled to fees only if the plaintiff's claim was frivolous, unreasonable, or groundless. So the question presumably becomes whether it was frivolous, unreasonable, or groundless to contend that these claims had been adequately investigated and mediated and filed within the limitations period, or frivolous, unreasonable, or groundless to contend that the EEOC had adequately responded to discovery. And the opinion does not appear to change the requirement that plaintiff obtain relief on the merits to be prevailing. Justice Thomas, concurring, adhered to his view that *Christiansburg* disregarded the statutory language and was wrongly decided.

Page 891. At the end of note 5, add:
    5. Preliminary relief. . . .
    The Ninth Circuit has held that a preliminary injunction based on a finding of probable success on the merits, followed by a settlement that permanently protects the rights temporarily protected by the preliminary injunction, makes the plaintiff a prevailing party entitled to fees. Higher Taste, Inc. v. City of Tacoma, 717 F.3d 712, 714 (9th Cir. 2013). The court noted that other cases had distinguished preliminary injunctions designed merely to preserve the status quo, without a preliminary finding on the merits.

Page 892. After note 7, add:
    7.1. Pushing the limit further. In Zessar v. Keith, 536 F.3d 788 (7th Cir. 2008), the court granted plaintiff's motion for summary judgment, holding a statute

unconstitutional, and asked the parties to submit proposed terms for a final judgment enjoining enforcement of the statute. Before any injunction was issued, the legislature amended the statute to conform to the summary judgment opinion. The court of appeals reversed a grant of attorneys' fees. The opinion on the summary judgment motion was only an opinion; the case was mooted by the amendment of the statute; and plaintiff was not a prevailing party.

National Rifle Association, Inc. v. City of Chicago, 646 F.3d 992 (7th Cir. 2011), was a proceeding on remand from McDonald v. City of Chicago, 561 U.S. 742 (2010). In *McDonald*, the Court upheld plaintiffs' claim that the Second Amendment applies to the states. Once that was established, the challenged local gun-control ordinances were obviously unconstitutional under the Second Amendment standards announced in District of Columbia v. Heller, 554 U.S. 570 (2008). Before a final judgment could be entered on remand, the defendant cities repealed their ordinances. A distinguished district judge denied attorneys' fees in reliance on *Zessar*.

This literal interpretation of *Buckhannon* was too much for the court of appeals. "If a favorable decision of the Supreme Court does not count as 'the necessary judicial imprimatur,' what would?" *National Rifle*, 646 F.3d at 994, quoting *Buckhannon*, 532 U.S. at 605. The common sense of that opinion is impeccable. But why doesn't common sense require the same result in *Hardt* and *Zessar*?

In *Hardt* itself, the Supreme Court reversed, but without reintroducing any measure of common sense to the prevailing-party requirement. Instead, it held that the ERISA provision authorizing fees for Hardt did not require her to be a prevailing party. 560 U.S. 242 (2010). The statute simply said that "the court in its discretion may allow a reasonable attorney's fee and costs of action to either party." 29 U.S.C. §1132(g)(1) (2012). Under that language, it was enough that Hardt achieved "some success on the merits," and the Court unanimously agreed that she had.

Page 892. At the end of note 8, add:
8. The reach of *Buckhannon*. . . .
The National Childhood Vaccine Injury Act creates a no-fault compensation system for persons injured by covered vaccines. Claimants are paid from a fund administered by the government. The Act prohibits attorneys from charging any fee to claimants. Instead it provides that the court "shall" award attorneys' fees to prevailing plaintiffs; for losing plaintiffs, it says that "the special master or court *may* award an amount of compensation to cover petitioner's reasonable attorneys' fees and other costs incurred in any proceeding on such petition if the special master or court determines that the petition was brought in good faith and there was a reasonable basis for the claim for which the petition was brought." 42 U.S.C. §300aa-15(e)(1) (2012) (emphasis added).

The Supreme Court unanimously enforced this unusual statute according to its terms. Sebelius v. Cloer, 133 S. Ct. 1886 (2013). The plaintiff filed a claim after new medical research linked her muscular sclerosis to the hepatitis-B vaccine. The Federal Circuit rejected her argument that the earlier lack of medical information should toll (delay the running of) the statute of limitations, and that issue was not before the Supreme Court. It seems likely that her argument for tolling was made in good faith and had a reasonable basis; that issue was left for the trial judge on remand. The

Supreme Court rejected some implausible arguments that the provision for fees to losing litigants should not apply when the claim was not timely filed. For more on tolling statutes of limitations, see section 11.E.

Page 893. At the end of note 5, add:
   5. Reasonable hours. . . .
   Trial judges can get away with impressionistic gross adjustments to claimed fees as long as nobody appeals. But if someone does appeal, the courts of appeals find it difficult to meaningfully review such adjustments. The Ninth Circuit recently described such gross adjustments as "an unfortunately common mistake," complaining that its "requirement that district courts show their work is frequently forgotten." Padgett v. Loventhal, 706 F.3d 1205, 1208-1209 (9th Cir. 2013). Plaintiffs in *Padgett* filed many claims and prevailed on one, recovering $1.00 in nominal damages and $200,000 in punitive damages. They sought $3.2 million in fees, and a stunning $900,000 in costs. The district court accurately summarized the controlling legal principles for fee awards to partially prevailing plaintiffs, and without further explanation, awarded $500,000 in fees and $100,000 in costs. On defendants' appeal, the Ninth Circuit remanded for further explanation.

B. Attorneys' Fees from a Common Fund

Page 900. At the end of note 2, add:
   2. Fees from common funds as restitution. . . .
   Section 30, cited here and also in note 5, became §29 in the final published version.

Page 902. At the end of note 3, add:
   3. The reach of *Dague*. . . .
The Supreme Court of New Jersey recently reaffirmed its commitment to contingency enhancements. Walker v. Giuffre, 35 A.3d 1177 (N.J. 2012).

Page 903. At the end of note 1, add:
   1. The choices. . . .
   The Supreme Court of California has held that trial judges in common fund cases have discretion to award fees based on percentage of recovery and to use a lodestar crosscheck. Laffitte v. Robert Half International Inc., 376 P.3d 672 (Cal. 2016). This formulation implies that there is also discretion to use the lodestar, but the opinion, which reviews the evolution of fee awards in both state and federal courts, plainly suggests that percentage of recovery is preferable. The court says that only Florida requires the lodestar in common fund cases. Justice Liu, concurring, urged more use of early fee agreements between counsel and class representatives.

Page 905. After note 8, add:
   8.1. Empirically assessing the PSLRA. A research team reviewed the case files in all 434 securities class action that settled in federal court from 2007 through 2012. Lynn A. Baker, Michael A. Perino, & Charles Silver, *Is the Price Right? An*

Empirical Study of Fee-Setting in Securities Class Actions, 115 Colum. L. Rev. 1371 (2015). A negotiated fee agreement was mentioned in only 41 of the motions to be appointed lead plaintiff and only 21 of the orders appointing lead plaintiffs. An agreement appeared in only 74 of the motions for fee awards. The authors conclude that fees in most cases are being set after the settlement by the same methods used before the PSLRA was enacted.

Judges awarded less than the fees requested in only 62 cases. Fee requests were smaller, and judges were notably less likely to award less than the amount requested, where there was a negotiated fee agreement. The authors found no evidence that lodestar cross checks accomplish anything. And despite the requirement of appointing the plaintiff with the largest claim, the lead plaintiff was an individual in 46% of these cases. They collect other empirical studies of fee awards in class actions in footnote 3.

Page 908. After note 1, add:

1.1. Disparities in wealth. There is a circuit split on whether courts have discretion to deny costs because of an enormous wealth disparity between the prevailing and losing parties. In Moore v. CITGO Refining & Chemicals Co., 735 F.3d 309 (5th Cir. 2013), the court said there is no such discretion; the cases are collected in the dissent. The court recognized discretion for indigent litigants, but these losing litigants were well paid individuals, far from indigent.

1.2. Except where a statute otherwise provides. Rule 54(d) is explicitly subject to contrary statutes; it would be subject to contrary statutes even if it didn't say so. The Fair Debt Collection Practices Act provides: "On a finding by the court that an action under this section was brought in bad faith and for the purpose of harassment, the court may award to the defendant attorney's fees reasonable in relation to the work expended and costs." 15 U.S.C. §1692k(a)(3) (2012). The Court held that this language does not provide "otherwise" than Rule 54(d) — that is, it does not require bad faith as a condition to awarding costs — because it does not state a rule for the case in which a plaintiff files a good-faith claim and loses. Marx v. General Revenue Corp., 568 U.S. 371 (2013). The Court viewed the bad-faith language as limiting the provision for attorneys' fees, and as not intended to implicitly change the quite different rule for costs. Justices Sotomayor and Kagan dissented.

Defendant in *Marx* claimed $7,779 in costs for a case with a one-day trial; these consisted of witness fees, witness travel expenses, and the court reporter's fees for deposition transcripts. The trial court allowed $4,543 of this. The district court opinion is unreported, so we get no details. I note the amounts because even $4,543 is significant for a plaintiff who was unable to pay her student loans and was complaining about unfair debt collection practices.

Page 908. After note 2, add:

2.l. Interpreters. The Court has held that the fees of "interpreters" includes only those who translate oral speech, and does not include the fees of those who translate documents. Taniguchi v. Kan Pacific Saipan, Ltd., 566 U.S. 560 (2012). This holding was based on the alleged plain meaning of "interpreters" as distinguished from "translators." *Taniguchi* is also being cited for the proposition that taxable costs have a "narrow scope," and "are limited to relatively minor, incidental expenses." *Id.* at 2006.

2.2. Electronic discovery. The Fourth Circuit has held that the costs of searching and extracting electronic files, making them searchable, indexing metadata, and preparing the files for conversion to non-editable TIFF or PDF files, all in response to allegedly overbroad discovery requests, are not taxable as "the costs of making copies of any materials where the copies are necessarily obtained for use in the case." Only the final steps of converting the files to TIFF or PDF and copying to compact disks for delivery to the plaintiff constituted "making copies." These final steps cost $218; the earlier steps cost $111,000. Country Vintner, LLC v. E & J Gallo Winery, Inc., 718 F.3d 249 (4th Cir. 2013). The court analogized the search and preparation costs to the cost of searching physical files and extracting paper documents, which also is not taxable. The court largely followed the reasoning of Race Tires America, Inc. v. Hoosier Racing Tire Corp., 674 F.3d 158 (3d Cir. 2012). A similar decision in the Federal Circuit also allows the cost of producing a mirror image of the original hard drive, a step that is often necessary to preserve metadata in the documents to be produced. CBT Flint Partners, LLC v. Return Path, Inc., 737 F.3d 1320 (Fed Cir. 2013).

But if the losing litigant specified details of how electronic information should be provided, the Ninth and Federal Circuits have held that the cost of complying with those specifications is taxable. In re Online DVD-Rental Antitrust Litigation, 779 F.3d 914 (9th Cir. 2015), quoting *CBT Flint Partners.* The district court in *Online DVD* had awarded $710,000 in costs against a class of Netflix subscribers. The court of appeals affirmed much of this, and set some of it aside in light of *Taniguchi*; the exact amounts do not appear in the opinion.

C. Ethical Issues in Fee Awards

Page 919. At the end of note 4.d., add:
   d. Assigning fees to the lawyer. . . .
   The Court held unanimously that the fees are payable to the client and that the government can offset the fees against debts the client owes the government. Astrue v. Ratliff, 560 U.S. 586 (2010).

Page 922. At the end of note 4, add:
   4. Reversionary settlements. . . .
   The Seventh Circuit rejected such a settlement in Pearson v. NBTY, Inc., 772 F.3d 778 (7th Cir. 2014). The claim was that defendants made fraudulent claims that a dietary supplement called glucosamine could cure joint problems. The settlement provided that consumers could recover $3 for each bottle of pills they bought, up to a maximum of four bottles, or $5 a bottle for up to ten bottles if they had receipts. Class counsel valued this provision at over $14 million, on the assumption that all class members would file claims. But the settlement website seemed to imply that receipts or other documentation were required for all claims, and it threatened prosecution for inaccurate claims. Only 30,000 claims were filed, for a total of $865,000.

Class counsel sought $4.5 million in attorneys' fees, which defendants did not oppose. The district court awarded $2 million, reasoning that this was less than ten percent of a $20 million settlement: $14 million in damages, plus $4.5 million in fees, plus the $1.5 million cost of notifying class members.

Judge Posner's opinion harshly condemned the settlement as the fruit of collusion between class counsel and defendants. He argued that the website and various other terms of the settlement seemed designed to minimize claims, that attorneys' fees and notice were a cost rather than a benefit to the class, and that the fees awarded were more than double the money actually paid to the class.

The Sixth Circuit has rejected *Pearson* as inconsistent with Boeing Co. v. Van Gemert, 444 U.S. 472 (1980), described at page 901 of the main volume, which upheld a fee award based on the total judgment in a litigated case, without regard to how many class members failed to file claims. Gascho v. Global Fitness Holdings, LLC, 822 F.3d 269 (6th Cir. 2016). Judge Clay dissented, relying in part on *Pearson*.

CHAPTER ELEVEN

REMEDIAL DEFENSES

A. Unconscionability and the Equitable Contract Defenses

Page 932. After note 2, add:

2.1. *Rent-A-Center*. The employer in *Rent-A-Center* required employees to sign a free-standing arbitration agreement. One clause of that agreement provided that the arbitrator would have "exclusive authority" to decide any question of "enforceability," including "any claim" that "any part" of the agreement is "void or voidable." Rent-A-Center, West, Inc. v. Jackson, 561 U.S. 63, 66 (2010). The employee, whose substantive claim alleged racial discrimination, claimed that the arbitration agreement was unconscionable because it applied only to claims the employee would raise and not to claims the employer would raise, it limited discovery, and it required the employee to pay half the arbitrator's fees.

As the majority applied the *Buckeye* rule to this agreement, all these issues were for the arbitrator. These were challenges to the validity of the contract as a whole, not challenges to the single clause providing that the arbitrator would decide questions of enforceability. A challenge to that clause would be for the court, but if that clause were valid, then all the rest was for the arbitrator. So the arbitrator would decide whether the arbitration clause is unconscionable. Justices Stevens, Ginsburg, Breyer, and Sotomayor dissented.

2.2. Preempting legal developments? In Nitro-Lift Technologies, LLC. v. Howard, 568 U.S. 17 (2012), the Court summarily reversed the Oklahoma court for declaring that covenants not to compete in an employment contract were void and unenforceable under state law. The contract also had an arbitration clause, and the legality of the covenants not to compete was for the arbitrator. The arbitrator is supposed to follow the law, more or less. But if all employers impose arbitration clauses, how will the courts make any law in employment matters?

Page 934. After note 6, add:

6.1. Federal preemption. The Supreme Court brought much of this law to a halt in AT&T Mobility LLC v. Concepcion, 563 U.S. 333 (2011). The Federal Arbitration Act expressly preserves state-law defenses that apply to any contract, and the Supreme Court has offered unconscionability as an illustration of that provision. See *Muhammad* at the top of page 926 of the main volume. But such a doctrine cannot be "applied in a fashion that disfavors arbitration." *Concepcion*, 563 U.S. at 341. And "California's courts have been more likely to hold contracts to arbitrate unconscionable than other contracts." *Id.* at 342. This is in some ways a disparate-impact opinion: the California law of unconscionability was preempted because it disproportionately affected arbitration clauses. The majority thought that class arbitration lost the advantages of arbitration — its informal and inexpensive nature — and that companies would not want class arbitration with no possibility of appeal, so that holding class waivers unconscionable defeated the purposes of arbitration. Justice Breyer dissented for himself and Justices Ginsburg, Sotomayor, and Kagan.

AT&T's arbitration clause was in some ways generous. AT&T paid the expenses for nonfrivolous claims, arbitration occurred in the customer's home county, and if a customer recovered more than AT&T's last written settlement offer, AT&T would pay a minimum of $7,500 plus double the customer's attorneys' fees. A customer could elect small-claims court instead of arbitration. (Why is this even an arbitration clause, and not just a class action waiver?)

But AT&T's clause did not solve the central problem of making small claims worth pursuing. In *Concepcion*, AT&T advertised free cell phones to those who would sign a two-year service contract. Then it charged $30.22 in sales tax on the free phones. So the Concepcions had a claim for $30.22. And if AT&T offered the Concepcions $30.22 before the arbitrator issued an award, then all they could recover was $30.22. This surely means that they could not hire a lawyer, and that it made no sense even to invest their own time in pursuing the matter pro se, and therefore, that AT&T need not worry about many consumers ever taking any effective action over its $30 deception. So AT&T would be safe from any claim where the damages were fixed or could be estimated in advance with reasonable accuracy. A viable claim for punitive damages would change this calculus.

Muhammad now serves as an illustration of state-court reasoning in the law of unconscionability. But its specific holding about the unconscionability of class action waivers embedded in arbitration clauses is no longer good law. *Concepcion* raises a different remedies issue: whether there can be any effective remedy for violations of consumer protection laws.

6.2. Another federal theory eliminated. Earlier Supreme Court cases upholding arbitration of statutory claims had consistently emphasized that the arbitration must be capable of effectively vindicating the statutory right. The drafters of form contracts could not require explicit waiver of a statutory right, and they could not achieve that result indirectly by requiring an arbitration process that could not enforce the right. But the Court has never found that standard violated. And in American Express Co. v. Italian Colors Restaurant, 133 S. Ct. 2304 (2013), the Court found no violation of the effective-vindication standard, even though both sides appeared to agree that plaintiff's antitrust claim was not viable in arbitration. The restaurants' individual damages were about $38,000, but to prove that claim would require an economist's expert report that could easily cost a million dollars.

The American Express arbitration agreement contains a class action waiver. It precludes joinder of more than one plaintiff. It contains a confidentiality clause that precludes plaintiffs in separate arbitrations from sharing evidence or experts. It precludes any shifting of litigation costs to American Express even on successful claims. American Express refused to enter into any kind of stipulation that would simplify the economic proof required in arbitration.

The Court did not deny that the American Express arbitration clause effectively barred the restaurant's claim. But it said that the Arbitration Act's "command to enforce arbitration agreements trumps any interest in ensuring the prosecution of low-value claims," and that the Act "favor[s] the absence of litigation when that is the consequence of a class-action waiver." *Id.* n.5. That would not seem to leave much of the effective-vindication principle, but formally the Court said that that principle applies only to the right to pursue a claim, and not to the ability to prove it.

Justice Kagan for three dissenters said that the Arbitration Act favored simpler and less expensive resolution of claims, not immunity from claims. And in the antitrust context, the Court's decision meant that a monopolist could use its market power to require customers to agree to an arbitration system that effectively waives their right to complain about the monopoly. Justice Sotomayor was recused, so the case was decided 5-3 on the usual ideological lines.

6.3. The end of class actions? For the view that *Concepcion* may not be as sweeping as these notes suggest, see Michael Helfand, *Purpose, Precedent, and Politics: Why Concepcion Covers Less Than You Think*, 4 Y.B. Arb. & Mediation 126 (2012). But that was before *American Express*, and so far, not much has come of the potential limits that Professor Helfand saw in the Court's opinion and in Justice Thomas's concurrence for the fifth vote. A survey of litigation post-*Concepcion* found many class action waivers upheld, very few struck down, and none of the latter yet final on appeal. Jessie Kokrda Kamens, *Post-Concepcion, Plaintiffs Chalk Up Few Victories, Look to Government for Relief*, 80 U.S.L.W. 1646 (May 29, 2012), also available at 13 Class Action Litig. Report No. 9 (May 11, 2012).

For the view that there is nothing to prevent corporations from including arbitration clauses with class action waivers in every consumer contract and every employment contract — and perhaps even in corporate charters or bylaws to bar shareholder class actions — see Brian T. Fitzpatrick, *The End of Class Actions?* 57 Ariz. L. Rev. 161 (2015). Class action waivers are widespread but apparently not yet universal, or even nearly so, in consumer and employment contracts. They have not yet appeared in corporate charters, partly because no one knows if they would be enforceable and partly because of resistance by the Securities and Exchange Commission.

6.4. Special rules for employee claims? The National Labor Relations Board has repeatedly held that a class action on behalf of employees is collective action protected by the National Labor Relations Act, 29 U.S.C. §151 *et seq.* (2012), and that a class action waiver in an employment contract is therefore an unfair labor practice. There is a circuit split on the question, and the Supreme Court has taken three cases to resolve it. Epic Systems Corp. v. Lewis, 823 F.3d 1147 (7th Cir. 2016), *cert. granted*, 137 S. Ct. 809 (2017); Ernst & Young LLC v. Morris, 834 F.3d 975 (9th Cir. 2016), *cert. granted*, 137 S. Ct. 809 (2017); NLRB v. Murphy Oil USA, Inc., 808 F.3d 1013 (5th Cir. 2015), *cert. granted*, 137 S. Ct. 809 (2017). The cases have been consolidated and will likely be decided under the *Epic Systems* caption; that was the first cert petition filed. The Obama Administration had been supporting the workers; the Trump Administration is now supporting the employers.

6.5. Quasi-governmental claims? California's Private Attorneys General Act (PAGA), Cal. Labor Code §2699 *et seq.* (LexisNexis 2006 & Supp. 2017), authorizes employees to file collective actions to recover civil penalties for violations of the state's Labor Code, with 75 percent of the recovery going to a state agency and 25 percent to the employees. The California court has held that these rights are not waivable, and that an arbitration clause that requires their waiver is unenforceable as against public policy. Iskanian v. CLS Transportation Los Angeles, LLC, 327 P.3d 129 (Cal. 2014).

The court distinguished *Concepcion* on the ground that a PAGA action is a law-enforcement proceeding on behalf of the state, and that the Federal Arbitration Act applies only to private disputes. It found support for this distinction in the absence of government cases in the Supreme Court's arbitration precedents and in the lone exception, Equal Employment Opportunity Commission v. Waffle House, Inc., 534 U.S. 279 (2002). *Waffle House* held that the EEOC could sue to recover back pay on behalf of an employee who had signed an arbitration clause. The Ninth Circuit also held that the *Iskanian* rule is not preempted by the Federal Arbitration Act. Sakkab v. Luxottica Retail North America, Inc., 803 F.3d 425 (9th Cir. 2015).

6.6. Other grounds for holding arbitration clauses unconscionable. The California court has held that unconscionability review of arbitration clauses survives *Concepcion* where the alleged ground of unconscionability is something other than a class action waiver. Sanchez v. Valencia Holding Co., 353 P.3d 741 (Cal. 2015). But on the merits, the court held the arbitration clause in an auto dealer's form contract not to be unconscionable.

The Ninth Circuit came to a similar conclusion in Chavarria v. Ralphs Grocery Co., 733 F.3d 916 (9th Cir. 2013). The arbitration agreement was procedurally unconscionable because it was imposed on all employees as a condition of keeping their jobs, and substantively unconscionable because it allowed the employer to choose the arbitrator and it required the employee to pay half the cost of the arbitration. The employer represented that the fees for an arbitrator would range from $7,000 to $14,000 per day.

6.7. A drafting glitch? Section 9 of DirecTV's agreement with its consumers provides for arbitration and prohibits class arbitration. And then it says: "If, however, the law of your state would find this agreement to dispense with class action procedures unenforceable, then this entire Section 9 is unenforceable." The California Court of Appeal invalidated the entire arbitration clause, because *California* law would indeed invalidate the class action waiver. Imburgia v. DirecTV, Inc., 170 Cal. Rptr. 3d 190 (Ct. App. 2014).

The Supreme Court reversed in an opinion by Justice Breyer. 136 S. Ct. 463 (2015). Recognizing that interpretation of the contract was a matter of state law on which the state court's decision was binding, the Court said that even so, the interpretation was suspect under California law and that it appeared that no California court would have reached that decision in any context other than an arbitration clause. A reference to state law would not normally be read to include invalid state law. And therefore, the state court's interpretation was preempted by the Federal Arbitration Act; it did not place arbitration contracts "on equal footing with all other contracts." *Id.* at 471. Justice Thomas dissented on the ground that the Federal Arbitration Act does not apply in state court. Justices Ginsburg and Sotomayor dissented on the ground that the state court had properly construed ambiguous language against the party that drafted it. The majority denied that the language was ambiguous.

6.8. Disclosure requirements? The New Jersey court has held that a consumer arbitration clause is invalid if it does not clearly disclose, at least in general terms, that the consumer is waiving his right to sue in court. Atalese v. U.S. Legal Services Corp., L.P, 99 A.3d 306 (N.J. 2014). The court said that all consumer waivers have to be clearly explained in New Jersey, so that its rule did not single out arbitration clauses. The arbitration clause appeared at page 9 of a 23-page form contract; inserting the disclosure would likely accomplish nothing going forward. The defendant in this case is a private "debt-adjustment" firm, not the federally sponsored Legal Services Corporation.

6.9. Empirical studies. Empirical studies of consumer arbitration are collected, and the largest study to date reported, in David Horton & Andrea Cann Chandrasekher, *After the Revolution: An Empirical Study of Consumer Arbitration*, 104 Geo. L.J. 57 (2015). Not surprisingly, they found no surge of small consumer claims into arbitration after *Concepcion*. They found 4,839 consumer claims filed with the American Arbitration Association in a four-and-a-half year period (2009-13). Of these, 30 percent were withdrawn and 38 percent settled on undisclosed terms; some of the withdrawals were probably also settlements. Twenty-nine percent were pursued to an arbitration award, and consumers recovered at least one dollar in 35 percent of those — or ten percent of the total claims filed. For those who prevailed, the average recovery was over $18,000 and the median recovery was over $5,000. The American Arbitration Association has special rules for consumer cases, which protect the arbitrator's independence and cap the consumer's liability for costs; the authors speculate that results might be worse in arbitrations with other organizations that lack such rules.

The Consumer Financial Protection Bureau has completed a massive study of consumer cases. *Arbitration Study: Report to Congress*, available at http://files.consumerfinance.gov/f/201503_cfpb_arbitration-study-report-to-congress-2015.pdf [https://perma.cc/J8RH-GC4E]. The study is 728 pages, but it has a helpful Executive Summary. The Bureau reviewed 1,847 arbitration cases filed in 2010, 2011, or 2012 and arising out of transactions subject to any one of six statutes for which the Bureau has responsibility. The average consumer claim was $27,000; the median was $11,500; very few presented claims of less than $1,000. So even if arbitration works for claims that are substantial from a consumer's perspective, it is not absorbing the small claims that would be aggregated in class actions. Companies won claims that they filed at much higher rates than consumers won claims that they filed, but that may be because the great majority of the company-filed claims were debt collection claims. At least a quarter of cases settled, but the Bureau did not have access to the amounts of these settlements.

The Bureau also reviewed class actions under the same six statutes, individual consumer lawsuits in federal court, and credit-card cases in a small number of small claims courts for which data was available on line. Small claims court was mostly a collection court in these jurisdictions; consumers filed something under 870 cases and companies filed more than 41,000 cases. Most class actions settled within a year or two of filing, and distributed about $540 million per year. This was a tiny amount per class member, but a significant amount per defendant.

Professors Johnston and Zywicki criticize the study on many grounds. Jason Scott Johnston and Todd J. Zywicki, *The Consumer Financial Protection Bureau's Arbitration Study: A Summary and Critique*, 35 Banking & Fin'l Servs. Pol'y Rep. No. 5, at 9 (2016), available on Westlaw. They say that the Bureau compared class action settlements to arbitration awards, giving arbitration no credit for all the money paid in settlements. The Bureau presented aggregate data on the class action settlements, so a few huge settlements make the totals look better. Few class members file claims in the typical class action settlement (but it appears that even fewer consumers file small arbitration claims). And they say that the fundamental question is whether class settlements have any relationship to the merits, or merely reflect defendants' desires to avoid the huge costs of class litigation; the Bureau study had no way to assess the merits of either class actions or arbitrations. The Bureau study included a consumer survey, in which few consumers said they would call a lawyer if their credit card issuer refused to remove a wrongful fee, but many said they would cancel the card and move their business. Johnston and Zywicki view this market discipline as a substantial incentive to compliance, and note that companies often give credits or refunds in order to keep the account. (This remedy works only for violations that the consumer can recognize on her own, without consulting a lawyer.)

If we think that consumer class actions are principally about compensation, then the reality is that many class members get nothing, because they do not file claims, and those that do file claims generally get small amounts. But if we think that consumer class actions are principally about deterrence, encouraging companies to comply with the law, then aggregating many small claims into one large liability performs a function that arbitration shows no sign of performing.

Based on its study, and an extensive notice-and-comment process, the Bureau has issued a final rule on Arbitration Agreements. The rule prohibits class action waivers in financial service contracts; it allows arbitration clauses for individual claims. And it requires companies to report arbitration claims and awards to the Bureau, where they will be made publicly available. The rule is available through a link at https://www.consumerfinance.gov/policy-compliance/rulemaking/final-rules/arbitration-agreements/, and will be codified at 12 C.F.R. part 1040.

Page 934. After note 7, add:
8. Personal injury. In Marmet Health Care Center, Inc. v. Brown, 565 U.S. 530 (2012), the Court unanimously and summarily reversed the West Virginia court's holding that pre-dispute arbitration clauses are unenforceable in personal injury and wrongful death cases. The case arose out of three allegedly wrongful deaths of nursing-home patients.

The state court had also held, in the alternative, that the clauses were unconscionable. But the Supreme Court thought that holding had been influenced by the state court's view that the clauses violated public policy. It remanded for further consideration of "whether, absent that general public policy, the arbitration clauses . . . are unenforceable under state common law principles that are not specific to arbitration and pre-empted by the FAA." Id. at 1204. On remand, the state court remanded to take further evidence on whether the contracts were unconscionable. Brown v. Genesis Healthcare Corp., 729 S.E.2d 217 (W. Va. 2012). No further proceedings are reported.

More recently, the Court considered two Kentucky cases in which relatives of nursing-home patients, acting under a power of attorney signed by the patients, agreed to arbitrate any disputes with the nursing home. The Kentucky court announced a clear-statement rule: a power of attorney does not authorize the attorney-in-fact to waive the right to jury trial unless it explicitly says so. The Court reversed, in an opinion by Justice Kagan, holding that this rule discriminated against arbitration clauses. Kindred Nursing Centers LP v. Clark, 137 S. Ct. 1421 (2017). Justice Thomas dissented, again noting his frequent view that the Federal Arbitration Act does not apply in state courts.

The Department of Health and Human Services has prohibited long-term care facilities that accept Medicare or Medicaid funds from requiring patients to sign pre-dispute arbitration clauses. 42 C.F.R. 483.70(n) (2016). A patient and a nursing home may agree to arbitrate a dispute after the dispute arises, but there are disclosure requirements, and the right to remain in the home and receive care cannot be conditioned on agreeing to arbitration. *Marmet* and *Kindred* appear to have arisen before this regulation took effect.

B. Unclean Hands and *in Pari Delicto*

Page 938. At the end of the first paragraph of note 1, add:
    1. Two defenses. . . .
    The cases on whether to apply unclean hands to actions at law are collected in T. Leigh Anenson, *Limiting Legal Remedies: An Analysis of Unclean Hands*, 99 Ky. L.J. 63 (2011).

Page 940. At the end of note 10, add:
    10. Comparative fault. . . .
    A lawyer who stole money from his client was much more at fault than the client, a medical marijuana dispensary in California whose entire business was illegal under federal law. Northbay Wellness Group, Inc. v. Beyries, 789 F.3d 956 (9th Cir. 2015). The surprising thing is that the bankruptcy court had gone the other way. The marijuana client's unclean hands did not bar it from asserting its otherwise straightforward claim that the attorney's debt for the stolen money is not dischargeable in bankruptcy.

C. Estoppel and Waiver

1. Equitable Estoppel

Page 946. At the end of note 5, add:
    5. Estoppel and fraud. . . .
    In Petrella v. Metro-Goldwyn-Mayer, Inc., 134 S. Ct. 1962 (2014), the Court rather casually characterized estoppel as requiring "intentionally misleading representations." *Id.* at 1977. There was no discussion, and the only citation was to a copyright treatise. The context was plaintiffs misleading potential defendants into believing that no lawsuit would be filed; probably the Court's statement should be limited to that context. *Petrella* is more fully described in the supplement to page 964.

Page 946. After the first paragraph of note 6, add:
    6. Estoppel and expectancy. . . .
    In CIGNA v. Amara, 563 U.S. 421 (2011), the Court described estoppel as an "equitable remedy" that "'operates to place the person entitled to its benefit in the same position he would have been in had the representations been true.'" *Id.* at 441, quoting James W. Eaton, *Handbook of Equity Jurisprudence* (West 1901). The case is more fully described in supplement to page 569.

D. Laches

Page 961. At the end of note 1, add:
    1. The special facts of *Harjo*. . . .
    A separate case with a new set of newly adult plaintiffs had already been filed while *Harjo* was pending. The Trademark Trial and Appeal Board again found "Redskins" disparaging and cancelled the trademark's registration. Blackhorse v. Pro-Football, Inc., 111 U.S.P.Q.2d 1080 (T.T.A.B. 2014). The district court affirmed. 112 F. Supp. 3d 439 (E.D. Va. 2015). (It was Congress that moved the venue to Virginia. 15 U.S.C. §1071(b)(4) (2012)). The district court rejected the laches argument on the ground that the new plaintiffs had not unreasonably delayed, and on the separate ground that the public interest in canceling the mark was a reason to override laches. The team appealed.
    Meanwhile, the Supreme Court held the ban on disparaging marks unconstitutional under the Free Speech Clause. Matal v. Tam, 137 S. Ct. 1744 (2017). At issue in *Tam* was an Asian-American band that calls itself the Slants. On June 29, the plaintiffs in *Blackhorse* filed letters with the Fourth Circuit conceding that *Tam* was controlling and consenting to a judgment in favor of the team. The laches issue had become moot.

Page 966. After note 6, add:
    7. *Petrella*. Petrella v. Metro-Goldwyn-Mayer, Inc., 134 S. Ct. 1962 (2014), was a copyright suit over the movie *Raging Bull*. MGM acquired the rights to the screenplay from the author, Frank Petrella, in 1976. The original copyright expired in 1991, but it could be renewed for an additional 67 years. And under a curious provision of the Copyright Act, the renewal rights belonged to Petrella's heirs, notwithstanding Petrella's attempt to assign those rights to MGM.
    Paula Petrella, the heir, renewed the copyright in 1991 and notified MGM of her claim in 1998, but she did not file suit until 2009. The statute of limitations was three years, running separately from each act of infringement. Petrella sought MGM's profits from sales in 2006 and later, and an injunction against further distribution of the movie. The Ninth Circuit held that the entire claim, and all remedies, were barred by laches. 695 F.3d 946 (9th Cir. 2012). The Supreme Court reversed.
    The opinion says many things, some with full explanations and some without. By barring all remedies for sales prior to 2006, the three-year statute of limitations fully protected most of MGM's alleged reliance. For sales in 2006 and after, MGM would get credit for its contributions to making and promoting the movie, citing Sheldon v.

MGM, in the main volume at 665. Laches cannot be applied to bar a suit for legal remedies filed within the period of a congressionally enacted statute of limitations; this statement is quite general but perhaps not quite absolute and universal. It clearly implies that the second paragraph of note 3 at 964 of the main volume is no longer accurate. But estoppel might bar legal remedies within the statute of limitations if a plaintiff intentionally misleads a potential defendant into thinking there will be no lawsuit and the defendant detrimentally relies.

And laches might completely bar some or all equitable remedies in extraordinary circumstances The Court cited two examples from the lower courts, each involving a demand for destruction of valuable tangible property created (books published; houses built, sold, and occupied) within the period of delay. More routinely, MGM's reliance could also be taken into account in crafting injunctive relief and in calculating MGM's profits from the infringement; the Court treated restitution of profits as equitable for this purpose. But the lower courts should closely examine MGM's alleged reliance, and among other things, take account of the protection MGM might have received by suing Petrella for a declaratory judgment.

There was evidence that Petrella delayed filing suit because the movie did not make any money until it was re-released in 2005. MGM attempted to portray this delay as plaintiff speculating at its expense. See note 6 at page 962 of the main volume. But the Court thought there was nothing untoward in waiting to see if the harms from infringement would justify the cost of litigation. Justice Breyer dissented, joined by Chief Justice Roberts and Justice Kennedy.

8. The Federal Circuit foiled again. The Federal Circuit convened en banc to decide whether *Petrella* required a change in its rule that laches can bar a claim to damages from patent infringement before the six-year limitations period has run. And it decided, 6-5, that no change was required. SCA Hygiene Products Aktiebolag v. First Quality Baby Products, LLC, 807 F.3d 1311 (Fed. Cir. 2015). The Supreme Court reversed. 137 S. Ct. 954 (2017).

It is hard to see any reason why laches in patent cases should be different from laches in copyright cases, and the Court rejected an argument that laches was implicitly codified in the Patent Act. The word never appears there, but there were court of appeals cases from before its enactment in 1952. Justice Breyer dissented, based on policy arguments and on a claimed consensus of pre-1952 cases. The majority claimed the consensus was the opposite; I made no effort to sort that out. The majority also said that it had no power to override Congress based on policy arguments. But of course Congress had not said either that there is a laches defense or there is not. Congress had enacted a statute of limitations and said nothing about laches.

E. Statutes of Limitations

1. Continuing Violations

Page 970. At the end of note 5.a, add:
    a. Hostile environment claims. . . .

The Court repeatedly distinguished the two kinds of violations in Petrella v. Metro-Goldwyn-Mayer, Inc., 134 S. Ct. 1962 (2014). With respect to the many acts of alleged copyright infringement in that case, the Court variously referred to "the separate-accrual rule," "[s]eparately accruing harm," "discrete acts, each independently actionable," and "separately accruing wrongs." *Id.* at 1969-1970 & nn.6-7, 1975 n.16. With respect to the cumulative violations illustrated by *Morgan*, it variously referred to "harm from past violations that are continuing," "conduct cumulative in effect," and "hostile-work-environment claims, cumulative in effect and extending over a long time." *Id.* at 1969-1970 & nn.6-7, 1975 n.16. The Court acknowledged that laches could bar claims within the period of limitations applicable to the latter category, conduct cumulative in effect.

Page 971. After note 6.e, add:
    6.1. Constructive discharge. If an employer discriminates by subjecting an employee to intolerable working conditions, and the employee resigns, the resignation is treated as a constructive discharge for which the employee can sue. The Supreme Court held that the very short statute of limitations (even shorter for federal employees, as here) runs from the date the employee resigns, and not from the last discriminatory act in the series of acts that provoked the resignation. Green v. Brennan, 136 S. Ct. 1769 (2016). This is an example of an issue about when a cause of action "accrued," and the Court invoked the general rule that limitations begins to run when the plaintiff "can file suit and obtain relief." *Id.* at 1776, quoting Bay Area Laundry and Dry Cleaning Pension Trust Fund v. Ferbar Corp., 522 U.S. 192, 201 (1997). And that requires that all events essential to the cause of action have happened. Plaintiff could not sue for constructive discharge until he actually resigned; it was not enough that he had adequate grounds to resign and claim constructive discharge.

Page 972. After note 7, add:
    7.1. ERISA. The Employee Retirement Income Security Act provides that suits against plan administrators for breach of fiduciary duty must be filed within six years of "the last action which constituted a part of the breach," or "in the case of an omission the latest date on which the fiduciary could have cured the breach." 29 U.S.C. §1113 (2012). Edison International included in its retirement plan six retail mutual funds, with high fees charged to employees, when it could easily have included institutional versions of the same funds with much lower fees. But the employees sued more than six years after some of the funds were selected. The Court noted that trustees have a duty to periodically review all of a trust's investments for appropriateness; it quickly and unanimously concluded that the statute ran from the

last breach of that duty to review. Tibble v. Edison International, 135 S. Ct. 1823 (2015).

7.2. The Establishment Clause. In Tearpock-Martini v. Borough of Shickshinny, 756 F.3d 232 (3d Cir. 2014), the borough erected a directional sign advertising and pointing to a Baptist church. The sign was in the public right of way in front of plaintiff's residence, and she claimed that the sign violated the Establishment Clause. It was not a very strong claim, however irritating the sign's location might have been to the property owner. But focus on Pennsylvania's two-year statute of limitations, which applied by analogy (see the next set of notes).

Plaintiff sued more than two years after the sign was installed. The Third Circuit held that the continued presence of the sign was not a continuing violation, but merely a continuing effect of the only alleged violation, which occurred when the sign was installed. This seems clearly wrong, and in a way that illuminates the distinction. If there was a constitutional violation, it was not a small bit of construction, but the borough's endorsement of the church. And if the sign were an unconstitutional endorsement, it was such an endorsement every day the sign remained. There is a decision going the other way in Gonzales v. North Township, 800 F. Supp. 676, 684 (N.D. Ind. 1992), *rev'd on other grounds*, 4 F.3d 1412 (7th Cir. 1993), and scores of cases that should have come out the other way if the Third Circuit were right.

Recognizing what it called "the long standing apparent exemption of Establishment Clause claims" from statutes of limitations, the court held that it would be "'inconsistent with federal law or policy'" to apply Pennsylvania's statute of limitations to the claim. 756 F.3d at 239, quoting Wilson v. Garcia, 471 U.S. 261, 266-267 (1985). The traditional rationales for limitations periods had "no persuasive force in this context," because plaintiff challenged "a still-existing monument that communicates anew an allegedly unconstitutional endorsement of religion by the government each time it is viewed." 756 F.3d at 239. And that is exactly why the court should have said it was a continuing violation.

Page 973. After note 6, add:
6.1. Contracting for a different limitations period. The Court has unanimously upheld a limitations period specified in an adhesion contract, provided that it is not "unreasonably short." Heimeshoff v. Hartford Life & Accident Insurance Co., 134 S. Ct. 604 (2013). The suit was for disability benefits under an employer-sponsored insurance plan subject to ERISA, the Employee Retirement Income Security Act, 29 U.S.C. §1001 *et seq.* (2012). ERISA has no statute of limitations for such claims; the most analogous Connecticut law said that the insurer could set a limitations period so long as it was not shorter than one year after the occurrence of the loss insured against. The employer's plan was more generous; it said that no lawsuit could be filed more than three years after the date on which the proof of loss was due. This provision tracked provisions in the insurance law of many states.

Plaintiff filed suit just short of three years after The Hartford denied her last internal appeal — that is, three years after her cause of action accrued, which is the usual date on which limitation periods begin to run. But of course, the conclusion of all internal appeals was considerably later than the date the proof of loss was due, so her lawsuit was filed way too late. Citing earlier cases on contractual rules concerning limitations, the Court held the plan provision reasonable and enforceable.

There are two things to note about the behavior of Heimeshoff's lawyer. First, he read the plan and found the three-year provision, but failed to notice when to start counting the three years. Second, his client was disabled and not receiving disability benefits, but he let her claim sit in his office for three years after the end of internal appeals, just because he was busy and he thought that no deadline was imminent. The statute of limitations is not the only reason to move claims forward promptly.

2. The Discovery Rule

Page 980. After note 1, add:

1.1. Multiple injuries from one wrong. A much-litigated issue in latent disease cases is what to do when defendant's wrongdoing causes one injury or disease early, and a much more serious injury or disease years later. Plaintiff suffers injury, and often discovers the cause of that injury, when the first disease is diagnosed. Early cases were divided, but the dominant rule has come to be that limitations runs anew with respect to the second disease. Some of the cases are collected in Pooshs v. Philip Morris USA Inc., 250 P.3d 181, 183 n.1 (Cal. 2011), where a long-term smoker contracted chronic obstructive pulmonary disease in 1989, periodontal disease in 1990, and lung cancer in 2003.

Page 981. After note 4, add:

4.1. The Securities and Exchange Commission. The Court unanimously refused to apply the discovery rule to claims by the SEC seeking civil penalties for fraud. Gabelli v. SEC, 568 U.S. 442 (2013). A quite general statute of limitations, dating to 1839, says that a claim for "any civil fine, penalty, or forfeiture" must be filed within five years after the claim accrues. 28 U.S.C. §2462 (2012).

The Court treated the discovery rule as having originated in fraud cases, and treated it as generally available in fraud suits by victims. But it said the SEC is different. Ordinary citizens do not spend their time searching for fraud; they have no reason to investigate until they discover facts suggesting a violation. But the SEC's principal task is to investigate for fraud. This statute of limitations applied only to government agencies, and it had never been subjected to the discovery rule. The Court concluded by emphatically urging caution in implying exceptions to statutes of limitation — a passage that will now be regularly quoted by defendants in statute-of-limitation cases.

Page 983. After note 10, add:

10.1. Other grounds for equitable tolling. In Holland v. Florida, 560 U.S. 631 (2010), the Court reaffirmed earlier cases holding that "limitations periods are customarily subject to equitable tolling." *Id.* at 646. Justice Scalia agreed with this presumption in his dissent. So he did not think that every exception must be set out in the statutory text and that none can ever be inferred. Rather, he appears to have thought that the discovery rule in particular is not an appropriate tolling rule.

Holland said that equitable tolling requires plaintiff to show "'(1) that he has been pursuing his rights diligently, and (2) that some extraordinary circumstance stood in his way' and prevented filing." *Id.* at 649, quoting Pace v. Diguglielmo, 544 U.S. 408, 418 (2005). On the facts, the Court held that the one-year period for filing petitions for post-conviction review under the Antiterrorism and Effective Death Penalty Act, 28 U.S.C. §2244(d)(1) (2012), may be tolled for some vaguely defined level of egregious malpractice by a prisoner's court-appointed attorney, although not by the mere negligence that is the usual reason lawyers blow the statute of limitations.

10.2. Applying *Holland*. In Menominee Indian Tribe v. United States, 136 S. Ct. 750 (2016), the Court held that the tribe had not alleged a sufficiently "extraordinary circumstance." The dispute involved the alleged underpayment of health-care funds due to the tribe. The tribe said it did not sue earlier because its rights were being asserted in a class action by another tribe. If one set of plaintiffs files a class action, the statute of limitations is tolled for all members of the alleged class. American Pipe & Construction Co. v. Utah, 414 U.S. 538 (1974). If class certification is eventually denied, the statute begins running again at that point. This rule means that class members do not all have to file their own lawsuits, just in case something goes wrong with the class action. The tribe also said that limitations should be tolled because the legal landscape was so bleak that filing suit appeared futile until a Supreme Court decision in 2005.

The Court unanimously held that neither of these circumstances was extraordinary. The tribe should have known it was ineligible to be part of the class action because it had not exhausted administrative remedies, and it was obliged to assert its claims whether or not they seemed promising. The Court therefore did not have to decide "whether an even stricter test [than *Holland*] might apply to a nonhabeas case." 136 S. Ct. at 756 n.2.

10.3. Rescission under the Truth in Lending Act. The Truth in Lending Act provides that in any transaction in which a lender acquires a security interest in the borrower's principal residence, the borrower can rescind the transaction in the first three days after the closing, or after he receives the required disclosures, whichever is later. 15 U.S.C. §1635(a) (2012). The borrower exercises the right to rescind "by notifying the creditor, in accordance with regulations of the Bureau [of Consumer Financial Protection], of his intention to do so." *Id.* If the lender never makes the required disclosures, the right to rescind "expires" three years after the closing. §1635(f).

The Supreme Court unanimously held that it is sufficient for the borrower to send his notice of rescission within three years; he can file suit later. Jesinoski v. Countrywide Home Loans, Inc., 135 S. Ct. 790 (2015). The lender can always force the issue by filing suit to foreclose the mortgage, to quiet title in foreclosed collateral, or for a declaratory judgment that the rescission notice is ineffective.

Page 983. After note 12, add:

12.1. Statutes of repose and class actions. The Court held that *American Pipe* (note 10.2 in this supplement) does not apply to statutes of repose. California Public Employees' Retirement System v. ANZ Securities, Inc., 137 S. Ct. 2042 (2017). The plaintiff, widely known as CalPERS, was part of a class action alleging fraud in the registration statements of securities that Lehman Brothers offered to the public shortly before it went bankrupt in 2008. As the outlines of a settlement began to emerge in the class action, CalPERS opted out of the class action and filed its own lawsuit.

The relevant statute of limitations says that no action can be brought more than one year after the fraud was discovered or should have been discovered, and "[i]n no event shall any such action be brought . . . more than three years" after the securities were issued. 15 US.C. §77m (2012), quoted in part in note 4 in the main volume. The Court held that the three-year provision was a statute of repose, not subject to tolling, a conclusion reinforced by the contrast with the one-year provision tied to the discovery rule and by the emphatic language "in no event." Perhaps the decision will be confined to statutes with this two-tier structure. Justice Ginsburg dissented for four. She thought the CalPERS claim had been filed as part of the class action and that its individual claim was just a continuation of its class claim.

12.2. Don't call them statutes of limitations. The Supreme Court has held that statutes of repose are sufficiently different from statutes of limitations that a federal statute preempting state statutes of limitations does not preempt state statutes of repose. CTS Corp. v. Waldburger, 134 S. Ct. 2175 (2014). The federal statute was aimed at environmental toxins with long latency periods, so this interpretation most likely defeats the statutory purpose. And the vocabulary for the two kinds of statutes was unfamiliar and unsettled in 1986, when the federal statute was enacted. But the vocabulary has become much more settled in the meantime. Justices Ginsburg and Breyer dissented.

12.3. Disclosure of short-swing profits. The Securities and Exchange Act requires corporate insiders to disclose their purchases and sales of their corporation's securities, and provides that any profits on securities held for less than six months must be disgorged to the corporation. 15 U.S.C. §78p (2012). The statute of limitations says that "no such suit shall be brought more than two years after the date such profit was realized." §78p(b). Defendants argue that this is a statute of repose, not subject to tolling rules, and alternatively, that it should be tolled no longer than the time at which plaintiff discovered or should have discovered the violations. The Ninth Circuit has long held that the statute is tolled until defendants make the required disclosures.

The Supreme Court split four-four, with Chief Justice Roberts not participating, on whether the limitations period is a statute of repose or subject to tolling rules. Credit Suisse Securities (USA) LLC v. Simmonds, 566 U.S. 221, 226-230 (2012). But the eight justices sitting unanimously rejected the Ninth Circuit's tolling rule. Defendants in *Simmonds* argued that they were not subject to §78p, so that they would never file the disclosure forms, and the statute of limitations would never run. But their actions were generally public (they were underwriters of initial public offerings), and plaintiff obviously knew about her alleged cause of action, because she had already filed suit. The Court remanded the case for further consideration under ordinary tolling rules.

Page 984. After the penultimate paragraph of note 13, add:

   13. "Jurisdictional" time limits. . . .

   In Irwin v. Department of Veterans Affairs, 498 U.S. 89, 95 (1990), in an opinion by Chief Justice Rehnquist, the Court said there is a "rebuttable presumption of equitable tolling," even in claims against the United States. *Id.* at 95-96. There were two dissents. On the facts, the Court held that limitations was not tolled by a lawyer's three-week absence from his office. That absence mattered, because plaintiff had only thirty days to file a lawsuit after he or his lawyer received notice that his administrative claim had been rejected.

   In Henderson v. Shinseki, 562 U.S. 428 (2011), a mentally ill war veteran missed the deadline for appealing a denial of veterans' benefits. In a unanimous opinion by Justice Alito, the Court said that "[f]iling deadlines . . . are quintessential claim-processing rules." *Id.* at 435. "Congress is free to attach the conditions that go with the jurisdictional label to a rule that we would prefer to call a claim-processing rule." *Id.* Congress need not use "magic words," but it must give a "'clear' indication" that it wanted a time limit to be treated as jurisdictional, quoting Arbaugh v. Y & H Corp., 545 U.S. 500, 516 (2006). Congress had not clearly stated any intent to subject veterans to a time limit with jurisdictional consequences.

   In Sebelius v. Auburn Regional Medical Center, 568 U.S. 145 (2013), another unanimous opinion, the Court repeated this clear statement rule for finding statutes of limitation jurisdictional. But it said that *Irwin*'s presumption of equitable tolling is for lawsuits in court; it does not apply to administrative appeals inside a federal agency. Auburn Regional claimed it had been systematically underpaid by a company hired by the government to process Medicare claims from hospitals, and that the contractor had concealed the violation by reporting only the results of its calculations and not the underlying data. The statute of limitations for seeking review of the contractor's decisions was 180 days; a regulation provided that the time limit could be extended "for good cause," but not for more than three years. The Court deferred to that regulation, holding that the extension up to three years was permissible because the statute was not jurisdictional, and that the three-year outside limit was not subject to further tolling.

Page 984. After note 13, add:

   14. The Tort Claims Act. The apparent agreement in these cases on suits against the government broke down entirely in United States v. Kwai Fun Wong, 135 S. Ct. 1625 (2015), on whether statutes of limitations in the Federal Tort Claims Act are subject to equitable tolling. The statute is 28 U.S.C. §2401(b) (2012), and it contains two time limits. The tort plaintiff must file an administrative claim with the responsible federal agency within two years of the alleged tort, and must file a lawsuit within six months of the agency's rejection of the claim. Two cases, one involving each of these time limits, were decided in one opinion.

   Justice Kagan's opinion for the majority started with *Irwin*'s presumption of equitable tolling. Rebutting that presumption requires a "clear statement" from Congress; there was no such clear statement here. The limitations periods did not appear in the statutory section that conferred jurisdiction. The statute said that untimely claims "shall be forever barred," but that was common language in statutes of limitations, especially older ones, and had generally not been given jurisdictional or substantive significance. The same language had been interpreted as jurisdictional in the Tucker Act, on suits against the government in the Court of Federal Claims, and that rule had been reaffirmed in *John R. Sand & Gravel* (note 13 in the main volume). But that decision was based solely on precedents going back to the nineteenth century, and not on the wording of the statute. The same "forever barred" language appears in the Clayton Act, and in other statutes, where it is subject to equitable tolling. The government had made no arguments against equitable tolling separate from its arguments that the statute was jurisdictional, so the Court treated the two issues as the same in this case, while acknowledging that they were theoretically distinct.

Justice Alito dissented for the four conservatives. *Irwin*'s presumption applied only after it was determined that a statute of limitations was not jurisdictional. The "forever barred" language was emphatic and unqualified, and it had always been interpreted as jurisdictional in suits against the government under the Tucker Act. Congress should be presumed to have relied on that. It is not apparent how this dissent fits with the conservatives joining in the cases in this supplement to note 13. Alito said that the limitations provisions in *Irwin* and *Henderson* were less emphatically worded, and that they referred to the person filing the claim rather than to the claim itself; the majority found these distinctions wholly unconvincing. Apart from the difference in wording, the Tort Claims Act is a broad, important, and explicit waiver of sovereign immunity, and that context apparently triggered the conservatives' concern with narrowly interpreting waivers of immunity. But all the statutes creating narrower causes of action against the government are waivers of immunity too, and *Irwin* explicitly addressed the argument that waivers of immunity are to be narrowly construed.

15. Returning abducted children. The International Child Abduction Remedies Act, 22 U.S.C. §9001 *et seq.* (Supp. III 2015), is the U.S. implementation of the Convention on the Civil Aspects of International Child Abduction, available at http://www.hcch.net/index_en.php?act=conventions.text&cid=24 [https://perma.cc/ET2R-6JBH]. The abductor in these cases is typically a parent seeking to avoid a custody decree, or the risk of custody litigation, in the child's home country. If the complaining parent sues within one year of the abduction, there is a very strong presumption that the child should be returned to the original home country and any custody litigation conducted there. After a year, the abducting parent can defend on the ground that the child has become settled in the new country to which the child was taken. The Court unanimously held that this one-year period is not subject to equitable tolling, even where the abducting parent conceals the child's location so that the complaining parent cannot know where to sue. Lozano v. Montoya Alvarez, 134 S. Ct. 1224 (2014).

The Court said that equitable tolling is a settled principle of American law, presumptively applicable to every statute of limitation unless the statute indicates otherwise. But equitable tolling could not be read into the treaty on this basis, because it is not a settled principle of the law of all the countries who agreed to the treaty. The Court also said that this provision is not a statute of limitations. It shifts burdens of proof, and allows a new defense, but it does not bar the claim. Three

154

concurring Justices emphasized that trial courts retain discretion in these cases, and that any misconduct by the defendant parent would be relevant to the exercise of that discretion.

CHAPTER TWELVE

FLUID-CLASS AND CY PRES REMEDIES

Page 1001. After note 3, add:

3.1. The reaction gains momentum. Courts of appeals are adopting the ALI standards and enforcing them vigorously. Some of the cases are collected in In re BankAmerica Corp. Securities Litigation, 775 F.3d 1060 (8th Cir. 2015). "Because the settlement funds are the property of the class, a *cy pres* distribution to a third party of unclaimed settlement funds is permissible '*only* when it is not feasible to make further distributions to class members' . . . except where an additional distribution would provide a windfall to class members with *liquidated*-damages claims that were 100 percent satisfied by the initial distribution." *Id.* at 1064, quoting Klier v. Elf Atochem North America Inc., 658 F.3d 468, 475 (5th Cir. 2011) and American Law Institute, *Principles of the Law of Aggregate Litigation* §3.07 cmt. a (2010). Paying out 100 percent of the amount due under a settlement formula is not the same as paying 100 percent of a class member's actual damages. Where a cy pres distribution is permitted, *BankAmerica* said that the court must identify the next-best recipient that most closely approximates the class. It is not clear who that would be for a nationwide class of investors.

In an example of the 100-percent-satisfied branch of the doctrine, the First Circuit has approved an $11.4 million cy pres distribution out of a $40-million settlement, where those class members who filed claims had already received full payment of their estimated damages. In re Lupron Marketing and Sales Practices Litigation, 677 F.3d 21 (1st Cir. 2012). Lupron is a cancer drug, and the cy pres distribution went to cancer centers for research on the cancers treated with Lupron.

3.2. The Third Circuit ups the ante. The Third Circuit joined the trend, and may have toughened the emerging requirements, in In re Baby Products Antitrust Litigation, 708 F.3d 163 (3d Cir. 2013). Plaintiffs' expert estimated that Toys R Us and its co-conspirators had inflated the price of certain baby products by 18 percent. The settlement refunded 20 percent of the purchase price, trebled under the antitrust laws, to any customers with some documentary evidence that they had purchased one of the products from Toys R Us. The settlement paid $5 to anyone who claimed to have purchased one of the products but had no evidence. Few claims with documentary evidence were filed, with the result that $3 million went to the class, $14 million to counsel, and $18.5 million to cy pres.

The court of appeals was troubled by those proportions. It approved cy pres settlements in principal, but vacated the district court's approval of this settlement. Noting that some of the products cost up to $300, so that 20 percent trebled would be $180, the court thought that the reason consumers failed to file claims must have been that the documentation requirements were too stringent. It remanded without suggesting what lesser documentation requirements might be feasible.

The court also said that cy pres distributions are less valuable than distributions to the class and should be discounted for purposes of awarding attorneys' fees.

Page 1002. After note 4.e., add:

f. AOL subscribers. Without disclosing that it was doing so, AOL added advertising at the end of every e-mail message sent by any of its 66 million subscribers. Damages were unquantifiable; unjust enrichment was $2 million, which would have been less than 3 cents per class member. The case settled for a promise of repeated disclosures at six-month intervals, with a right to opt out of having advertising attached to one's e-mails, and charitable contributions of $110,000, principally directed to the Legal Aid Foundation of Los Angeles, the Boys and Girls Clubs of Santa Monica and Los Angeles, and the Federal Judicial Center.

The court of appeals disapproved, because two of the charities were local but the class was national, and because none of the charities had anything to do with the underlying claims. The court rejected the parties' argument that the class was so diverse that no more appropriate charity was available. "The parties should not have trouble selecting beneficiaries from any number of non-profit organizations that work to protect internet users from fraud, predation, and other forms of online malfeasance." Nachshin v. AOL, LLC, 663 F.3d 1034, 1041 (9th Cir. 2011). And if no such charity could be found, the district court should consider giving the money to the government.

g. Facebook subscribers. The Supreme Court declined to review a decision upholding a dubious cy pres settlement of a case arising out of one of Facebook's more outrageous privacy violations. See Lane v. Facebook, Inc., 696 F.3d 811 (9th Cir. 2012), *cert. denied* as Marek v. Lane, 134 S. Ct. 8 (2013). Chief Justice Roberts filed a separate statement, agreeing that this case was not a good vehicle, but flagging the issue of cy pres settlements and saying that "this Court may need to clarify the limits on the use of such remedies." *Id.* at 9.

h. Securities fraud. Additional cases are collected in In re Bankamerica Corp. Securities Litigation, 775 F.3d 1060 (8th Cir. 2015). The court held that no cy pres distribution is permitted if an additional distribution to the class is feasible, and that where a cy pres distribution is permitted, the court and counsel must search diligently for a charity that serves the interests of the class. A legal aid society could not receive any cy pres distribution when there were organizations devoted to securities fraud as their issue, "such as the SEC Fair Funds." *Id.* at 1067. Fair Funds are created from judgments or settlements in SEC enforcement litigation and are to be distributed to victims of the fraud that triggered the SEC lawsuit; Fair Funds can also accept contributions. 15 U.S.C. §7246 (2012).